There is No Bad Truth

Second Edition

The Search for Self

Charles D. Leviton, Ed.D.

KENDALL/HUNT PUBLISHING COMPANY
4050 Westmark Drive   Dubuque, Iowa 52002

Illustrations by Preston Tharp

Copyright © 1990, 1995 by Charles D. Leviton

ISBN 0-7872-3687-X

All rights reserved. No part of this publication may be reproduced,
stored in a retrieval system, or transmitted, in any form or by any
means, electronic, mechanical, photocopying, recording, or otherwise,
without the prior written permission of the copyright owner.

Printed in the United States of America
10 9 8 7 6 5 4

Table of Contents

"Being Somebody" is much harder than **"Doing Something"**. It is not enough to ACT differently or even correctly - to function in a manner equivalent to that of a healthy individual - to perform behavior in such a way as to earn the plaudits of society and the approval of my parents or church.

Don't ACT healthy - BE healthy.

Don't ACT appropriately - BE appropriate

The search for self is the search for truth. This is also a quest for equality and balance, for integration and appropriateness. There is no bad truth because truth is not selective, judgmental or moralizing. Truth just IS. How we perceive and react to truth determines its goodness or badness. The pursuit of happiness is really the happiness of pursuit - the elusive but constant quest for Self. There is no truth without self. There is no self without truth.

In the beginning there is a self. In the end there is a self. Life is what happens in between. In a very real sense, Self is our only reality - all that we own and all we are responsible for. My job description is to be the best me I'm capable of being and share that responsibly with my world. If I want to love and be loved, I must start with love of self and share that love so that it can be received and returned by others.

We are all changing emotions, roles and components. It is not that we really change but rather that we express different aspects of ourselves at different times These are called subpersonalities and can be seen much like the characters, sets, script and staging of a play. They each have their role and play off each other.

The Director of the play is the true self who has total responsibility for the proper blend of ingredients that make the play a congruent and meaningful whole.

Guided imagery, also referred to as guided daydreams or visualizations, are important tools for experiencing, confronting, understanding and changing subpersonalities. This chapter gives simple steps for mastering this technique and using it for yourself.

Achieving a sense of self means looking at what it means to be a man or a woman. How are we different? How are we the same? What are the elements of parenting and society that help shape our sexual identities and how we feel about them? What does every man and woman need to be healthy and have good sexual identity? How will it affect you not to get it?

How does the sex act itself affect our self image, identity, feelings of power or helplessness as well as bring feelings of loving and being loved? Blending the intellectual and physical expressions of being is one of the best prescriptions for living a healthy life. Listening to the body, interpreting the messages correctly, acting them out appropriately is the ultimate expression.

A look at Father and Mother as the ultimate masculine and feminine symbols. What each is supposed to share with us and how it affects us when they do or don't.

Two things that every child needs from his parents, suggestions on approaches, what to do if not successful. All of us need to be healthy - with or without our parents' cooperation.

All of us are deprived to some degree. No parent is perfect or even perfectly aware of what your needs are or how to supply them. Five steps are presented here for healing the past feelings of a deprived child. Also, many examples of how imagery can be used in this process.

Part I was concerned with knowing the self. Stop, look and listen - accept, evaluate and understand. Part II is more concerned with the acting out of this knowledge; sharing the self with others in a way that brings the best possible results.

Some people are avoidant personalities, needful of intimacy and love but who can only receive it or give it in painfully sparing dosages. It's too naked, vulnerable and dangerous to put themselves on the line, presenting the other person with material that could later be used against them. We present seven blocks that often keep people from sharing the self, how these blocks affect their relationships and how the partner can use this information to help remove the blocks and open new areas of communication.

What we call anger is often poor communication skills. We don't feel the right to our feelings or their expression for fear of alienating others, so we hold them in until there is an explosion or express them indirectly and hurtfully.

Here we list ten "types" or "labels" for expressing anger (or deeply important emotional feelings) in an abusive or hurtful way, along with suggestions for dealing with these people appropriately and providing a safe environment for all of us to change.

Who would not want to declare self as authentic and genuine? Yet to be such requires at least two principles - to know who you are and to appropriately express who you are. Very few of us qualify in this respect. Is it possible to find a balance that is neither selfless or selfish, that gives to self without limiting others, that expresses feeling without demanding compliance? We present 13 examples of what authenticity is and how it should be expressed, along with the expected outcomes.

Will we ever find the solution to the man-woman dilemma? FACT: Men and women NEED each other, SEEK each other out, FEEL INCOMPLETE without each other. Society has always held this out as the ultimate success. Then why is it so difficult?

Leviton's five hypotheses about compatibility. A look at negative attractions and how they can be broken. What are positive attractions? How do values and interests come into play? Two different "self tests" are supplied for yourself and prospective partner to see how you measure up and why. A fun approach to an often perplexing dilemma.

Most of life turns out to be "silent, demand expectations and confused, guess work response".

There is a way to be honest, open and authentic without being demanding and self-centered. It is my obligation to both of us to be real and yours to respond to that realness with your own. It doesn't have to be in a spirit of alienation or competition. Step-by-step examples are provided for changing and improving the way in which you communicate needs and feelings and the way you perceive the communication of self and others.

Romantic love and the battle of the experts. Trying to find a definition of love that fits, makes sense and is approachable. Much of what we "call" love ranges from horniness to indigestion. What is the real thing and why do we seek so strongly for it?

It is not enough to understand the semantics of love and the theory that supports love. How do we work through the stages? In what manner can we locate and utilize the passion within us? On what basis can we effect commitment: The nuts and bolts of intimacy and the struggles of achieving it as we look at seven vital aspects which help create intimacy in a relationship.

People and relationships change when they get married. Marriage is a powerful institution that tends to bring out the closet craziness in us. A look at cultural expectancies and how they shape and affect us. Why marriages succeed and fail and some suggestions for making yours work.

Once one is free to be, one is free to love. What king of couple could we expect from this maturity? What type of interaction, mutual support and interdependence would emerge? I believe the effect is enormous. We need each other - not to survive - to abound; not for dependence - for abundance; not for basics - for the ultimate. Twelve attributes or examples of what the self-actualizing self-sufficient and satisfied loving couple would be like.

Think of the total self as a house supported by seven strategically-placed pillars in perfect balance and harmony.

These areas combined, contain all that you need to be a healthy self. They are the sum of all we have tried to present in this book. They are not of equal importance and will require various shiftings of priorities as to time and energy invested in them, but it is still essential to maintain a balance of growth patterns in all seven areas to keep "the roof of the house on straight and true."

Worksheets A, B, C.

Specific exercises for yourself and spouse to work on to improve your relationship.

The Self

They tried so hard to teach us
   The things that are not true
The lessons that we learned so well
   The sundry things we do.

"Survival of the fittest
   Will cost you lots of friends
Don't rock the boat that floats you
   Just smile and make amends.

"Don't be honest with your feelings
   For folks will take offense
Be tactful - not dishonest
   Walk that lonely picket fence.

"Just **Be Nice** my mother taught me
   No matter what the cost
A good example for the neighbors
   Never mind the painful loss.

"**Fit in** and people like you
   Agree and smiles abound
Always do what is expected
   Never throw things out of round."

Now there's nothing wrong with niceness
   It's OK to just fit in
Tactful is delightful
   Being gracious is no sin.

But the question that I ponder
   Of this niceness that I share
Are the feelings **really** truthful
   Am I honest, do I care?

What good is tactful niceness
   That doesn't tell the truth?
Politeness doesn't get it
   If I'm lying to myself.

Being hurtful or rebellious
   Is not my basic theme
I'm not asking that you lash out
   Blowing off your vicious steam.

If they like you 'cause you're phony
   Where's the gain in that?
But truth that rips and shatters
   Will not bring you what you want.

Things extreme that are described here
   Often seem our only choice
There is more for us to choose from
   There is honest, that is nice.

Be yourself in all your feelings
   See and know and be and do
Then express with your uniqueness
   What you've seen and felt and been.

This is all you have to offer
   For yourself and to mankind
Folks can then be free to love you
   As you search and as you find.

Share yourself just as you find it
   True to feelings understood
True to self and true to others
   Free from those who pressure **shoulds**

Teach yourself a new beginning
   Teach the lesson that is TRUTH
Give yourself in all your realness
   Loving gift for all the world.

Introduction

Sitting in group therapy with a confronting mixture of unsympathetic and rather challenging adults was a very painful experience for me. They didn't seem to understand me (or care to, for that matter), and the more I explored or clarified my feelings and behavior, the more I felt ripped apart, undressed, vulnerable, exposed and WRONG.

After a few weeks of hearing that my judgment was distorted, my behavior adolescent and being not the victim but the causal agent of every negative happening in my life and in my relationships, exasperation, torment and desperation exploded all at once. In a rage of frustration and anger, I lashed out in verbal fury at my tormentors.

"You all seem to be experts at what's wrong with me. I haven't said or done one thing right in my life according to you. You take great delight in explaining in detail the mistakes and stupidity but no one yet has been smart enough to suggest what could have been done better. If you are so smart to know where I am wrong, kindly be so generous as to tell me what I should have done. TELL ME WHAT TO DO AND I'LL DO IT!"

The room became very quiet. No one seemed to respond to my tirade of pain and desperation. Finally the therapist broke the silence with a murmur of amusement at my discomfort.

"DON'T JUST DO SOMETHING, CHUCK. **BE** SOMEONE!"

I shook my head in confusion and disgust. "They're all crazy - even you, my therapist." I didn't understand a word he said.

It was several months later before those words began to take on meaning in my life. "BEING SOMEBODY" is much harder to conceptualize and bring to fruition than "DOING SOMETHING". That was over 30 years ago and much of my life since - as an educator, therapist, and sometimes husband, father, child and person - has been spent learning to BE or processing my BECOMING.

It is not enough for me to ACT differently or even correctly - to function in a manner equivalent to that of a healthy individual - to perform behavior in such a way as to earn the plaudits of society and the approval of my parents or church.

A sociopath can do that. A person with no special conscience can learn the rules of the social game and play them exceedingly well, by rote, by rule, by conditioning.

I don't want to ACT healthy - I want to BE healthy.

I don't want to ACT appropriately - I want to BE appropriate.

I don't want to please others by giving them what they believe in - I want them to be pleased because they believe in ME.

What I DO is NOT what I am. It is a symbol of what I am. It my be a hint of what I am or an expression of some part of what I am, but it is NOT what I am.

So then this book will attempt to answer my own desperate cry for help -

"Tell me what to DO and I'll DO it!" "Tell me how to BE and I'll BE it!" In all fairness I'm not sure this can be done. Eric Fromm started "THE ART OF LOVING" with the proclamation that "Love could only be experienced and could never truly be defined" and then spent 200 pages trying to define it.

Such is the folly of psychotherapists (sometimes psychos for short) who have this need to make sense of life and share with others. It's easier to tell you what's wrong. Hindsight as to why something didn't work is a paradise of wisdom. Criticizing one's behavior because "it didn't work", which simply interpreted means "didn't bring the results it was designed to", is judgment by the wrong person, for the wrong reasons, set up by a faulty criterion.

Motive and intent are the measurements of BEING.

Who are you?

What do you feel?

What are your REAL NEEDS?

What will bring you ultimate JOY?

What is truly best for you? **This** is integrity and morality - not some discussion over the validity of war, or a new definition of pornography, or whether or not to eat red meat.

This is ultimate simplicity but most of us have a need to make it distorted and complex.

Am I a product of all of my yesterdays? a clone of my parents values and belief systems? a victim of society's inability to love?

Am I DNA and heredity, passing Universal life and wisdom from generation to generation? created personality and predetermined truth? reincarnated karma striving for ultimate perfection?

Am I all the above or none of the above?

YES! and NO!

"Does anybody REALLY know what time it is? Does anybody really CARE?"

WHO AM I?

A psychiatrist by the name of Roberto Assagioli, who created PSYCHOSYNTHESIS, summarized it very nicely in the following:

"I have a body but I am NOT my body. My body may find itself in different conditions of health or sickness, it may be rested or tired, but that has nothing to do with my real SELF, MY REAL 'I'. I value my body as my precious instrument of experience and of action in the outer world, but it is only an instrument. I treat it well, I seek to keep it in good health, but it is not my SELF. I HAVE a body, but I AM NOT by body.

"I HAVE emotions, but I am NOT my emotions. My emotions are diversified, changing, sometimes contradictory. They may swing from love to hatred, from calm to anger, from joy to sorrow, and yet my essence - my true nature - does not change. 'I' remain. Though a wave of emotion may temporarily submerge me, I know that it will pass in time; therefore I am not this emotion. Since I can observe and understand my emotions, and then gradually learn to direct, utilize, and integrate them harmoniously, it is clear that they are not my SELF. I HAVE emotions, but I AM NOT my emotions.

"I HAVE a mind but I am NOT my mind. My mind is a valuable tool of discovery and expression, but it is not the essence of my being. Its' contents are constantly changing as it embraces new ideas, knowledge and experience. Often it refuses to obey me. Therefore, it cannot be myself. It is an organ of knowledge of both the outer and the inner worlds, but it is not my SELF. I HAVE a mind, but I AM NOT my mind. I have desire, but I am NOT my desires. Aroused by drives - physical and emotional - and by outer influences, desires too are changeable and contradictory, with alternatives of attraction and repulsion. I HAVE desires but they are not myself.

"After disidentifying myself from the contents of consciousness, such as sensations, emotions, thoughts, I RECOGNIZE AND AFFIRM THAT I AM A CENTER OF PURE SELF-CONSCIOUSNESS, A CENTER OF WILL. As such, I am capable of observing, directing, and using all my psychological processes and my physical body.

"Who am I then? I am the permanent factor in the ever-varying flow of my personal life. I am that which has a sense of being, of permanence, of inner balance. I am a center of identity and pure self-consciousness. I AFFIRM MY IDENTITY AS THIS CENTER.

"I recognize and affirm that as this center I have not only self-consciousness, but also creative, dynamic power. I recognize that as this center, I can learn to observe, direct and harmonize all the psychological processes and the physical body. I will to achieve a constant awareness of this fact in the midst of my everyday life, and to use it to give increasing meaning and direction to my life. I AM A CENTER OF IDENTITY, SELF-CONSCIOUSNESS AND WILL."

Another method of expressing this is to see oneself as the director of a play. The play has many parts just as the body does. It has a script, sets, actors and dialogue. It is the director's responsibility to put it all together and make sense of it. You SEE the finished product, impressed by the significance of the sets, touched by the sensitivity of the dialogue, moved by the power and authority of the actors, but you never see the director behind the scenes making it all work. If it happens, you walk away with a total experience, it not, you struggle with the incomplete parts of an uneven performance.

YOU ARE THAT DIRECTOR. The essence, the core, integrity, truth, purity and character - WHO YOU REALLY ARE.

Unfortunately, you can live out your lifetime with very little recognition or experience of your inner self, bouncing off walls, carried by society's currents, functioning to expectations, all with minimal contact or knowledge of your true being. The fortunate part is that you don't need 100% constant contact with the director of your play. You can shave, shower and get to work on time without even engaging the brain, let alone the integrity.

But the more you access the self ... to truth ... to character...the more true you will be to your personal nature and to the world you live in, the more success, happiness and joy you will experience for yourself and others.

This book is written for those who do want to experience life differently, who are willing to go out on a limb where they've never been before, who will choose to search their inner being for inner truth ... and finding this truth, will be strong enough to act on it ... to discover a scary but exciting new way in which to live.

If your DOING has left you with feelings of being unfulfilled and incomplete, come along and explore the concept of BEING for awhile.

"IT COULDN'T HURT!"

"TRY IT, YOU MIGHT LIKE IT!"

What is Truth?

What is Truth? Eternal question,
  What is real and genuine?
What is honest, what is earnest?
  Is there truth that is divine?

Is there truth to calm the masses,
  Are there laws to fit each case,
Is there justice we can count on,
  Or does confusion regulate?

Is there good truth, what of bad truth
  Who determines or defines?
Truth is fact in simple context
  Not embellished or denied.

"What exists or what just happened"
  Recorded in the sands of time
Not to judge or run away from
  Not of morals to define.

Truth just **IS** - in total being
  Nothing more and nothing less
You may hate it or distort it
  Nothing changes none the less.

There is no good truth.
  There is no bad truth
Truth exists for all to see
  Know the truth that lights the darkness
  Know the truth and be set free.

Chapter 1

There Is No Bad Truth

Today I saw a "rocking horse" in front of a department store, rocking away with no one on it or around... Somehow, that seemed to speak loudly of the life most of us get stuck in or settle for. Life is out there "rocking or happening" and most people are too preoccupied with side issues or survival to see or to bother to climb on for the ride.

In trying to determine a course to follow or the best ride to pursue, we often get caught up in the vacillation of extremes.

Historical tradition gave us the seduction of selflessness

- ◆ Spirituality thru denial of self
- ◆ Love thru martyrdom
- ◆ Control by guilt and obligation

In essence the message came to us that it was not spiritual to love oneself, that the self was a pesty and bothersome fraud to be delegated to some back room and ignored or forgotten. To be truly spiritual was to be selfless or thru the denial of self by putting the needs and feelings of others first and foremost. The expression of love then was to sacrifice (or martyr) yourself and your needs in favor of the one you love. What could be more evidence of your devotion? The secret payoff that no one acknowledged out loud is that by giving this selfless, sacrificial love you put the other person under severe guilt and obligation to please you - or at least not disappoint you - thereby achieving indirect but ultimate control over the relationship.

AN INFLATED EGO

*IS ONE THAT IS TOO SMALL
TO SUPPORT THE PERSON WHO
CONTAINS IT.*

TOP
BANANA

The Human Potential Movement over the past 40 or so years responded to this historical tradition with the opposite doctrine that your first obligation was to oneself and that in order to "give" a self you must "be" a self and meet your needs first. From this would come expressions of love and generosity toward others **but** each is committed and obligated and responsible to and for only himself in the long run.

The 70's reacted with "Mature Selfishness" taken to the extreme stupidity of

♦ Do your own thing
♦ Lack of personal responsibility
♦ Exploitiveness
♦ Alienation and divisiveness

As with any truth or doctrine there are always people who will stretch it all out of proportion and distort the meaning to justify selfishness, avoid responsibility and exploit others. In the 70's this came to a head and we now refer to that decade as the "decade of selfishness". With each of us fearfully protecting our own interests, alienation and divisiveness occurred.

The 80's cried out for an "US" generation but no clear cut direction or definitive clarity has emerged to answer that cry.

We became painfully aware that neither extreme has worked and we have nothing to replace or improve them. There has to be a way to be an "US" - a method or manner of relating that enables each of us to be responsible for and meet our own needs, without taking from, hurting, rejecting or depriving the other.

There Is No Bad Truth: The Search for Self - is presented as an answer to this need. The need for equality and balance - integration between

- ◆ Male and Female
- ◆ Parent and Child
- ◆ Group and Individual
- ◆ Assertive and Receptive
- ◆ Self and Others

It must be obvious that there is no easy solution. There can be no book of rules that spells out the perfect equation or balance between the above list of polarities. Giving to one side necessarily deprives the other. We all have **rights** and we all have social **responsibilities**. In a win-win situation the solution is not static but constantly moving and flowing back and forth, seeking the highest good, the greater need, the utmost truth for the moment.

Under the chauvinistic tradition of our culture someone had to have the power to unblock the impasse. This power has legally and traditionally been given to the man. If a family lived in California and the man were offered a job opportunity in New York it was HIS decision alone. Of course he respected and listened to the input of wife and children and if they said they did not wish to move and he did wish to, THEY MOVED. If the wife chose not to, he had grounds for divorce on the basis of abandonment. Today, with two working partners, the situation is often reversed. **BOTH** have good jobs in California and the WIFE is offered a promotion or better position in New York. The husband would have to uproot himself and follow.

YOU REMEMBER
CHAUVANISM...

THAT'S WHERE MEN
OPEN DOORS FOR LADIES
PICK UP CHECKS AT
RESTAURANTS
LIGHT THEIR CIGARETTES
PROTECT THEM
SUPPORT THEM
POSESS THEM
CHEAT ON THEM
PAY ALIMONEY TO THEM

USUALLY IN THAT ORDER

Does **either** partner have the right to demand this? Does either partner have the right to DENY this?

Yes, each is responsible to do what is best for self and meet his own needs.

Yes, if you love someone you do not want to stand in their way of success.

No, I do not want any success at severe cost to my partner. That goes **against** my need. I have a personal need to take care of self. I have an equally personal need to please and respond to the true needs of my spouse.

Is there a solution? Not an easy one. Not one that can be printed in a book for all to follow and proclaim as truth. The solution is personal and individual to each couple involved. I'm not here to tell you what to do. I would like to be here with suggestions for approaches, understanding and resolving such problems so that each of us have some tools and abilities for laying out the options, considering the risks and arriving at the conclusions that make sense and work best for **you**. That is what this book is about.

The search for equality and balance, for integration and appropriateness is a true SEARCH for SELF. Find the SELF - the true, genuine, complete and absolute Self and you will find all the above.

The Search for Self is therefore the search for TRUTH and THERE IS NO BAD TRUTH. Truth is not selective, judgmental or biased. Truth simply is.

TRUTH FOR MOST PEOPLE

*WHAT YOU WANT
TO BELIEVE*

*WHEN YOU WANT
TO BELIEVE IT.*

The goodness or badness of Truth is our emotional response to how we perceive it affecting us - not the truth itself. If I were to lose my arm in an accident, the truth is simply stated, "the arm has been lost" - fact only. How I feel about that loss is the goodness or badness. Denying my arm is gone to avoid the grief or pain of loss will not make the situation better, or bring my arm back but will actually delay my need to grieve and emotionally heal from the loss and forces me to live (or try to) in a world of distortion and lies.

Truth is what is. To deny a wall in front of my path will not remove the wall but will cause ME to be broken upon the truth I have denied.

Truth does not change from our refusal to acknowledge it. Truth is the one absolute. It does not relate to us. WE MUST RELATE TO TRUTH. The sooner we understand this principle, the sooner we can consistently look at SELF and LIFE without denial or distortion, see things from a factual point of view, decide how this relates to us and act appropriately in response. The lack of what I just described is essentially the cause of all neurosis, psychosis and "sin".

In the most simplistic terms: the ability to see and relate to TRUTH in a direct and appropriate fashion is the best definition of mental and spiritual health.

"You shall know the TRUTH. And the TRUTH shall set you free."

But what is TRUTH? IS there such a thing as truth? Can truth ever be identified, separated, clarified? Can the experts ever agree to its definition or description? How can we find answers when we aren't even sure of the questions?

And if truth is to FREE us - from what does it free us—

TO what does truth free us?

TRUTH FREES US **FROM** the restrictions of an incomplete or distorted perception of self...

Truth frees us **TO** fully comprehend, perceive and experience the deepest aspects of authentic, genuine, real Self...

And finally truth provides us the freedom to share that Self with others in mutual respect, admiration and caring, meeting the deepest, spiritual needs of all in the ever-evolving growth of love and life.

What does that mean? If there is an aspect of myself I can't accept as Truth, such as: A. I occasionally tell lies; B. when frightened I viciously attack; C. when at fault I totally deny guilt; then I am forced to lie to myself and deny the above realities to protect my perception of self as a good person.

When I can admit the above Truths about myself as aspects I don't like but are still true about me, along with more favorable or acceptable facts, then I am freed (by Truth) from the restrictions of an incomplete or distorted perception of self. I can now see and acknowledge the total self - good and bad - acceptable and nonacceptable.

Once freed from restrictions, I am now able to fully comprehend fears or feelings that bring about this behavior and how I truly feel about myself afterward.

This is a true look at the deepest aspects of my authentic, genuine, real self. That self is not composed only of the very best and acceptable parts but the negatives, as well. To acknowledge all of me brings the freedom to learn what I did, why I did it, and the consequent results. The next step is to evaluate if that was the best possible behavior under the circumstances or how I could have responded more appropriately and with better results, both for myself and the significant others involved.

And finally, because I don't have to protect myself from the judgment of self or others because I admitted the Truth to myself, I am now free to share this Truth with you so that we both can profit from the new information.

This will help both of us to meet our needs, and also enjoy our relationship at a higher level.

Our forefathers proclaimed "Life, Liberty and the Pursuit of Happiness"...

THIS IS SELF - THIS IS LIFE - THIS IS MEANING.

The pursuit of happiness is really the happiness of pursuit! It is the elusive but constant quest for **SELF**.

Who am I? Why am I here? For what purpose was I born?

TO FIND THE TRUTH

TO FIND THE SELF

There is no Truth without Self

There is no Self without Truth

You can create a new Self by simply uncovering and discovering real Truth - basic Truth - the Truth of WHAT IS!

God said - "I am what I am - without distortion or self- consciousness."

"I AM," I SAID!

LET THERE BE SELF!

LET THERE BE TRUTH!

I AM!

The search for truth is the search for self. The search for Self is the search for Truth. They are inseparable. Is there universal Truth? Only to the extent there is Universal Self.

In many respects, we are as one - Universal man. But even as no two snowflakes or fingerprints are alike, even so no two individuals and perhaps no two Truths. This is the great mystery and paradox - a SEEMING contradiction that can never be fully explained or truly understood.

So then each of us is only accountable for our own Truth - our own Self.

AND YOU SHALL KNOW THE TRUTH - AND THE TRUTH SHALL SET YOU FREE. AND YOU SHALL KNOW THE SELF - AND THE SELF WILL TEACH YOU TRUTH.

Most of us don't want to do this. We are totally sure there are parts we can't or won't accept within us. To admit these is to admit we are not worthy of living or at least of friendship or respect. We suffer from programmed judgmentalism that is unforgiving. Forgiveness and love are the basis for life and relationships. NO ONE IS WITHOUT FAULT. NO ONE CAN CAST THE FIRST STONE. WE ALL NEED THE UNCONDITIONAL ACCEPTANCE OF THIS TRUTH. If we don't like our fault, CHANGE IT, don't DENY it. We can't and won't change what we deny exists.

This all may sound overwhelming and a little confusing right now. I have attempted to reveal THE PROBLEM in Chapter One. The problem has been with us for a long time. Of course, there is no easy answer and at times it seems impossible. From this point I will attempt to break the Truth into smaller parts, easier to digest and understand. The more of self and others we know and understand, the clearer our options, the simpler the solutions. Come, let's explore the TRUTH together.

The Dilemma

I want what I've got, I must keep it;
If I move on ahead I might lose it.

I can't make up my mind, it's driving me blind.
Do I risk or protect? I can't choose it.

My heart aches to grow.
It's pushing me so,
But my fear stands firm in my way.

If I dare to leave home,
I can't feel secure.
I don't know I can win, anyway.

it's boring to stay
to hoard and decay,
I'd rather be stretching for life.

But life's an unknown.
I have what I own;
I might find only heartache and strife.

The answer my friend,
brings confusion to end:
You've based your protection on things.

Life is in living
not hoarding and hiding -
you've got to take risks to explore.

True safety in living
is trusting one's being,
believing "I am" my supply.

No one can rob you
of what is within you,
That will be yours till you die.

You are the essence.
You are the value.
Safety and peace you employ.

So seek out the future
with courage and fervor
Life's best is for you to enjoy.

Chapter 2

Granting Permission to Love the Self

What does it mean to BE somebody? What is the purpose of life in general? For what specific purpose was I born? Is there a specific purpose other than the accident of birth? What is successful living? What creates ultimate happiness and joy, is there meaning beyond just making it through the night, is there a Supreme Being that really cares what happens to me?

Psychologists regurgitate terms such as SELF ACTUALIZATION, SELF REALIZATION, and EXPERIENCING ONE'S HIGHER CONSCIOUSNESS. Does that really exist? Is anyone really happy, or satisfied or content?

Religion preaches faith in God that will bring deep inner peace which surpasses understanding. Is this lip service, wishful thinking, or reality? Is hope just the opiate of the neurotic? The promise of tomorrow usually soothes and calms beyond just the reality of today.

It doesn't require a genius IQ or a "Philosophical Master" to ponder these questions. I believe the answers are out there in the Universe and we all have intellectual belief systems that keep us sane and attempt to make sense of our lifes. Yet none of us can really stand on the summit, pound our chest and say THIS IS TRUTH.

So life then is the journey, the ultimate search for truth. Since we can't reach the "end", let's concentrate on enjoying the "means" to that end, the process that compels us. Perhaps there IS an end to reach, a perfect culmination of varying perceptions that when in perfect alignment allow us to see and experience the ultimate and infinite.

Perhaps that will propel us into a higher level of being, far beyond what we are capable of comprehending in this existence.

I believe it was Teddy Roosevelt who when referring to the Bible, stated, "It isn't what I DON'T understand that scares me, it's what I DO understand."

The eternal questions challenge us all and scream to be addressed, to bring meaning and focus to our lives. Yet it's easy to bury ourselves in the unanswerable to avoid the inevitable.

IN THE BEGINNING THERE IS A SELF
IN THE END THERE IS A SELF

No matter what happens in between and who we relate to or how - there is no other reality but self. I was born with senses such as taste, touch, feeling, hearing and vision for the express purpose of perceiving, experiencing and making sense of the world which contains me. But I am NOT that world and can at best only learn how to cooperate with it. I have a difficult enough time just understanding ME.

So while we are cruising the highway of eternal philosophy, or the pathway to ultimate wisdom, let's share some simple, basic truths to ponder.

Since there IS A SELF and SELF is really all we have to work with, let's concentrate on you, which seems like a good place to start.

LOVE YOURSELF. Why not? If you won't, who will? If you don't, who SHOULD?

This book is BY the self -
For the self
ABOUT THE SELF

Perhaps you are not ready to do that just yet - LOVE THE SELF. Can you at least begin with an agreement to stop DISLIKING the self? If that is a little scary, just be willing to suspend negative judgement for the time being - at least until you finish reading this book. You DO know how difficult that is, don't you? All of us have intimate, private, personal knowledge, unavailable to others, which creates extreme negative reactions about our thoughts, feelings, behaviors and attitudes. These negative reactions are based on information that violates our code of ethics and morality, or at least the code we were conditioned to accept as our own by the society that influenced and shaped us while growing up.

Literally dozens of clients over the years have confessed at some point in their therapy that there was a "secret" bit of information in their past they had never shared with anyone. Obviously they did not intend to share with me either, but had some need for me to know this terrible truth about them existed. I never ask what the truth or information is. I do ask what would happen to them or how they would feel if the information were revealed.

It would be more than they could handle. Once the truth were spoken out loud it would be as though the entire world now knew this person to be corrupt, evil and without social redemption. It would be a hardship from which they could never recover.

Almost all of them during the course of therapy eventually revealed "this terrible hidden truth". One woman had systematically stolen clothes from a department store she worked at as a teenager. The total theft amounted to less than $400. She treated this as though it were millions - "theft is theft, sin is sin, evil is evil and cannot be forgiven."

A man spoke of having sex with a small farm animal at 12 years of age. Another of incest with a sister as a teenager; others of drug use, being a "peeping tom" or indecent exposure. Some were so simple as to be laughable that anyone would treat them so seriously, others were crimes of serious nature.

How can we withhold this judgement? How can we NOT be critical? Is it moral to love a self containing and often expressing such negativity?

Let me give you some simple hope. Jesus said judgement cannot be made on the basis of a concrete act or behavior but rather on the reason or motive behind that act.

Suppose I mentioned in passing that I killed someone on the way to work this morning. I'm quite sure that would create a vivid reaction within you. In all probability, there would be intense curiosity and desire to know the facts and learn the circumstances surrounding the incident. The fact that I killed someone is hardly enough information to be simply received and accepted as "passing information" about my morning. "And, how has your day been going?"

If I tell you that some stupid drunk cut me off on the freeway and I pulled him over and shot him, you'd be horrified by my psychotic behavior. If I said some man tried to pick up on my wife or made a vulgar remark so I beat him to death, you would undoubtedly question my overaction and violent outburst (perhaps not to my face) and also wonder at my sanity and stability. In both cases, the law would prosecute me for murder.

If I mentioned that I caught a man raping my daughter in her bedroom and in the process of rescuing her, we wrestled over his gun and I managed to turn it on the rapist and kill him in our defence, you **and** society would probably see me as a hero. There would be no trial for murder and I might even get a citation for bravery.

Not the act, but the motivation, reason and circumstances of the act, determine its morality.

Society and individuals, in spite of our knowledge and good intentions, still tend to **judge** ourselves and others on the basis of concrete labels and laws, rather than trying to understand the provocations that set those actions in motion.

Examples: divorce is immoral, anger is never acceptable, commitments can never be broken, driving over 55 miles per hour is a criminal offense.

I'm not asking you to condone anti-social or criminal or even negative behavior. I'm not a "bleeding heart" who blames society and parents for all crime and individual rebellion, and wants to coddle the criminal and underprivileged to overlook their acts because it is NOT their fault. I believe in being accountable. I believe people have to be responsible for their own lives, actions, successes **and** failures. What I'm suggesting is that you suspend judgement until you have all the information necessary to fully understand what happened, the circumstances contributing, the feelings and emotions involved, and the attitudes and motives behind what was done.

I DON'T MIND BEING TOLD OF MY FAULTS . . .

IT'S THE DELIGHT IN THEIR VOICES THAT BOTHERS ME.

At this point, rather than judging the PERSON (yourself or another) as being of bad character and therefore beyond redemption, judge THE ACT, and correct accordingly.

This is very much the role of the therapist. A person (client) comes in with problems and tells the therapist all the negative, terrible, unacceptable thoughts, feelings and actions that are literally making him ill - both psychologically and physically, and ruining his life and his relationships. Is the therapist to then play judge and jury?

"Yes, you are right. You are guilty as charged and sentenced to ten years in Hell, followed by eight years on parole in Purgatory."

Or - "No, you are wrong. I find your behavior acceptable under the circumstances or I'm a nice guy and I'll let you get away with it or I condone and accept whatever you do, no matter who it hurts."

OF COURSE NOT!

We listen in a caring, non-judgmental manner and try to understand all those actions in the context of current conditions and historical background. We care that the person is in pain and acting out that pain. We are concerned that the behavior IS negative or antisocial and thereby endangering self, others and relationships. We have an obligation to protect society and the individual. We are no more in the business of condoning sickness than we are in judging it. There is an implied contract with the client that he wants to **change** and get better, and enlists our help to achieve this. Helping the client (in a safe, non-judgmental environment) to see, understand and explore all the feelings involved, offers opportunity to see and try new options. Many times, the client feels he **has** no other option and is shocked to discover alternatives. Or he views those other options as not acceptable for various reasons. New insights and understanding often change that.

The biggest change may very well be to stop judging yourself as bad, and understand your own feelings. Whenever BAD (or unacceptable) feelings are explored and better understood, they often CHANGE and so do our needs and actions. It would be impossible to illustrate all the possible reasons people change and become more reasonable in both their feelings and actions as a result of therapy, but I hope you get the message that the therapist **doesn't** judge or condone but rather facilitates positive change - in behavior - AND the feelings supporting that behavior. The best therapy not only does this FOR the client, but teaches the client to do this for himself.

What happened to the clients who made these "confessions"? They already had judged and condemned themselves as bad people of rotten character for committing these acts. The expectation then was for anyone who found out to be shocked, upset and critical of them as well - thereby confirming the guilt and badness.

The first result was always relief that they took the chance and cleared their conscience, regardless of the outcome. Confession is good for the soul in the same way vomiting is good for the stomach - it removes poison that is toxic and constantly making us ill. Having negative thoughts and feelings tends to exaggerate and enlarge them, giving excessive power to make us literally ill. Exposing then removes this power in the same way exposing a blackmailer to the police, takes away the power of the blackmailer.

The second result is that the therapist was not shocked, judgmental or critical. He expressed sympathy and concern for the feelings of the client rather than judging the behavior. "What was going on in your life at the time that contributed to this behavior? What did you learn from it? How did it affect you? How do you feel now that we've discussed it? What keeps you from forgiving yourself? Many people say that God forgave them years ago but they could not forgive themselves. Are you more spiritual than God? Are you so arrogant that your standards are higher than God's? Forgiveness is the essence of religion, of life, of love. "GOD SO LOVED, HE **FORGAVE**!" No one is without sin, neurosis, mistakes, negative or counterproductive behavior. Therefore we **all** need forgiveness - to BE LOVED IN SPITE OF OUR IMPERFECTIONS. Not to give that to self is the ultimate crime against self.

HOW TO BECOME AN OBJECTIVE OBSERVER

You must start by stepping back and just identifying what you DO, SEE, FEEL and EXPERIENCE, without JUDGEMENT of good or bad, right or wrong.

This is called "the objective observer" or "fair witness" - someone whose only interest is "telling it like it is" - the facts of the situation - without regard to protecting anyone's feelings or special interests. To the extent you can achieve this, the personality's need or tendency to self justification no longer stands in the way of clear vision.

For example: wife to husband - "You hurt me." There are only two standard, defensive reactions to that kind of attack:

1. I didn't do it! (denial) or

2. I had a right to, because...(justification).

What exactly are we defending against. "You hurt me" implies more than it says.

Actually, the more correct manner of expressing the truth involved - both in terms of the English language and psychological accuracy would be, "As a result of the following behavior, I felt hurt." But, that involves taking responsibility for one's own feelings and who wants to do that?

Stating "You hurt me" implies INTENT on your part. You hurt me because you wanted to hurt me. You are a hurtful person and I am solely a victim of this dastardly act. So, if you admit you hurt me, you admit to doing a bad thing. Bad things are done by bad people with bad characters who are not socially redeemable. The true emotional reaction to "You hurt me" is -

"I AM NOT A BAD GUY."

We are not clever enough to figure all that out in a moment of defensive reaction, so it generally comes out of our mouths as..

"I DIDN'T DO IT" (I'M NOT A BAD GUY)
or
"I HAD A RIGHT TO DO IT BECAUSE..."
(HENCE, I'M NOT A BAD GUY)

From the kid caught with his hand in the cookie jar to the husband caught in the act of adultery, we get the ridiculous sounding "I didn't do it - are you going to believe ME or what you see?" What is really meant is, "I'm not a bad person of bad character for what I just did, but if I admit I did it, both of us will believe I AM bad."

The truth is that even good people make mistakes, have poor judgement at times, and yes, do BAD things. A lie does not make one a liar, anymore than one drink makes one an alcoholic, nor being in a garage makes one an automobile!

THE OBJECTIVE OBSERVER DOES NOT JUDGE BEHAVIOR OR CHARACTER! Then what does it do?

1. **It observes.** What a surprise. To observe is to see what really happened - to quote back "just the facts, Ma'am". Example: husband and wife in heated argument over where to put the glasses in the dishwasher. He puts them on the bottom and she has told him repeatedly to place them on top. He is upset by her nagging criticism and she is upset that he refuses to learn and do it right. This is an observation of what is happening, with no judgement of who is right or who is wrong - a statement concisely reporting the facts.

2. **It evaluates.** What's really going on here - what are the real or deeper issues involved?

   A question you can ask that often cuts quickly to the hidden issue is this. Finish this sentence: "If you really loved me, you would..."

   Husband:

   "... appreciate and see what I do around here and not demand perfection from me."

   "She doesn't appreciate what I do around here. No matter what I do, it won't measure up to her perfect standards so why try? I don't want to do the stupid dishes anyway, but it's unfair to admit that to her. She overwhelms me with her nagging and logic, and I can't take her on directly."

Wife:

"If he really loved me he'd listen to me an do it right so my life would be easier."

"He says he wants to divide the chores equally, but won't do them correctly. Even a child could learn that much. He does this deliberately to get to me. I have to nag and punish him to keep him from winning."

3. **It defines cause and effect.** Husband puts glasses in wrong place and this aggravates wife to reaction. Wife's aggressive and angry reaction makes husband feel degraded and unappreciated.

It is sometimes amazing and amusing when a simple statement of cause and effect is shared with a quarrelling couple. The logical sharing of how each one's behavior elicits the other's response and that in turn creates another response often tends to remove the hurtful aspects of the interaction. Simply repeating a summary of "this is what just happened between you" with no judgement of right or wrong in the voice of the therapist (the objective observer) gives permission for the clients to neutralize it as well.

"Now I can see why my spouse acted that way." With no judgement it's easier to understand the partner's point of view and not just see her (or him) as mean and destructive.

It's what I often call PASSING INFORMATION. Not hurtful information - something to be used against you later - just information. Information is the basis for knowledge and action.

4. **It tries to understand motives.** From the information we have, the husband is apparently using a passive-aggressive reaction to this wife's aggressive demands. He sees her as overwhelming and impossible to satisfy so he "wins" by withholding what she demands but does it "unconsciously" so he can deny guilt or responsibility. He feels unloved and unappreciated but can't deal with it directly.

The wife also feels unloved and unappreciated due to the husband's seeming inability to cooperate and do it right. The more resistive he becomes, the more she feels a need to demand, nag and punish. If she can get him to conform she'll "win", and therefore feel loved.

The key to the above explanation is the lack of judgement. Neither person is on trial. It is not important who is right or wrong. There is no right or wrong. It is only important to understand the motives and feelings of each.

BITTER

*IS BEING ACUSED
OF SOMETHING YOU
DID NOT DO . . .*

*BY THE PERSON
WHO DID IT.*

WHY they feel correct, which explains why they act in the manner they do. Each interprets the other's behavior according to his own values and frame of reference, and responds accordingly.

So, each is "right" in his own framework. Understanding WHY someone does what he does removes the need to judge. It clarifies what happened, why it happened, and what options may be available in the future.

Often in this type of situation I will ask one spouse or the other, "What do you feel was the REAL motive for what your spouse did?" The answer is generally, "How should I know" to negative, "Because he's vicious and wanted to hurt me."

"What are three or four possible motives for ANYONE acting in this manner?"

"Because they want to hurt you and enjoy doing that - because they don't know any better - because they are scared, defensive or trying to protect themselves."

"Let's go over each one and see which one you feel fits your partner."

The spouse generally winds up saying, "My spouse is not a vicious person, sometimes he's not aware, if reacting to defend himself obviously he must feel I attacked or hurt him."

With this most of the anger is removed.

Before you can play the role of objective observer in your own relationships with others, you must first be able to examine your own feelings, actions and motives in this light. Long before you make decisions or choices, it is incumbent - to just LOOK, EXPERIENCE, and ACCEPT the total truth about yourself - seeing the various parts - strengths, weaknesses, potentials and fears - and accepting them all as reality, truth - what IS. Then, without judgement, trying to understand, making sense of it all. Again, therapy provides a good example: providing a safe environment (an objective observer) of acceptance and love within which the therapist can hold up a mirror to the client for self examination and disclosure. This is what you do, these are the factors that caused your feelings, here is the cause and effect that brought about a particular behavior or activity. Once understood, there is no further need for judgement. What were the results and how did they effect us and others? How can we improve on that or make it better to bring more satisfaction?

In the case of the woman who stole clothes as a teenager, what is the value of continued judgement and condemnation? In her mind condemning and not forgiving is a sign of good moral character and spiritual values. To forgive and act as though it did not happen is to condone criminal activity. Even the criminal serves his time, pays his debt to society and is set free "forgiven". She is giving herself eternal punishment for petty theft. The punishment doesn't fit the crime.

Give money to the store, pay for the clothes, confess the crime and go on with your life. To essentially STOP LIVING at the point of the crime is ridiculous. Some people use guilt as a sign of spirituality. "At least I feel guilty for being a drunk, a liar or a thief. If I did not feel guilty I'd **really** be bad."

How about cleaning up the behavior, changing to more productive living and forgiving the past, and LEARNING from the past. Learning from our mistakes turns them into positives.

It is the externalized norms, standards, expectations and values of the important others in our lives - such as parents and society - that cause the internalized judgements of right or wrong, good or bad, with subsequent guilt or defensive rationalizations to avoid the guilt. Prejudging distorts it further. Being objective is to remove society's standard or guide of the norm, and just BE in pure essence.

If we can step aside from that standard of society in order to look for information to better understand ourselves and our behavior, we have less need to defend and more ability to see clearly without self protecting distortions. This brings freedom for true change and mutual benefit for ourselves and others.

When we don't judge ourselves, we are more free to LOVE ourselves - even the unlovable parts - feel sorry for, care about and comfort those parts so that they can be free to be more appropriate and thereby more loveable.

Treat yourself like you would treat a good friend. Put your arm about the part of you that goofed up and express love and sympathy. "I'm sorry you're in pain." "I'm sorry you had a need to do that." "I love you anyway and I want to be here for you and help you learn from this and not have to repeat the same mistakes."

The ultimate benefit of this is the ability to take control of our own authencity, rather than allowing circumstances to control us. Make our own direction and let circumstances follow us, rather than the other way around. This is the essence of integrity.

Society really holds paradoxical and ambivalent points of view regarding love and relationships. One side proclaims "to thine own self be true" while the other calls that selfish and insists we put the needs and desires of others first as the true statement of generosity, giving and love.

Meeting one's own needs cannot truly be separated from meeting and responding to the needs of another. True love is born from the loins of an individual who is expressing his own need TO LOVE - NOT TO BE LOVED. Of course, that love requires a respondent or it falls somewhat incomplete.

The theme of this chapter is that it's OK to love self. I have taken you through several steps: at least don't DISLIKE your self, withhold or suspend judgement with your self in both its behavior and character. We do this by separating behavior from character. behavior is what you DO. Character is what you ARE. Behavior may "reflect" character, but does not automatically define it.

Patterns of behavior may more accurately define character and may also define a person's M.O. (Modus Operandi - methods of operation) that speak more often of a biased belief system, a defensive habit of reaction, or even a distortion of reality. To understand the logic and reasoning behind a pattern of behavior is to make sense of it. If the pattern is based on distortion or incorrect information, it is far easier to correct the distortion and take away the need for that continued pattern.

If I believe my sister constantly finds ways to hurt me and puts me down in front of our parents (the pattern of behavior) because she hates me, feels I am inferior, and wants me out of the family, it is easy to see why I'd be angry and try to hurt her back. If I discover the TRUE reason for her behavior to be that she feels our parents favor me, and therefore she feels angry and rejected by them and me, my view of her behavior changes. I now understand her motivation to be that of raising her stature in the eyes of our parents so she can be more loved and respected. She does this in two ways: by trying to make herself look "more" good and by showing that I am "less" good.

The pattern of behavior remains negative towards me, HOWEVER understanding that I am dealing with a HURT sister is very different than an EVIL sister. I feel differently and certainly act differently towards a person perceived in HURT and PAIN than one perceived as MEAN or EVIL. It is easier to understand and forgive someone acting out of PAIN or need, than anger and greed.

Have you ever experienced a situation where a family member attacked you viciously with total anger, but for some reason you did not get frightened or defensive or feel a need to fight back? This time you saw through the vicious words and attitudes and before you was a frightened little child. For that moment, it was as though a curtain were parted and you saw BEHIND the anger; a frightened child literally scared to death and fighting for its life. You felt within you a rush of softness, love and caring for the child instead of your usual anger toward the attack. You are no longer afraid of the attacker, but sympathetic to the fearful child. In a soft and concerned voice, you hear yourself say, "Wow, you really seem frightened right now."

The family member burst into tears. "Someone saw through my facade - someone sensed my fear and vulnerability, and instead of taking advantage of it to finish me off (which I was sure would happen if they knew the truth) reached out in love and concern, ignoring the attack and caring about my true feelings - that's love. Someone in this scary world understood my fear and I am no longer ALONE."

If that has never been your experience, you've missed out on something special. If it has, you've had a glimpse of what I'm trying to illustrate - the behavior we perform is not always reflective of what we feel, experience and ARE on the inside. We often act angry when we are scared, aggressive when we'd prefer to run, withdraw when we want to fight, act superior or correct, when we feel inferior or to blame.

Looking at behavior without judgement enables us to see factual truth without having to rationalize or distort our reasons. If what we do is going to be judged (by ourselves or others) than we'd better dream up some damn good justifications that we had a right to do what we did. If our character is NOT going to be judged on the basis of what we did and the behavior will be examined for the purpose of understanding - NOT judging - good or bad, then we have little or no reason to justify, rationalize or distort.

This may sound difficult to do, to see behind someone's behavior to read unspoken motivations. The ONLY way to learn this is to start with SELF.

STOP JUDGING SELF AND CHARACTER AS GOOD OR BAD

STOP JUDGING BEHAVIOR AS A DIRECT INDICATOR OF CHARACTER

Legitimate guilt is a feeling that comes when you violate your own integrity. Without it you are a psychopath.

Neurotic guilt, by far, more common, comes from the standards and judgements which we are TOLD throughout most of our lives to believe, yet is inappropriate to our integrity.

WITHOUT DISTORTING, DENYING OR JUSTIFYING, LOOK AT WHAT YOU DID: THE FACTS.

NOW, ASK YOURSELF: "WHAT WAS I REALLY FEELING WHEN I DID THAT? WHAT WAS THE DEEP TRUTH ABOUT WHY I DID IT?"

If you aren't afraid of the consequences, and have given yourself immunity from prosecution, YOU CAN TELL YOURSELF THE TRUTH.

When the truth is known, distortion clears up and the need to behave as before is no longer present. As understanding and needs change, so does behavior. There are new choices or options and they are more appropriate to REAL needs, not defensive ones.

As each person becomes proficient in doing this for self, a wonderful and unexpected bonus occurs. You find yourself, you stop judging others and you can SEE THEIR REAL TRUTH by putting yourself in their shoes and asking yourself how you feel. It's amazing how accurate you will be regarding the feelings of others.

Experiencing, feeling empathy for, knowing, understanding and loving the self IS THE ONLY PATHWAY to experiencing, feeling empathy for, knowing, understanding and loving the important others that we so desperately desire to be close to.

"Do unto others as you would have them do unto you." "Love thy neighbor as thyself." We would interpret that to mean, "Be unto others as you would have them be unto you," with the emphasis on my responsibility for my beingness. While treatment of the others is important and necessary, we can't lose track of ourselves through making the others more important than us in the transaction. How can one "love another as thyself" until that love is experienced by the self?

"Love thy neighbor as thyself" pre-supposes that it is OK to love yourself first and use that for a model of how to love others. Somewhere through social history that notion got turned around so that we are taught to believe love for others is good and self-love is bad!

Individuals can create together, a way or language in which their innermost beings - experienced as individual personalities - can function undisturbed and unmanipulated, on the basis of mutual respect and mutual self-love.

Mary states, "I'd like to go to a movie tonight."

Dave replies, "Gee, I'm not sure I'm in the mood for a movie, what did you have in mind?"

A simple, everyday situation where many people have intense difficulty just being honest and open with their feelings for fear of hurting someone, being rejected or not feeling they have a right to disagree. In the above example Mary made no demand, just stated a preference or a suggestion. Many people will "hear" it as a demand - "if you want it, I have to do it."

Dave, on the other hand, didn't say he **wouldn't** go, but that he wasn't necessarily in the mood. Both are now free to throw it back and forth between them. How important is it to Mary, perhaps she will suggest a movie Dave wants to see or perhaps Dave will make a better suggestion that would also please Mary as much as a movie. This is what is meant by mutual respect and self love. Neither is more or less important than the other. Both needs must be expressed and weighed.

This type of life-giving change is available to anyone who wants it, anyone who is willing to first understand and view his own needs without distortion, and be objective to the needs of another. The purpose of learning a new language is to enable you to communicate facts, feelings and needs more accurately and more easily and to be understood. It is not the other person's primary responsibility to sort through the muck and mire and try to figure out what you're saying, it is **YOUR** responsibility to be clear. Hopefully, the other will care enough about you to ask questions and make it easier to clarify your thoughts, but the primary responsibility for clarity rests with you.

Don't play games and expect the other to read your mind. Wife blurts out to husband, "If you loved me you'd buy me flowers. You haven't bought me even one rose in ten years of marriage."

"I had no idea you wanted flowers. You've never mentioned this once in ten years."

"If I have to **tell** you what I want it isn't love. I want you to bring me flowers because it's **your** way of expressing love."

Can you see the logic in both their reasoning and yet this is crazy-making. Flowers obviously are NOT the husband's way of expressing love, but it IS the wife's way of feeling loved. So then it is her responsibility to both of them to express that - "Receiving flowers once in a while makes me feel thought about and loved."

Then it become the husband's responsibility to spontaneously act on that information and send flowers. He can't even say "no" if he doesn't know the need or desire.

Too often, we try to predict the response of the other in advance and that determines what we say. Usually, that involves our telling them what we think they want to hear, rather than the truth of how we feel.

There seems to be a universal fear that if we tell our true feelings we will be rejected or not loved or look selfish as though telling true feelings is a DEMAND FOR A

PARTICULAR RESPONSE THAT WILL COST YOU DEARLY. So we desperately try to read our partner's mind, guess what the appropriate answer might be and then tell him what he wants to hear so we will be admired, loved and appreciated.

If we both tell the truth about our feelings and desires - WITHOUT DEMAND FOR A PARTICULAR RESPONSE - we now have the information necessary to make an informed decision.

The real need for a "new language" is to express how we really feel and who we really are in a non-defensive, non-attacking, straightforward and informative way. And to encourage and expect a similar response! While we cannot control the response of others, this direct approach has by far the best "track record" in any sort of relationship exchange.

*YOU ARE WHAT YOU **EAT**.*

*YOU ARE WHAT YOU **THINK***

*YOU ARE WHAT YOU **DO***

*YOU ARE WHAT YOU **WEAR***

WE'RE IN TROUBLE

Chapter 3

True Me Vs. Lots of Partial "Me's"

Subpersonalities:

Can We Give Up Our Roles Long Enough To Be What We Are?

Are we more than the roles we play? In his book, **Pairing,** George Bach talks about the problems of "thinging" and "imaging" in relationships. When asked, "Who are you?" we generally answer in terms of roles or "things". "I am a teacher, family counselor, spouse, parent, child, etc." If we wish to impress the other with who we are, we may tend to exaggerate or at least reveal everything we think will be impressive. That's "imaging" - raising our image in the eyes of the other, trying to be what we feel will make them like us and want to be with us.

While a healthy self-image cannot be separated from satisfaction in what we do or accomplish in the various roles we play, it is also true that we are many other things as well. "I am happy, sad, timid, bold, angry, depressed, loyal, cruel, alert, sincere, tender"...the list is endless. In all of this, "I am me. There are many parts of me...some I like and some I don't...but all are me."

A client complains, "My husband is a Jekyll and Hyde. One day he's loving and kind, the next day he's angry and cruel. He's constantly changing."

It's not that we really change. It is rather that we express different aspects of ourselves at different times. Which is the real person - the sober or the drunk one? The truth is that he is both. When sober, the shy, timid side is in control and when drunk, the inhibitions become lowered and an angry, abusive side emerges.

James Vargiu, in his "Synthesis" magazine, refers to these various states as subpersonalities:

> There are in each of us a diversity of these semi-autonomous subpersonalities, trying to express themselves. And when any of them succeed in doing so, we then play the corresponding role. But, during that time, the other subpersonalities are cut off. Yet they are still very much present even though we may be unaware of them and they are likely to create a lot of inner conflict. They may also have some very beautiful, useful qualities that we may need, but not be in touch with. So, one of the easiest and most basic ways to facilitate our growth is to get to know our subpersonalities. As we understand them better, we can regulate and direct their expression according to all our needs and goals, making them our helpers and our allies, and bring them increasingly close to each other, toward greater harmony and integration.

The Transactional Analysis approach also talks about subpersonalities in terms of the Parent, Adult, and Child ego states within each of us. These categories can be broken down into sub-groups such as overprotective or punitive parent, rebellious or adaptive child, etc. Gestalt therapists talk about the "Top Dog" and "Under Dog" in all of us.

In the past few years, I have worked with several female clients, usually in their mid-thirties with several children, generally "happily" married, but a little bored, often with a dominating husband. Then one day, these women enrolled in school to fight boredom and get back into the swing of life. After a year or so, the "women's lib syndrome" caught hold and they felt the need for abrupt change. They found it impossible to be both individual and wife; free and committed. Having to justify their new-found needs (subpersonalities) for independence, strength, freedom, and growth, they felt compelled to reject "all" the old - often blaming their husbands for abusing and misusing them.

There is really no need to make that choice. Both the sensitive, compassionate wife and mother and the independent, free individual can dwell together in peace and harmony if both are recognized to be legitimate and important parts of the total person. Each has a place; each has a role.

We can certainly identify and work with these various parts of ourselves on a conscious level, and one of the major thrusts of therapy is to help clients become comfortable with "every" part of themselves, to own and acknowledge all of their feelings. When they do this, the parts they dislike become less threatening. When they don't, the ones they deny or attempt to repress seem to get out of control and take over their lives.

As we move toward the goal of being an integrated personality, we become increasingly able to choose, at any moment, which subpersonality we want to express. Until then, we are controlled by whichever subpersonality we are identified with at the moment, and thus "limited" to its particular good and bad qualities. But as the integration proceeds, every quality within us, every aspect becomes available to us. When they are "on call", we have then the greatest freedom of expression: whatever is in us can be brought out and actualized.

The psychosynthesis approach speaks of a "higher order center", the "I" or "I-ness' around which the synthesis of subpersonalities can occur, which is the harmonious and effective means of expression for the self-actualized human being.

In therapy sessions, I refer to the "higher order center" or "I" as the "Inner Mind" or one's "Spirit", the inner core of your "beingness" of your integrity, wherein lies absolute truth.

The subpersonalities are various aspects of self that represent the scared, protective, defensive side of you that won't trust the **inner mind's** sense of faith and adventure. While the subpersonality is often expressed in a negative, hostile fashion, it is sometimes there to protect us from inner fear, imagined dangers and pitfalls.

Carl Jung referred to the "SHADOW" in all of us - the "hidden, negative side of one's nature" that needs to be "tamed" and brought back into appropriate relating. Subpersonalities often express themselves in this negative fashion, much like a kid brother with whom we carry on a love-hate relationship. At one point, the brother speaks of loving and protecting, and in the next moment is spewing hatred and hostility. It is very difficult to love an angry, acting out, rebellious child. But the less we love, the more deprived, angry and acting out, the child becomes. He prefers negative attention to no attention at all.

In an hypnosis or guided imagery state, the therapist helps the client to talk to these subpersonalities in some type of symbolic form. If you choose to deal with your ANGER subpersonality today, you could ask it to take symbolic form outside yourself and talk to you. It might come as a huge lion, menacing and snarling before you. You often have to confront, argue with, or reason with a self-centered, defensive and totally unreasonable entity that claims to know how to be mean and hurtful because it was created by you for that purpose and knows nothing else. It must be responded to as a good parent responds to a demanding or unreasonable child - with firmness and strength, good authority and loving concern.

In contrast to this demanding, aggressive, attention seeking subpersonality, the INNER MIND is usually not aggressive or demanding and even reticent to reveal itself. Often it must be convinced that you really want help, desire to change and will cooperate before it really shares. There is always (no matter what "form" it takes) a quiet and confident strength and a feeling of love, BUT also a need for evidence that its help is really wanted. Until convinced, it won't participate. Many clients are afraid of change and resist help even when they are in therapy. There is an inner struggle going on as to whether or not they want to experience the "major surgery" of the therapy that roots out the deep problems and corrects them or to just place a few strategic bandaids around or to do a little cosmetic cover-up. Once you are able to make contact with the various subpersonalities (whether in your everyday intellectual awareness or through the more explicit confrontation within the scope of a guided daydream) you are prepared for the process of integration or congruence. James Vargiu calls this "the process of harmonization of our subpersonalities".

The Five Phases of Harmonization

He described the process in five phases: recognition, acceptance, coordination, integration, and synthesis. The following is my version of these phases.

Recognition of the existence of a subpersonality is obviously the first step. As long as you deny or distort unpleasant reality within, you can never have the power or choice of change. You must first be prepared to recognize and identify the particular problem or "child" of the moment. Most people do not want to experience this for obvious reasons. It is painful to look at and admit to negative aspects of self. To do so is to admit being a "bad" person who does "wrong" things, and deserves extreme punishment. Ignoring undesirable parts of self doesn't make them go away, however.

A simple admission of TRUTH, "this is a part of who I am and what I feel", is a giant, first step toward changing what is undesirable. You can't change what is denied or not admitted to.

The next step is **Acceptance** of this subpersonality as a part of yourself. It requires experiencing and owning those feelings no matter how distasteful, which can then be transformed into more positive ones. ("I feel sorry for this "dictator" part of me that keeps scheming for control when all he really needs is love.") To most people, "accepting" a negative part of self is giving it permission to be destruc–

-tive and encouraging a total takeover of the personality. "If I accept the 'killer' part of self, I am saying that it is OK to kill people and I will find myself doing that on a consistent basis. This is not acceptable to my moral belief system. It is NOT acceptable to feel the anger I feel."

It is not acceptable to KILL. It **is** acceptable to know that you feel angry enough to kill and to fully understand why you feel that way and, furthermore, to sympathize with those feelings, and the part of you that feels them. Someone who is **that** angry and is **that** hurt deserves a lot of understanding and love.

Feelings must not be judged as moral or immoral. They are to be understood and responded to appropriately. When this is done, the desire to kill goes away. The deprived child wants to kill because it feels rejected. Accept it's right to LIVE and feel anger and the anger goes away and the behavior becomes more appropriate. Loving the child within you does not include giving that child the right to destroy you or itself.

Coordination is a central aspect of the work with subpersonalities. It consists of reaching from the external demands of a subpersonality to its core, its inner needs; from its actions to the meanings of its actions, and the causes behind them; from what it says it "wants" to what it truly "needs". In practically every situation, even if a subpersonality initially appears ugly, mean, in deep pain, hostile or a complete hindrance, once you reach its core, you find that its "basic quality" is good. You see that it is not only acceptable, but useful, and at times, badly needed; that it can be harmonized with the other qualities, and that distortions and conflicts were produced largely in the frustrated efforts to express and actualize the fundamentally good quality. So, the first step of coordination is to establish clear and open communication .

The true purpose of anger is to protect. Feelings serve as an inner signal or message to the brain that danger is dose at hand. Anger can protect you in a terrible, abusive and totally defensive manner, or it can do so by being assertive, firm, strong and appropriate.

There **is** a true purpose of goodness in every subpersonality. Usually, it is to protect or warn us from perceived danger. The purpose of coordination is to seek out the true nature, to bring it to conscious awareness, and to find appropriate expression.

Integration is the process by which subpersonalities interact with each other and establish increasingly harmonious relationships. Hence, in combining all these subpersonalities, eventually one whole, healthy, integrated personality will emerge. Similarly, a physical body that is not integrated would find its various parts (hands, feet, mouth, or fingers) each going separate ways. Like a well functioning basketball team, each has an appropriate role to play and the finished product, the integration, is beautiful to behold. The opposite is chaos.

Synthesis is a term to indicate the last phase of the harmonization process and concerns primarily the personality as a whole, and is essentially the culmination of individual growth. While personality integration is intrapersonal (within oneself), "synthesis" is basically interpersonal (between oneself and others) and transpersonal (similar to Maslow's "peak experiences", mystical experiences or a higher conscious ness beyond our human understanding). As a result of this interplay, the life of the individual and his interaction with other human beings becomes increasingly characterized by a sense of responsibility, caring, harmonious cooperation, and altruistic love. It leads to the harmonious integration of the human being with others, with mankind, and with the world.

Talking with Subpersonalities

You can talk to your subpersonalities and ask them what they want, why they are angry, etc. They can negotiate with each other. When one dominates, the other is ignored. Somewhat like children in a family situation, each seeks its proper place and acceptance.   In a real sense, you are acting as your own therapist by experiencing the feelings of the client (subpersonality), identifying with those feelings to better understand them, then providing love and acceptance and caring that they hurt.

Here is an example of a woman who confronted a very frightening part of herself in a guided imagery. Remember that all symbols in dreams or guided imagery can be interpreted two ways: objectively and subjectively. In the objective interpretation, all the images represent your outside environment. A monster might represent a parent or a spouse. In the subjective interpretation, all the images are parts of you...your subpersonalities.

Irene had been suffering from nightmares for several weeks and was unable to clarify or even remember them well. Her fear was overwhelming at times. In a therapy session, she was encouraged to try to go back to sleep to continue the dream the next time she was awakened at night. The following is what she reported.

"I awoke feeling terrified and overcome with anxiety. Staring me in the face was this ugly crippled monster with bulging eyes threatening to destroy me. I was convinced he could. My immediate feeling was to run away crying for protection...but somewhere down deep, I felt I must "speak" to this monster before he destroyed me. Our conversation went something like this:

Irene:	What is your name?
Monster:	My name is anger.
Irene:	What do you want with me? What have I done?
Monster:	I want my share of glory and recognition. I'm tired of being in the background - ignored and denied. I behave in this destructive manner, yelling and screaming because it's the only way I can be heard. I have to attack you to get your attention. You're always trying to control me and pretend I don't exist. Well, I do! I'm equally important. If it weren't for me, you wouldn't even know how you felt about anything...I'm like a thermometer; I keep you in touch with reality.
Irene:	I apologize for not recognizing you. I'm sincerely sorry you are in so much pain. I will try to recognize your "needs" and "voice" more often and allow you to speak. I agree, you are important and I want to honor your presence. I want to become your friend and understand you.

"As I did this, the monster began to cry and shrink into a little mouse and ran away. I couldn't believe my eyes."

This client had been suffering from the impression that it was in poor taste or even wrong to express anger. Her need was to appear calm and together, with never a ruffled feather. Irene was so out of touch with her feelings, the only way it was possible to deal with them was through intense dreams. At first it seems foolish to try to have a conversation with the various subpersonalities and symbols of our dreams. This client was absolutely amazed at her conversation with the monster, particularly when experiencing it in the twilight hours of sleep. This is consistent with the pattern we have found: monsters cease to be monsters (actually changing shape and form) when confronted, listened to, and offered love.

Before we can get where we're going to be healthy, self-actualizing people, we must **know** who we are and secondly, **love** who we are.

The more deeply we can experience and understand our feelings, needs, motivations, fears, anxieties, goals, and aspirations, the less need we will have to judge or condemn ourselves. The more we can believe in ourselves, the more we are capable of deep love for ourselves. If I understand what I feel and do and see it as appropriate, reasonable and realistic, I will like it and therefore like myself - the one who is feeling, doing, and experiencing.

The Guided Daydream

The most common method of harmonizing our subpersonalities, and thereby integrating ourselves, is the European technique often referred to as a "visualization" or "guided daydream", as created by Desoille. This is similar to hypnosis, meditation, yoga or prayer. The purpose of all of these is to relax both the mind and the physical body so that it can literally release tension and stress, filter out the excess outside stimuli bombarding the senses, and thereby focus more total awareness on the inner self. This true inner world of feelings, thoughts, emotions, intuition, and intellect is the only real world, the only real truth - the truth of what **is** for all of us.

Some people resist what is called hypnosis or condemn it as giving up control to another person, who can then brainwash or program them to his own image and belief system. To the contrary, a true hypnotic state is giving up control - from your conscious control to your inner or subconscious control. From the **outer** you to the **inner** you - not to another person. Your therapist is a facilitator to help you get there in a safe environment to protect you (with understanding, love and comfort) when what you experience is discomforting.

Some people think hypnosis is being asleep and you wake up with no conscious awareness of what happened. Instead, it is an enhanced awareness that allows you to shut out the world and focus more clearly on one subject or experience. You **know** you are in a therapists's office and you **know** you are somewhere else experiencing yourself as a six year old arguing with your mother. Part of you **is** the six year old having the experience and part of you is the adult watching a movie in your head.

The interesting part of guided imagery is that it can be done in a deep, hypnotic trance, a slightly relaxed state, or with no relaxation and eyes wide open. If I ask you to "see" yourself having breakfast with your parents in their kitchen, the instant image is there right now. Then I can "guide" you to continue either a spontaneous experience or very structured one. As we get more deeply involved, the imagery takes on a spontaneous life of its own and soon becomes a movie in your head that you are sharing in the details as it happens, rather than deciding what to do next.

Basically, three things are accomplished through the visualization or guided imagery process:

First, the process invariably relaxes a person at a very deep level of the inner being, usually far beyond one's conscious awareness. (For the person who is highly nervous and upset, this can be very effective.) Because the body is relaxed and less able to cut off subconscious feelings, these feelings come more readily to the surface. Muscle relaxation is correlated with lessened "anxiety". The imagery can last anywhere from thirty minutes to one and one-half hours. Because it has been a very pleasant and relaxing time, the person becomes less afraid of his deep inner feelings, the things that are "buried" inside of him.

This leads to a second step, "catharsis", the releasing of more repressed images and materials. Often, for the next week or two, after a visualization, the person will be much more congruent with his feelings and remember more of his dreams. He is instructed to write these dreams down and bring them in for further interpretation. The dreams would not necessarily be a continuation of the imagery, but simply a clue that more buried emotions have been released to the awareness level and the person is repressing fewer items.

The third thing that happens, occasionally, but not always, is that specific material from the past will come into a visualization and will be relived and reenacted by the person. On occasion, I have had clients relive terrifying and very traumatic experiences at a very deep emotional level. They are re-experiencing the emotions of an event that happened to them as a child, but now with the strength and endurance of an adult. At the end of this traumatic experience, they are invariably exhausted, yet very much at peace with themselves.

Even though the experience has been frightening to relive, the result is deeply peaceful and relaxing. This in itself, is reassuring to them as they no longer need to defend against any of their deep, innermost fears. Thus, psychotherapy helps people to find and be more comfortable with the meaning of their everyday experiences.

This visualization technique can also be used for what is called "Behavioral Rehearsal", an acting-out of what is expected to happen in the future (i.e., confronting one's boss for a raise) to help extinguish much of the fear and anxiety which could normally be connected with the anticipated event. What really happens is the practice of the good results extinguishes the fear of the bad or negative results.

Probably the most common focus of imagery is the process of confronting, looking at, and acknowledging subpersonalities that we have tried to deny in our conscious state. They often start out as monsters, witches, dragons or worse; but once accepted, experienced, and even loved as a "legitimate part of yourself", only acting out feelings of rejection and deprivation, the monsters usually cry, shrink and become less ugly and frightening. It is as though they take off their masks and costumes and let you see who they really are.

Whether the visualization is a traumatic one or a pleasant "romp in the meadow", the experience puts you in touch with your deepest feelings and you become very relaxed in the process.

The following guided imagery sessions are detailed examples of the visualization technique. In both cases, the clients are asked to bring forth a symbol representing their lives at the moment. These symbols could be dealt with as subpersonalities in general (as we did here) or as a diagnostic tool to show their present state of being. As you can see, it is possible not only to diagnose but to help change the present symbol and self image.

Therapist: I would like you to visualize a symbol that represents your life right now, at the moment.

Client: I see garbage. It's waste, crumpled papers in a shopping bag.

Therapist: Dump the contents on a table. What is there?

Client: T.V. dinners, old clothes (my wife's), money, crumpled up bills, baby bottles, and more clothes.

Therapist: Anything valuable?

Client: Outlines of notes from school. I discarded them; they didn't bring me happiness...would like to salvage something.

Therapist: You are standing next to a recycling machine. Dump it all in and see what comes out.

Client: I see myself at home when I'm younger. Glad to be home. The kids are small and running to greet me. I'm picking up my daughter. She's small...it feels great!

Therapist: Now pick up your son.

Client: Feels good. He's hugging me back. My wife is at the door.

Therapist: What does she look like?

Client: Soft and white. I'm reaching out to her. I feel good about her. Soft and warm, she's responsive. I'm glad to see her. We go into the living room and share experiences. We're happy to share with each other. We'll eat in a little while...now we are all eating a nice meal together.

Therapist: Now it's after dinner and the children are in bed. Where are you?

Client: On the couch in front of the fireplace. I feel warm and sexual, but I'm concerned about the kids.

Therapist:	They won't wake up.
Client:	We're embracing, making love.
Therapist:	Feel your bodies melt into each other and become one.
Client:	Feels great.
Therapist:	Enjoy the afterglow.
Client:	I feel satisfied, warm, thankful.

Here was an impotent, angry man, who saw his life as garbage, who was able to re-experience it in a new and positive way.

Our other session involves K.T., a successful business woman; she is going through a divorce and has one child.

Therapist:	I would like you to visualize a symbol that represents your life right now.
Client:	It's a huge cable-like rope in a knot. It's big and brown, a very neat knot, a couple of inches in diameter and is cut at one end and pulled apart at the other. Not much rope. It's lacquered and neat. It would make a nice wall decoration.
Therapist:	Pick it up.
Client:	It's heavy and large. I wouldn't want to untie it. I either accept it the way it is or throw it away. The edge is not lacquered. It's fresh rope. The other edge is pulled and rippled. All torn up, but lacquered.
Therapist:	Become the knot.
Client:	I am the knot. I feel tight. The side with the lacquer I give or show to others; the other part is soft. The soft side is not as attractive or formal, but more comfortable to the touch.
Therapist:	Which would others prefer?
Client:	It depends. If you want pretty, you'd want the lacquered. If you like the rope and what it symbolizes, you'd like the soft side.
Therapist:	Which do you prefer?

Client:	I like both. One's attractive and one's comfortable. It brings back thoughts and it's better to be comfortable. when I first saw the cut edge, I didn't like it. Felt loose, and loose ends hurt. They are still sharp from the lacquer. I feel hurt from those edges; I have to be careful.
Therapist:	You could break the lacquer off the end to be less sharp.
Client:	That helps a little. My self-image is as uncomfortable as the rope. It's lifeless.
Therapist:	It could come to life by changing forms.
Client:	All I see is me casually dressed. The knot symbolizes my heart...all tied up.
Therapist:	Remove the lacquer as one piece. Now look at the rope.
Client:	It's soft. I like it better with the veneer. It could still be a decoration.
Therapist:	Become the knot again.
Client:	The knot can now move. It's not stuck and more flexible. It's still a hard, tight knot, but it's supposed to be that way. It's not hurting the fibers and doesn't feel vulnerable. It actually feels stronger; a working knot now.
Therapist:	Let's leave the lacquer off for now.

Evidently, this young woman has two distinct images of herself; the lacquered, successful, well functioning front she gives the public and the softer, more relaxed, more natural side, which seemed rather vulnerable. She is comfortable with both but really doesn't feel people would accept the softer part of her.

Part of her is "cut off" but unlacquered. She is divorced and cut off from a relationship, and feeling hurt. A part of her is ripped and torn but lacquered, leaving sharp edges that can protect her from outside invasion, but actually wind up hurting her. This is the defensive side of us that says, "I won't let anyone close enough to hurt me again." It also keeps people from being close enough to love us again.

At this point in her life, she is unsure of her real function and value. She can be a wall decoration or be thrown away. The knot gave her structure and security and didn't want to be unravelled. However, she feels a little "too" tight.

She does not believe her soft, natural self is as attractive to others as the lacquered form she presents to the business world, but admits that if someone really knew the soft side, it would be liked, too. When she is able to discard the lacquer and be her soft self, it is relaxing and she feels even more functional and even stronger than before.

GUIDED IMAGERY:

INSTANT ACCESS
TO THE HIDDEN SELF

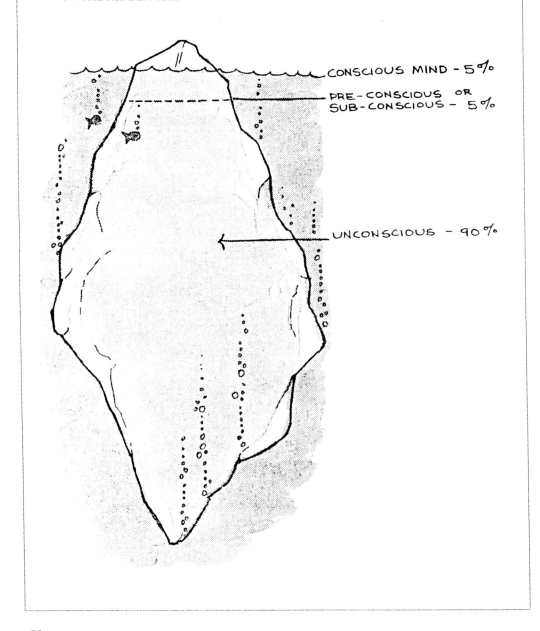

CONSCIOUS MIND - 5%

PRE-CONSCIOUS OR
SUB-CONSCIOUS - 5%

UNCONSCIOUS - 90%

Chapter 4

A Simple System for Creating Guided Imagery

You can try some guided imager for yourself in the privacy of your home; the process is really quite simple.

1. Relax yourself in a comfortable position either in a chair or on a bed, making sure your arms or legs are not crossed. Crossed limbs cut off circulation flow and tend to tighten muscles rather than relax them. Sometimes it can take three to five minutes to reach a state of relaxation, but often just by getting comfortable and closing your eyes the symbols come rather easily.
2. I suggest you start with three deep, slow, cleansing breaths.
3. Then make a deliberate decision to let go of all your body weight and allow the chair or bed to totally support you.
4. Now imagine yourself being totally immersed in a blanket of peace and tranquility, or focus for a few seconds on listening to your body breathe, simply go with the experience. That should be enough to prepare you. (To illustrate how easy this is: Stop right now, and visualize your car, where you parked it. Walk to it, get in, start it and drive off. That's a visualization. It's that simple.)

5. Now, spontaneously let a symbol appear for whatever you want to experience (your life, spouse, parent, job, something you fear, whatever). Try to stay with the first symbol that comes, even if you don't like it or it seems inappropriate to you. Symbols can be anything, by the way - animals, plants, things, geometric forms - it doesn't matter. Many times our critical judgement gets in the way and wants to censor feelings before they have a chance to develop, for fear of learning something negative that we are afraid to look at. The purpose of this exercise is to learn truthful information for greater clarity and understanding, so we must leave the judgement out.

If a symbol doesn't readily come, you may deliberately create one, but it is surprising how easily they will appear for most people.

6. Be aware of the setting or background your symbol is in. Be aware of all the details of the symbol itself and how you feel about them. Explore, look at or have an experience with the symbol.

7. Try to become the symbol. What does it feel like to be this symbol?

8. How does the symbol feel about you?

9. Have a conversation with the symbol. Often the symbol will answer back - or you can switch back and forth playing both roles.

10. Feel free to change the symbol any way you want and then put it anywhere you want.

11. As soon as you open your eyes, write the experience down. This is a must; describe on paper in the simplest and most basic form how you felt about that symbol and what you experienced. If the symbol is a horse, write all your feelings about that horse (strong, weak, good for plowing all day, a fragile but fast race horse, swaybacked, mean, powerful, etc.)

If you have no feelings about that horse, describe how you feel about horses in general - love them, hate them, afraid of them, beautiful, ugly, whatever.

12. When you finish writing your feelings, including those of the symbol, look at the things in the symbol you changed. Where did you put it?

By now, you should have a clear picture of how you feel about whomever the symbol represents. If it doesn't fit your conscious feelings about that person (i.e. "I think I have no negative feelings toward my spouse but my symbol is a horse and I despise horses and think they are dumb"), perhaps you are repressing a lot of anger you don't wish to feel. Wherever there is a discrepancy between conscious awareness and imagery, I'll go with the imagery every time. Remember, it is your subconscious bringing out the symbol and its corresponding feelings. Symbols are the language of the unconscious and are used to by-pass the intellect and go directly to the source. Trust them.

In the experience of guided imagery, you can address many different issues: through symbols, you can speak with the various subpersonalities within you, or confront situations in your life which are causing emotional, as well as physical pain. While in this relaxed, non-judgmental state, for example, talking directly to a chronic headache or a cancerous tumor, can bring a client tremendous insight as to why the pain is there, the lessons that can be learned from the pain, and lastly, help in soliciting the physical body to begin the healing process. The same body that created the discomfort, the tumor or whatever, can also create the energy to heal it.

The word Healing itself seems to raise controversy and conflicting feelings in many people. Some define healing as a special miracle of God, outside the expected or predicted actions of nature. Others may perceive healing as the natural recovery of the body from illness or the removal of symptoms that irritate. Still others, the removal of the disease itself, by way of surgery or drugs; or finally a discovery and removal of the psychological cause of the illness to begin with.

All these definitions have merit. Healing - much like the word LOVE - has many aspects and connotations of usage.

This is a multi-sided, difficult subject to discuss.

There is both psychological and physical illness. They are woven together in such a way that we often are handicapped in establishing cause and effect between them.

As a young child I had hay fever and asthma and lived in Chicago where the pollen count was printed on the front pages of the daily newspaper. Every year from the age of four I got hay fever symptoms starting August 1st when ragweed came to a certain development stage and asthma on August 15th at full bloom of the plant. I had serious attacks daily until the first frost, which killed the plant and brought relief. This continued like clockwork yearly until at the age of 12, my family moved to Arizona and no ragweed.

No one could call that a psychological illness and yet hay fever and asthma have been described as 75% emotional and psychological. As I grew older attacks would be triggered by emotional stress as well as pollens or dust.

Some psychologists say that asthma is a child crying out for Mother. I was an adopted child (from the hospital at birth) reared by a rather negative and frightened woman who was at her best and most loving when I was ill. Interesting coincidence.

The point is we cannot separate psychological cause from illness. People "choose" their diseases by weaknesses of their bodies. All my children have inherited my bronchial weakness and tendency to allergies but none are asthmatic.

Therapy is a healing process acting on many levels. The majority of those seeking a therapist are looking for symptom relief. "Solve my immediate problem, take away this acute pain, give me some advice and direction, comfort and understanding and I'll be O.K." That is a healing, much like getting over the common cold or a flu bug.

As a hay fever sufferer I have found that when I am unable to get relief from a runny nose I get irritated and upset, my symptoms get worse and last longer, sometimes I even get more ill, possibly developing the flu. If I can catch the symptoms early enough I don't "feel" sick, and therefore I can remain emotionally relaxed and recover quickly. My conclusion is that the body heals itself more quickly when relaxed and unstressed. So symptom relief is not only acceptable but desirable. Pitchers in baseball have been known to "blow out their arms" favoring a sore ankle or pulled muscle in the leg.

Another step in healing is to remove the physical cause of the problem. We can surgically remove a tumor, reset a broken bone, or psychologically remove a parent problem by going back to the parent to resolve the necessary issue. As we have pointed out previously, many marital issues go back to a cause unresolved in the relationship with a parent. If Father is the cause of your anger towards men then it must be resolved at the level of the Father.

In the healing of marriages many times therapy must work on dual levels. The cause is usually rooted in the individual and his own particular defense mechanism, but if there is no symptom relief, no negotiation in today's living conditions, the marriage might not last long enough to enable the therapy to cure the cause.

Where does one begin? At the point of the squeaky wheel. Go with the greatest pain. If one partner is in individual pain and discomfort which makes him unequal in every aspect of the relationship, concentration will have to be applied to healing that first before marital therapy can be approached.

Hypnosis and guided imagery are wonderful tools for both dealing directly with immediate relief and also digging out original source or cause, and changing that as well.

If a client comes with a tumor in the arm, causing great pain and emotional distress, there are two approaches. The first is to ask the person (in a relaxed or hypnotic state) to "go inside" his body and look at the tumor. He may describe it as to size and shape and coloration. Often this description turns out to be scientifically correct even if the client has no medical knowledge of the inner body. Other times what the client sees is symbolic. For instance, I asked one lady who had a sudden migraine headache during a session to go inside her head and tell me what she saw. She saw a metal band surrounding her skull which was being tightened more and more until the head would break open. Then suddenly the band became a circular, tall wall around a courtyard and she was sitting inside, protected by the wall. This was obviously symbolic and there was no metal band there or high walls. As it turned out she realized the migraine headaches were her walls, her protection from hearing or experiencing what she wanted to avoid. She subconsciously created a headache when under stress. Once she realized it was her wall and her decision and she was not being attacked from outside, the headaches went away.

In the case of the client actually describing a tumor, it might look red and inflamed or black and dead. I then say I am handing him a salve or ointment that is a "magic" solution made up of chemicals from his own body that will "heal" the illness. He is then asked to take this medication and rub or spray it on the inflamed spot or tumor. As this is done, various possibilities occur. Sometimes the dead skin disintegrates and falls off. Sometimes it looks like running paint being stripped away. Eventually, there is always improvement. The skin looks pinker and more alive in the area, a tumor may shrink or disintegrate entirely, and major change is seen.

I do believe the body has all the chemicals necessary to heal itself. With the help of symbolic gel or salve, I am asking the body to use its own chemicals to effect the healing. Infections have cleared and tumors have literally vanished with this kind of treatment, often spontaneously after one session, or gradually after repeated applications. The least that happens is a decrease in pain or discomfort.

A second step we can take is to "talk" to the tumor or infection or disease and ask why it is there, what the client is to learn from it. How we can change it now. The illness usually appears as a subpersonality and does talk to us. We handle it as we discussed in the previous chapter on subpersonalities.

The tools of guided imagery and hypnosis therefore give us the methods to reach the inner aspects of self, where all personality battles are going on, to help the client understand why his body has created this particular situation and how it can be changed.

I see all problems or illnesses - physical and emotional - as the body's way of crying out for help.

"Pay attention to me." When we listen and obey and do meet the REAL need of the individual, healing can take place on all levels.

Behavior change heals from the outside - in. As a result you feel different (better) about yourself, others respond more favorably so you therefore "feel" different, become different and less defensive and angry. Imagery works from the inside - out. Imagery enables us to quickly go to the source, fight it out at that level and change inner feelings and perceptions. Because of this change, we behave more appropriately and get the same results. Doing both at the same time speeds up the process.

Both the outer and inner problems are symptoms and symbols of each other.

Both the outer and inner healings are reflections of each other.

Healing and peace to you all.

To be feminine is emotion
    Masculine is brain
Feminine is softer
    Masculine is brawn

The female is submissive
    The male should dominate
These are dictionary definitions
    To which we all relate

But if men have all the answers
    And women all the tears
Why do men have strokes and ulcers
    While their wives
    Live on for years?

Chapter 5

Self and Sexual Identity

Sexual Identity as an Expression of the Self

One of the truest and most important aspects of loving oneself is an acceptance and realization of sexual identity. We are born with sexual identity: male and female. We are related to by society according to that identity with subsequent expectations and pressures for certain performance and attitudes. Furthermore, the performance is being constantly judged by others and ourselves and the standard of judgement is just inconsistent or confusing enough to leave us insecure about the results.

To show how deeply ingrained chauvinism is in our culture, even some therapists - who are supposed to be aware of such biases - are not immune to its lure. The Broverman study, a recent survey of clinical psychologists, asked this question: "What do you consider the qualities of a mentally healthy person?" The study also asked them to identify the desirable qualities of male and female. Going directly to Webster's Dictionary, the professionals equated healthy males with qualities defined as masculine and healthy females with those defined as feminine. Healthy males were considered aggressive, assertive, non-emotional, and objective. Healthy females were agreed to be non-aggressive, passive, dependent, and very emotional. But the traits of the male and the healthy human being were almost identical. Evidently, a woman could either be a healthy female or a healthy human being. She could not be both. Under these definitions, neither male nor female could qualify as healthy. All of us are both masculine and feminine and possess all the qualities of both. To the extent we are unable to experience and express these qualities in appropriate ways at appropriate times, we are not mentally sound or functioning well.

THE DICTIONARY DEFINITION
OF FEMININE
DESCRIBES ONE OF
THE CHARACTERISTIC QUALITIES OF WOMAN AS
"WEAKNESS"

WEBSTER OVIOUSLY DIDN'T UNDERSTAND WOMAN

A healthy man would be aggressive and assertive as the need requires, and so would a healthy female. Moreover, it is foolish to believe that a healthy man is non-emotional and only objective. People are a combination of the intellectual, emotional and spiritual. To be a truly self-actualized, fully-functioning human being requires an integration and synthesis of the full range of these qualities. One's emotions and intellect must work in harmony with each other for the fullest benefit. A non-aggressive, passive, dependent, and very emotional woman would not be treated in a therapeutic setting as having reached an ideal psychological state, but as a woman with a serious problem who was a drain on her husband and family and a handicap to herself.

There is an appropriate time and place for the experiencing and expressing of all these traits for both men and women. But, there is also a place for independence, assertively taking one's needs seriously and objective decision making, based on listening to what one's emotions have to say.

Women may often be stereotyped as "castrating bitches, "histrionic, manipulative and seductive", or "hysterical" and "depressed". Counseling experiences indicate that

*DOES THE BITCH
CREATE THE
NICE GUY?*

*OR THE NICE GUY
CREATE THE BITCH?*

these women do exist and are usually found married to aggressive, self-centered nonemotional, intellectualizd men who: 1) talk them out of their feelings; 2) run away from any emotional exchange; 3) cannot communicate on a personal level; and 4) know nothing about intimacy, tenderness, compassion, or understanding.

When a woman is taught how to take her needs seriously and how to present them assertively, she has little need for hysteria, manipulation and bitchiness. When men are taught not to be afraid of emotions (both theirs and hers) and how to communicate feelings on an intimate, revealing, non-defensive level, women have less need for destructive tactics and men less need to run away or withdraw into silence. One of the goals of therapy for women is to help them have equal access to all aspects of their being. Women receive (from society) a tremendous amount of support and encouragement to be nurturing; to nurture their friends, husbands, and children. But they draw the line at themselves because they have also been taught to be self-sacrificing.

The result is a martyr who does not know or experience her own self-worth. All mature, nurturing love for others includes and is based on nurturing love for self and an expectancy of receiving this nurturing love from others as it is needed. We suggest that such a woman consider three steps toward becoming more balanced:

1. take the compulsion off nurturing others;

2. begin to nurture herself; and

3. begin to express all her feelings - especially anger.

While society expects women to be intuitive and have a lot of feeling and emotion, it often devalues and degrades women for experiencing these same things. An interesting contradiction in the Broverman Study is that the stereotyped female qualities of nurturing, intuitive understanding, perception, and concern for others are also seen as the qualities that make a good psychologist. Since most therapists are men (and one would hope most therapists are "healthy"), then a healthy male-therapist should be in good touch with his inner feminine self. This paradox is often overlooked.

Talk uni-sex all you want and argue that the only difference between men and women is the ability to bear children but we still seem to prefer our women soft and loving, and our men strong and virile.

The truth is we are BOTH masculine and feminine - all of us - and need to comfortably accept this beautiful truth:

ALL OF US NEED TO BE STRONG, ASSERTIVE, INDEPENDENT, INTELLECTUAL, TAKE CHARGE LEADERS, WITH ELEMENTS OF LOVING, KINDNESS, SUPPORTIVE, CARING, NURTURING AND WITH SUBTLE EMOTIONS.

As such, we can truly be INTER DEPENDENT - which is the best of both worlds: the ability to survive and take care of ourselves under all conditions, combined with the ability to cooperate and share, give and receive, take care of and be cared for.

This identity is the basis for our sexuality. We are born both sensual and sexual. Much has been made of the factual information that baby boys have erections and baby girls lubricate even in their mother's womb, and this phenomenon continues every ninety minutes of sleep time the rest of their lives. For many, its every 90 minutes while awake, also.

To be sensual means to be in touch with one's bodily sensations - tuned in, responsive to, experiencing and enjoying. It includes sexual feelings and desires, but is certainly not limited to them. Anyone who has experienced an infant is aware of a purely sensual entity, totally immersed in the delight of his own appetites, sensations and bodily functions. Delighting in sight, touch, taste, feel and smell. No one teaches a child how to touch or respond to touch; how to love or be loved. In an emotional sense or from a psychological perspective, we say that a child learns to love by BEING loved and there is no other way to learn it.

However true that may be, the child is also born with an innate ability to reach out and touch someone and do it right. NO ONE IS SO PURELY SEDUCTIVE AS A CHILD. That is their job description: to seduce the world by purely being themselves as an innocent expression of the total joy of BEING. The loss of this pure joy of being may be the most important and damaging loss growing up fosters upon us.

It may be threatening to see this in print but this seductive nature is the major cause of child molestation. Freud's biggest mistake was to place an adult's thoughts, motives, and desires in the body and mind of an innocent child.

This is exactly what happens to a mixed-up, neurotic, sexually and emotionally hungry adult who experiences the child being flirtatious, sensual, touching and seductive, and sees this as a sexual come-on. Either he interprets the child as deliberately coming on to him in a sexual manner or finds that no matter what the child's motives, he can't resist the pure sensual energy.

Even if the child is precocious and sexually curious, there is no way for the child to totally understand the full consequences of what is going on in the relationship. A little girl gets her sexual identity of what a women is from her mother. "Mother is a woman - I am a woman in bloom. What she is, is what I am to become. I identify with her many roles in life and how she plays them out (either liking or disliking what I see) and I try them on for size. I dress in her clothes, act out her roles, use her words and voice intonation, and generally mimic what I see."

Part of this acting out is to experience a woman's relationship with a man. Mother's primary man is the husband-father in the home. This is also daughter's primary man.

In a very real sense, daughter's job as a daughter is to "seduce" her father: flirt outrageously, love and touch, without restraint, compete shamelessly for attention. All this for the express purpose of receiving a response that proclaims: "You are beautiful, loving, loved, adorable, admired. I see and respond to what you totally are and I approve of it all."

EVERY WOMAN NEEDS A WARM, LOVING, PHYSICAL, AFFECTIONATE, ACCEPTING, KIND AND SENSUAL RELATIONSHIP WITH FATHER - THAT IS NOT SEXUALLY THREATENING TO EITHER ONE OF THEM.

To the extent she receives this she will grow to be a warm, sensual and sexual woman, relating warmly, openly and comfortably with men in both casual and intimate relationships. To the extent she does not get this, she will be handicapped in these relationships.

Father is the key here.

Daughter is "doing her thing" with little concern for ultimate consequences. She will not be threatened unless father is. If the father is threatened by his daughter's sexuality, if he is afraid he might have sexual intercourse with her, he may pull back or run away, and the daughter feels this anxiety and experiences it, too, but without necessarily conscious understanding of why. Consciously or unconsciously, she feels her sexuality so powerful even her own father can't handle it. If father is overwhelmed so am I, and all the little boys my age can't handle it either.

If father does molest or have intercourse with his daughter, an even worse thing happens. Now she has beaten mother at mother's adult game, and again, does not know the limits of her own sexuality. She is burdened also with the guilt of what she has done and usually grows up feeling totally responsible for the act. It seems very difficult for the daughter to accept the fact that father might be to blame. She goes on in life feeling the only way one can satisfactorily express love to men is sexually. She may like or dislike this and react accordingly.

For instance, as a result one girl may be totally turned off by sex and have difficulty giving herself to any man. On the other hand, her twin sister might become a nymphomaniac who cannot get enough sex. Each woman has a deep sexual problem but expresses it with exactly opposite symptoms.

Of the clients I've treated who were sexually molested by father, another intriguing stereotype emerges. Most find they are even more angry with mother than father for several reasons.

1. How can a small child compete and "win" over a fully sexual adult? If mother were meeting dad's sexual needs, this would not have happened. (Not always, but usually a correct assumption.)

2. Mother did not find a way to protect me from father. She's the adult and should have picked up on what was happening.

3. I can't tell mother or go to her for help because:

    a. She'll blame me

    b. She's too dependent to leave him and then I'll really be stuck

    c. She won't believe me

    d. She'll divorce him and I'll be responsible for breaking up the marriage and she'll hate me for that.

Unfortunately, all or part of the above comes true, more often than not.

A good father understands his daughter's role-playing seductiveness and responds with warmth, love and appreciation. He is taking care of his adult sexual needs in an adult, sexual manner and has no need to use or abuse his daughter in this fashion. He is not threatened, does not pull away, but helps orchestrate the relationship in a supportive, caring way. This gives daughter what she needs: validation, love and physical affection that is normal and appropriate. Whether we like to admit it or not, most sexuality traits of women can be traced directly to their relationship with father.

Society has given women and men very different cultural messages about sex. Religion, in particular, and the culture in general, have given both a generalized statement historically that sex is bad and therefore should be reserved for marriage and adulthood. Dictionary definitions of sensual, for instance, include terms such as preoccupied with bodily or sexual pleasures, lustful, licentious, lewd - rather negative connotations. Masturbation has been put down as "self-abuse" or sinful to both sexes until the past few years.

BUT IT'S ALWAYS BEEN MORE NEGATIVE FOR GIRLS THAN BOYS. THE SIMPLEST KEY AS TO WHY IS - GIRLS GET PREGNANT, BOYS DON'T.

So, the culture has prescribed part of the ritual of growing into manhood as an ever-increasing, dominant and insatiable lust for women. BOYS ARE SUPPOSED TO DEMAND AND PUSH FOR SEX WITHOUT RESTRAINT.

*ALL MEN'S DAUGHTERS ARE **VIRGINS***

*ALL MEN'S SONS ARE **STUDS***

THEREIN LIES A HELLUVA PROBLEM

GIRLS ARE SUPPOSED TO SAY NO.

This is why most men have difficulty believing in the concept of rape. "She must want it as much as I do - she's been programmed to say 'no' - I'm programmed to overcome her resistance because she really wants me to. If she admits this, she is a slut or a whore, so she has to play the game."

The irony is we tend to believe this contradictory, inflammatory, stereotypical and degrading concept of male and female sexuality even in the sophisticated '90's.

*IF IT'S TRUE THAT
"WOMEN GIVE SEX
TO GET AFFECTION"
AND
"MEN GIVE AFFECTION
TO GET SEX"*

*...THEN WE ARE NOT
REALLY PARTICIPATING IN THE SAME EVENT.*

Men and women have historically accepted the stereotype that men are sexual predators. "Men cannot control themselves sexually, this is their nature, sex is primarily to satisfy and please men, men are by far, the more sexual creatures, they are driven by their sexual nature and calmed only by proper sexual release."

So, we learn to tolerate man's adultery or sexual infidelities as bound to happen to the best of us from time to time.

At the same time, we hold our women up as pure and chaste, above the sexual clamor of life. She has no such low life animal instincts and needs but is sexually turned on by romance and love and mostly pleased by the satisfying of her mate. If you believe this has no application to life in modern society, explore your deep, inner feelings. We may have learned a lot intellectually over the past 25 years or so, but it's difficult to give up emotional feelings rooted in centuries of belief systems.

How many men do you know who still chase women into the bedroom, only to dismiss them as whores or sluts the next day. As a college professor, I hear that from my students constantly.

I once listened to an angry new client spew hate about his ex-wife after losing a child custody case to her in a bitter courtroom battle. He spent over 30 minutes cursing her as a "slut, whore, loose woman, who could screw anything that moved."

When he paused for a moment to catch his breath, I casually inquired about HIS current sex life.

*IF MAN IS REALLY
A SEXUAL ANIMAL
SEEKING CONQUEST . . .*

*HOW COME IT'S THE WOMAN
WHO HAS MULTIPLE ORGASMS?*

There was an instant smile, the body sat up straight and a satisfied expression defined his face. "Oh, I am very sexually active."

"That's very interesting. Your ex-wife is a whore and YOU are very sexually active."

"My God, I did say that, didn't I?"

CHAUVINISM IS ALIVE AND WELL IN CONTEMPORARY SOCIETY.

Women are well aware that they still to some degree, play the sexual tension game. She is allowed to tease and encourage and play the man like a fisherman with a great marlin on the reel - slow enough to keep him interested - not too much to look desperate or easy. "Do I have to kiss him tonight to get another date tomorrow?" has become "How soon do we have sex to keep his interest?"

To some degree, aggressive women have turned this around and swapped roles with the men, leaving both sides confused. "Do I open a door, light a cigarette, pick up the check for a lady or will this offend her as weak and incapable?"

THE TRUTH IS WOMEN ARE BY FAR THE MORE SEXUAL OF THE SPECIES, ALWAYS HAVE BEEN AND ALWAYS WILL BE.

Our society has long known of the sexual limitations of men such as refractory periods after orgasm, when it takes time to recharge the penis to erection for a second orgasm. For men to have an ultimate limit on how many orgasms they can have in a period of time, regardless of stimulation. There is a limit for all men. There is no refractory period or limit for women, healthy women who have learned how to be sexual, with no self-imposed limits.

God in His infinite wisdom, decided that man was too stupid to learn to be sexual, so He hung the plumbing where man couldn't miss it, hung the arms at an appropriate level so that contact was inevitable, and charged up the battery with 500 million new sperm each day - fussing to be free. Then came the message that a woman's body is beautiful and soft and greatly to be desired visually and kinesthetically. Orgasm was automatic; a gift of puberty and proof of emerging manhood. All this to overcome man's built-in limitations.

Woman, on the other hand, was not so lucky and this may have been God's greatest mistake (with a lot of help from His friends). A woman's sex organs are not as freely available. Some women who have been married and having sexual relations for years still haven't discovered them. She must learn to be orgasmic. It is not an automatic switch turned on at puberty. All she gets at puberty is the ability to become pregnant and a 30-day "changing of the guard".

Orgasms are not automatic and it is very possible for a woman to go through her entire life without having one - even if she is having consistent intercourse. This is not possible for a man. We can only assume that the ability to become pregnant and the limitless potential of female sexuality were so strong and scary to Society, she was left on her own to discover and explore her potential, while being discouraged on all sides.

We have had a sexual revolution for the past 25 years. Sex has become more open and accepted in our society. Appropriate sexual information is available and widely disseminated for general use. Women have benefited the most from this. In the days of the Kinsey surveys about four times more men were having sex before marriage than women. (A small group of women had a monopoly.) Now, it's almost dead even. Women have been given permission to lust after men's bodies. They now masturbate

A NYMPHOMANIAC

    IS ONE WHO GETS
    *MORE SEX THAN **YOU** DO*

    *AND **ENJOYS** IT MORE*
    THAN YOU DO . . .

BUT NOT AS MUCH AS SHE SHOULD!

and explore their own sexuality and routinely learn to be orgasmic. They actively and openly pursue men and initiate sexual contact.

Yet, it is disturbing to me that many sophisticated, successful, sexually active women of all ages still have not become comfortable with their sexuality. I do therapy in California, the cutting edge of permissiveness. If these women are having trouble with sexuality, what about the rest of the country? All of these women need to hear the message that within their bodies they have full access to the ultimate secrets and pleasures. The epitome of this problem was a 24-year-old, beautiful, sexy client of mine, extremely educated, who partied every night, scared to death she was going to miss something. She used drugs and alcohol to feel good and be socially acceptable, desperately desirous of men lusting after her, however totally overwhelmed and frightened when they always did.

A mass of contradictions who had never had an orgasm nor could she even bring herself to look at her sex organs with a mirror or touch herself for sexual pleasures.

Woody Allen said it to be funny, but it is a natural and beautiful truth:

"Masturbation is making love to someone who really cares."

Learning about one's self by trial and error of personal exploration and arousal is an important step toward sexual maturity for both men and women.

BOYS AND MOTHERS

What does a boy need from mother? Is his sexuality as fragile and directly connected to mother as his sister's seems to be to father?

IT IS SAID THAT SOME MEN BECOME HOMOSEXUALS BECAUSE THEY HATE WOMEN

THAT IS ALSO TRUE OF SOME HETEROSEXUALS

I would believe that it is at some deeper level, but the application is more subtle and indirect. Because of the supportive parenting of society giving strong pressure to act out sexuality as a ritual of manhood, as well as nature's daily prodding for orgasmic relief, most men are going to be sexual and certainly orgasmic. How they express it and use it to relate to women is more difficult to interpret at times.

A boy gets his sexual identity of what a man is from father. "This is what a man is and what I am supposed to grow into." He literally crawls into his father's body in a spiritual or fantasy sense to experience manhood. Then he acts it out with mother, practicing what it means to be a man with his primary, safe woman - MOTHER.

Every boy needs the same warm, loving, physical, affectionate, accepting, kind and sensual relationship with mother that the girl needs with father, but in our culture, it is more common for mother to give that kind of love to both children than for father to do so. That's why we call unconditional love "Mother love" and conditional love "Father love".

Unconditional love: I love you because you exist and need no other reason to love you. Nothing you may do can stop me from loving you. This is pure emotion and feeling, symbolic of the feminine side of life, identified as pure mother.

Conditional love: I love you because you meet my conditions, obey me, share my values, make me proud of you, and follow in my footsteps. This is more intellectual than emotional, and based on responsible living in a real, adult world.

Again, mother is symbolic of the love, nesting, nurture, food and protection. Father is symbolic of the outside world, risk taking, growth and adult responsibility.

There is a difference between mother and father as **symbols** and mother and father as real people. Real mother and father need to give both kinds of love: a balance of "love regardless" and an "expectancy of being responsible".

What I feel boys need from their mothers in learning to relate to women in an adult fashion is ANGER. Boys need to learn how to fight with mother, experience and express both love and hate and find that neither of them are destroyed by this full range of emotions. We can fight and still love each other. "Mother cannot castrate me and my anger cannot destroy her. She has the power and authority, however, to discipline and control without the help of dad."

If there is a consistent weakness in men-women relationships, it is that men cannot deal comfortably with emotions - their own - and especially a woman's emotions. The only emotion a man is given permission to feel is anger and he can't express that to a woman. If the woman becomes upset and either cries or yells, the man generally runs away. So many competent, efficient, leadership-oriented men cannot bring these skills home from work and apply them to personal relationships.

There is actually a feeling of panic and many men report **terror** when a woman raises her voice or breaks down into tears. They seem to have no resource supply of choices - what to do, how to respond. Their feelings literally go numb, the machinery shuts down as though to avoid exploding or making a mistake, and they either physically or emotionally run away.

Learning to fight appropriately with one's mother is the best preparation for marriage. This involves mutual respect - the mother must give her son the right to his feelings and the right to express them with intensity. Intensity does not imply disrespect or attack. The mother who leaves the anger, discipline and punishment to father, with father "protecting" her with "You can't talk to your mother that way" is giving a message to the son that women are weak and fragile and you can't take them on. This is a disservice to both men and women. I deal with this more fully in another chapter. However mother must provide a consistent model of behavior for her son. If mother swears and curses at him, she should expect the same in return. She sets the standard. If mother can get angry and express that anger directly, she also can expect and demand the same back from her son. From this, the son learns several things: "Mother is strong and I had better respect her," "Mother respects my feelings and allows me to express them and disagree with her if I do it appropriately," and "Mother is not fragile and/or weak." Mother can also teach her son that it is O.K. for her to cry and be vulnerable and upset and it is O.K. for him as well to experience these feelings. This should carry over to his adult relationships.

Going back to our original symbols - Father is the symbol of anger and strength for both boys and girls with Mother the symbol of love and protection.

FATHER	MOTHER
ANGER	LOVE
STRENGTH	PROTECTION
BOY	GIRL

The boy sees what he is supposed to be. As a young, growing man, he identifies with Father's anger and gets love from Mother.

The girl identifies with Mother's love and protection as an example of her destiny and experiences anger and strength from Father.

NOW, each needs to know if they can cross-fertilize. The girl gets love from Mother, can she ALSO experience it from Father? Father protects me, can he also LOVE me? The boy gets anger from Father, can he ALSO fight with Mother and experience HER anger as well as the love? This is how a normal, healthy child develops **both** his masculinity and femininity - by identifying with those qualities in BOTH parents and by experiencing those qualities in interaction with both parents.

To the extent a boy experiences his Mother as strong and assured, with a full range of emotions from vulnerable to anger, able to express it all without destroying or being destroyed AND able to grant the same to her son, the stronger, kinder and more loving man he will grow to be. To the extent he sees his Mother as loving but weak, or dominant and castrating, he will grow up fearing, resenting or being uncomfortable with women and his own feminine emotions.

The fact that society is in transition with the symbolic line between the roles of men and women blurring and less traditional, doesn't change the above truth. This is not an old-fashioned, outdated, chauvinistic appraisal of men and women. Definitions of masculinity and femininity have not changed - the way people express or live out those definitions is what is in the process of change. Our chauvinistic heritage has consistently robbed men and women of great portions of self-hood. Men can remain masculine and still experience the full range of femininity (softness, love, vulnerability and receptiveness) that is ALSO theirs and makes them complete and appropriate without being labeled effeminate.

Women can remain feminine and experience the masculine qualities (assertiveness, leadership, anger) that make them balanced and complete without being labeled bitch.

In our new society, that promotes equality, and inter-changeable sexual role models, the child can experience the best of both worlds - interchangeable parents that are appropriate to whatever the situation calls for and who give permission (by word and example) for the children to do and BE the same. If fathers are truly

IF TO BE FEMININE IS TO BE
GENTLE, WEAK, DELICATE AND MODEST . . .

AND A FEMINIST IS ONE WHO ADVOCATES
FEMINISM . . .

ARE FEMINISTS REALLY
ADVOCATING THAT WOMEN
SHOULD BE   GENTLE,
*   WEAK,*
*   DELICATE*
*   AND MODEST*

masculine and mothers truly feminine, but also able to cross roles, the children will have stronger sexual identity, not confusion about who they are.

We are obviously aware that most parents aren't that healthy and don't do the best job of rearing children. Are we therefore doomed to loveless relationships and sentenced to three years each of intensive therapy to become well? Not really!

To the extent our own child needs were met while growing up, we find our social relationships to be an extension and validation of positive life experiences and we will continue to use them to grow. To the degree they were not met, we will use these social life experiences to "reparent" ourselves and meet those child needs as we also meet the adult challenges and growth requirements of life.

"HOW'S MY **WHAT** LIFE?"

Chapter 6

Sexuality and It's Expression of Self

Touching, caressing, enjoying, realizing the full potential of sensual joy and sexual fulfillment is an important step in discovering the SELF. The infant child first experiences love through the body - physical contact - skin to skin. Contact that says, I love you, admire you, you are special, I delight in the experience of you.

There is a physical, emotional and spiritual need, that we never lose - the love touch. The infant cannot experience his own body in the fullest sense - all the sensations of pure exuberant, unadulterated JOY, PLEASURE, HAPPINESS, EXCITE-MENT - without being touched. Children DIE if not touched - and so do adults - it just takes longer.

The child discovers SELF - IDENTITY - through the body. Touching and being touched, being loved and loving back.

The ultimate purpose of life is to fully know, experience and fulfill one's SELF. What else can be important - how else can it be said? All our DOING and BUSY-NESS really comes out of that need.

The sad truth is that we get so busy meeting obligations, making a living or trying to have fun that we never get around to the essential ultimate task - to know SELF. We are also experiencing a generation of selfish, self-centered, hedonistic, drug addicted, "feeling good" enculturated young people who are trying to get the maximum pleasure out of self and life, and they are missing the point as much as their uptight, work-ethic parents.

The older generation looked to work and the satisfaction of being productive, using and experiencing talents and energies to know the self, build confidence and self esteem. And it worked. When we stop using ourselves productively and creatively, we lose self. But in accomplishing this the older generation left out an equally important ingredient - not only left it out but ridiculed and degraded it - perhaps out of fear of personal need for it. The ingredient was pure sensual experience and pleasure. This is also an important aspect to fully knowing the self.

Young people delight in rejecting parental values. Perhaps the funniest example of childhood rebellion is in watching the offspring of pot-smoking, communal living, politically radical anti-everything hippies becoming hard core, right wing Republicans. The ultimate retribution. The battle cry of parents has always been "Just wait - your kids will do to you what you've done to me" and it happens.

Part of discovering the self is in what we do, accomplish, intellectualize and experience in the outside world. The other half is in experiencing the inside world of emotions, feelings, sensations and reactions to that outside world. People who take a totally hedonistic, instant pleasure route, with no desire to be productive or responsible, asking the world to take care of them while they stay in an infantile state, are also missing the point.

Happiness, joy and ecstasy are products of experience, natural consequences of our behavior and actions, creative, productive and expressing aspects of who we are. Using the artificial means of drugs and alcohol produces an artificial high, joy, happiness based on the effects of the drug - not truly tuning in to one's own feelings and emotions. There is no substitute for the real

thing! Artificial highs result in artifical lows - neither based on any reality other than a change in bodily chemistry and certainly not connected with true feelings or emotions, true self image or self worth. A balance of focus that evokes us to see, experience, recreate and validate the true self is an ultimate blending of emotions and intellect, productivity and pure, raw elation.

The intellect supplies the reason and rationality of behavior and living, while the emotions report back to us a feeling response of how we are being affected by the consequences of these thoughts and actions. The intellect, in turn, interprets the feelings and evokes us to understand their origins, listen to their messages and make appropriate decisions for further action.

How does all the above apply to our sexuality and how we express it? A healthy human being first of all grants himself permission to fully experience and express all his emotions, feelings and sensual experiences without guilt or embarrassment, accepting this as an appropriate and necessary product of the true self. The reason he can do this without discomfort is that he trusts himself and has proven himself to be a reasonable, trustworthy person that functions easily within the concepts of his own morality and judgement.

A man sees a beautiful woman and becomes sexually excited and interested in pursuing his feelings. He gives himself permission to "know" how he feels without guilt. He turns to his intellect for the options on how to approach her. It is **not** appropriate to grab, fondle, rape or be crude. It is appropriate to strike up a conversation and try to know her well enough to see if there is a basis for further relationship. Or he may decide to just enjoy the feelings without acting on them.

There was a period of time in psychotherapy when the edict was to FEEL at all costs. People were seen as too much into their heads and controlling through intellect. "Turn off your head and feel." Telling a neurotic, psychotic, psychopath or anyone who has ben totally out of touch with his true self and integrity to trust his feelings is equivalent to handing a loaded pistol to a five year old so we can play "cowboys and Indians" together. YOU play with him - I'm going to lunch!

We learn to trust our feelings slowly, carefully, tentatively, by trial and error, hopefully in a safe environment (a mature parental love, a therapist's office, or with a loving spouse), so if we fall or fail, there is someone to pick us up, comfort us and kiss it well. This is dealt with in more detail later in the book.

One of the most impactful emotions we experience is our sexual identity and all that it entails. There is no way of ever measuring or knowing how deep the sex act, along with the encompassing mating rituals we perform, effect our BEINGNESS and sense of total self worth. The act at worst represents some positive feelings of power, loveability or well-being. At best it is the ultimate expression of every aspect of our physical, emotional and spiritual being. Positive experiences of sexuality confirm the self as a truly sexual entity, capable of experiencing the utmost in physical and emotional pleasure and generously bringing this same pleasure to a partner. Sexuality brings the opportunity of combining our own inner perceptions of the sexual self with those outer perceptions of the sexual self and with those outer perceptions of how others see us. This helps to finely tune the focus of who we are, bringing confidence in ourselves and how that being fits in society's frame of reference.

This affects not just our romantic involvements, but all our relationships: from soul mate to child, to associate, to friend. With this confidence comes strength, security in who we are and feeling good about it. One step further into this security is the recognition of our body, our mind, our gender to be an equal entity to someone else.

The true focus of who we are creates a comfort level to accept the very material, biological necessity of being sexual. To enjoy the pleasures of our own body and enjoy satisfying the needs of the one we are with is the truest affirmation and for that matter confirmation of our own confidence and identification. To accept this as a bodily need, a need the same as for food or water - for the psyche - to satisfy and fulfill this need for both the self and the other - sharing - is one of the fundamental aspects of what it means to be a human being, helping to create the total picture, the total self.

The sexual drive, the biological as well as psychological desires, should remain objective as well as subjective and be integrated into the total scheme of daily living.

The more we share ourselves in various relationships (with or without the sex act), the more we are adding to the clarity of our own sexual identity. Sexual awareness and identity therefore help to perfect the focus of our inner self and the overlay of outer reality to more completely share with a soul mate or someone of similar vibrations for a moment - a day - or a lifetime.

Touching, caressing, caring and sharing who we are, the drive and assertiveness to know our OWN need, seek that need and fulfill that need is more than just selfish clamoring for sexual pleasure, BUT THE URGENT desire to fulfill the sexual pleasure of our mate, as well. I dare say the greatest satisfaction of the ultimate loving individual in a true blending relationship is the ability and joy of satisfying the partner.

Drive and sexual identity go far beyond making love. Being seen by the outer world as attractive and desirable, as a beautiful, sexual entity combines with many other facets to complete the package of self worth and well being.

At 16 years of age, my first sex manual instructed me that it was not fair to make love like a rabbit. It was a man's responsibility to be certain the woman was satisfied first. To quote the great sexologist, Leo Durocher, "Nice guys finish last." A man must therefore "earn" his orgasm by giving her one first and not just selfishly use his partner for gratification. Most women would agree with this philosophy of not being selfish and rightfully so, but in all honesty, it does put an insidious pressure to perform on both sexes.

The man has this pressure to prove he is a good lover by staying power and technique, with her climax as the ultimate proof or reward. The woman had better cooperate, however, by always having one, or he feels like a failure. Years ago I had a very sexual couple in therapy in their late 30's, second marriage for both, very much in love and sexually aggressive. Her one sexual complaint was that even though she loved sex and was very orgasmic, she wasn't always in the mood to work that hard. She was always in the mood to make love and enjoy sharing and pleasing each other, but did not always need an orgasm to feel complete. Her husband always ended by asking if she had "come" in a little boy voice, asking for approval. If she said "no", he went into great personal recrimination of not being a good lover, not deserving her, being no good, etc.

She asked me to explain to him how ridiculous that was, and that he WAS a good lover, he DID please her it wasn't necessary for her to have an orgasm each time they made love. When we discussed it at length, and I asked if he understood the principle, he replied, "Yes, I understand. She is a selfish lover."

The man is primarily responsible for his own sexuality, pleasure and satisfaction. The woman is primarily responsible for her own. The world's greatest lover cannot guarantee success with a sexually turned off partner. Demanding your partner (male or female) to have an orgasm so you have proof you are a good lover is as selfish as not caring at all. The sex act is an exact metaphor for love and life and vice versa. Each of us is responsible for our own actions, pleasures and personal results. Each of us is responsible to our partner only to be the best person we are capable of being. It's a mutual inter-dependence and inter-relationship that requires both to be complete.

Because the man tends to be more visually excited or attracted (though, that is becoming less and less true) the mating ritual might start with his seeing an attractive woman and saying to himself, "I'd like to look at, touch and make love to that beautiful woman." He is NOT saying, "Boy would she love for me to touch her," but rather, "The thought of touching her, making love to her is exciting to me."

Even in our era of sexual revolution, it is disappointing and exasperating to hear how few men really know how to make love or that the kissing, fondling, caressing, and skin to skin contact is the actual love act. What we call "foreplay", the play that goes on BEFORE the sex act, IS REALLY THE SEX ACT!!! Intercourse and other stimulation of the genitals are and can be part of the total experience. It's NOT a contest to see how quickly one finishes nor an endurance test to see who can "last" the longest. Orgasm for both is the dessert to cap the meal.

But I have gotten ahead of myself. The man approaches the woman for the primary purpose of pleasing himself, with the pleasure of exploring her body. If she finds him attractive and there is mutual interest, the woman is usually turned on by his expression of desire for her. Lest you fear this "pickup" is too quick and morally loose, it does no damage to the illustration to have them married (to each other!). Once the love making starts the man begins to enjoy the pleasure of what he anticipated, revelling in the delights of her lovely body in his arms. Of course, it is extremely important to the man that she desires him also, and takes pleasure in his advances. What good is a desirable body that does not respond to YOU? So, the man is being sexually excited by his making love to the woman. His excitement can be turned off or enhanced immediately by her response. As she reacts by her own sexual response and excitement from his touch, he becomes even MORE excited.

Because she is pleasured and excited by her partner, the woman feels a need to reciprocate - not just to pay a debt, but she has her own need to please and stimulate the man. She also takes delight in touching, caressing, kissing and holding HIS body. Not primarily because he wants or needs it, but to please and pleasure HERSELF. Of course, she would be a fool not to want him to want it and enjoy it. As you can easily

OVERHEARD ON CAMPUS . . .

"ALL MY BOYFRIEND WANTS IS SEX - SEX - SEX . . .
WHAT'S IN IT FOR ME?"

"OH, AREN'T YOU PLANNING TO BE THERE?"

see, this COULD BE two totally selfish and self-absorbed individuals, completely lost in their own worlds, oblivious to their partner's needs and responses. What was described could be identified as "masturbation by use of a partner", not making love.

While each partner's PRIMARY interest and concern is doing what he enjoys doing because it brings him pleasure, MOST of the pleasure he receives comes from the responses and excitement of the partner, which send back the message that HE IS A GREAT LOVER. So a secondary and compelling interest is in the satisfaction derived by the partner as a result of pleasing both. Pleasing one, pleases the other. So each partner has to be just as tuned in to the other's reaction as to his own or the whole experience collapses. As they take turns pleasing each other, giving and receiving, building the mutual excitement, both become totally satisfied and the experience is complete. If sex is acted out as selfish, it is little more than masturbation and physical relief. It is immaterial who the partner is or how the one feels about the other, and leaves both partners feeling empty, though the selfish partner is usually too stupid to know it. Both partners have been cheated because so much more was available to both.

If sex is acted out as a selfless gesture of good will you get the same result. Worse yet, imagine two partners, each actively sacrificing his own pleasure and concentrating totally on the other. THERE IS NO RECEIVER. BOTH FAIL MISERABLY. BOTH FEEL CHEATED. (I am aware there are exceptions to all rules and at times one partner will simply please the other because you choose to for a variety of possible reasons. What I have illustrated is sex at his highest functioning.)

The purpose of sexuality - to each individual - is balance and focus - the fine line of sanity and happiness. Without happiness and balance we have no real reason for living. Many (perhaps most) people walk around really dead - dead inside - missing all the sunsets of life, the rainbows of their being. Don't let this be your experience. Open your eyes - look at life with all the tender joy of loving - YOUR VERY BEST FRIEND - YOURSELF. Experiencing your sexuality brings into full focus and awareness the confirmation of inner and outer layers of truth - validating your true BEING.

Loving yourself will joyfully enable you to bring the full value and benefit of that loving, peaceful experience to a soul mate - a life partner, who loves self as you do and thereby both of you have that exciting something EXTRA and special to bring to your love relationship - YOURSELF. What greater gift can you bring to another. And the receipt of and response to this gift adds to the dimension of the gift itself - A POSITIVE AND ENLIGHTENING SELF FULFILLING PROPHECY.

Take time each day - a simple exercise of sitting quietly for inner focus, centering oneself, relaxing the mind, totally yielding the body to be perfect and well, and in tune with the vibration of inner peace and serenity. Heart open and mind a sieve through which tension and frustration can be dispelled, retaining only a balance of I AM GOOD - I AM WISE - I AM SENSUAL - I AM SEXUAL - I AM COMPLETE.

"YOU SEE, IT DIDN'T HURT"

Chapter 7

Impact of Parents on the Self

A classic text in the area of biofeedback and the mind-body connection of illness is aptly entitled: *Mind As Slayer, Mind As Healer,* and demonstrates that just as all physical illness originates in the mind from unresolved stress and distorted perceptions, all healing also starts in the mind, and as discussed in Chapter Four, anyone with the power to negatively activate that body has the same power to heal it.

Sometimes I'm tempted to write my own sequel to that book - ***Parents As Slayer, Parents As Healer*** for the same general truths prevail here. No one has the intense power to maim and inflict pain nor the amazing healing touch as one's parents.

Perhaps more has been written on the subject of parent-child relationships in psychological literature than any other and I hesitate to add to the confusion. But, how does one write about the SELF without including the impact of the parents? Parents are the original contact lenses through which we view, interpret, understand and relate to all the world that comes thereafter. The universal symbols of Mother and Father are closely tied to our universal meanings of masculine and feminine. MOTHER represents the feminine attributes of life: soft, receptive, emotional, caring, nurturing, womb, love, security, and unconditional love. Our original view of all the above is filtered through the way we perceive our particular Mother figure.

FATHER represents the masculine attributes of strength, anger, discipline, courage, penetration, aggressiveness, logical intellect, the outside world, work, career and

CHILDREN —

YOUR SECOND CHANCE TO MESS IT UP

YOUR OWN CHILDHOOD
WASN'T BAD ENOUGH?

conditions that account for both success and conditional love. Our original view of this world is filtered through the actual Father with whom we relate on a daily basis.

As you can see, the symbolic representation is not necessarily close kin to what we experience in the real world growing up. For one thing, both sexes need and ARE **both** masculine and feminine, strength and softness, Mothering and Fathering, discipline and love, home and the outside world. We no longer have the sexual stereotypes of yesterday to fall back on.

It is my opinion that children need and fight for SPIRITUAL POSSESSION OF BOTH PARENTS. By this I mean they literally want to crawl inside each parent, feel what they feel, do what they do, and test out for themselves in the safe, limitless world of fantasy what it means to be a man, to be a woman, to be an adult.

Boys crawl inside Dad to get their personal identity of what a man is. Then they must act out this role of man with a safe, primary woman - Mother. In order to fully understand Mother's role as a woman, respondent to the masculine attention, they crawl inside her for a look on the other side - to feel what they are relating to.

Girls experience the same in reverse with Mother and Father, getting their sexual identity from Mother and "testing it out" with Father, but must also experience what

Father is like to know the other side. Good parents see, understand, and encourage this. Both parents become a safe environment to be explored, experienced and defined by each child.

MOTHERHOOD:

A LIFETIME OF PUNISHING FOR WHAT HE DID TO YOU AT CHILDBIRTH

A Job Well Done!

   Selfish, childish parents who never felt fully loved and appreciated themselves by their parents while growing up, tend to resent the demands and expectancies of parenthood. They compete with their children, on a child level, fighting for the attention of the spouse, feeling deprived and resentful of the love given to the child, feeling it as a great loss to themselves. This leaves the child confused. How can a boy relate to or get inside a hostile father who competes and resents, is not loving or warm. Then, when the boy desires to crawl into or experience Mother, the father becomes doubly dangerous and threatening. "Don't tread on my territory, kid, or you'll get trampled." It is tough to exercise your fantasies with either parent in these extreme conditions.

If the child is allowed to grow up without fulfilling the need to experience and relate to both the masculine and feminine aspects of the parents, which in essence is the formation of his own self integration, he cannot mature. His need for parenting continues into adulthood, creating dependency, hidden hostility and demands on a spouse or even his children, to "make up" for the parenting he missed. Talk about perpetuating the problem!

For years, psychotherapy has wrestled with the problem of what to do with one's par-

FATHERHOOD:

AN 18 YEAR SENTENCE FOR A ONE NIGHT STAND

ents. One side of the coin, Freudian or dynamically-based therapy, tends to blame parents for all the client's inadequacies and goes to great length to disclose and uncover hysterical traumas from which could be traced present symptoms. This process has often led therapists to be described as those one visits to "cop-out" on their parents, the dumping ground for all blame. Much of the client's growth seems to stop at the point of the parents, and accepts the client's "right" to hate them for their failure toward him and thereafter giving him "permission" to limp through life with the credo "What do you expect from a man with a broken leg?" Leaving a man a legacy of hate and an excuse to be lame hardly constitutes the summation of therapeutic growth. The only value in hate is to use it as motivation to win freedom to be truly your best self. (That will be more fully explained in the chapter.)

The other side of the psychological coin reflects the ideas of the modern-day therapists, ranging from Carl Rogers' Client-Centered Therapy to Behavior Modification, and from George Bach's Creative Aggression to Albert Ellis and Rational Emotive Therapy, including Gestalt and encounter groups. While their methods vary and are often diametrically opposed, they agree that history and parents have little real place in the therapeutic growth of today. In short, it doesn't matter what the cause of your difficulty, you have long since been divorced from that cause, and must change

*IF AT FIRST YOU
DON'T SUCCEED . . .*

*CRY A LOT . . .
AND BLAME SOMEBODY*

*IF IN THERAPY . . .
WHINE A LOT
AND BLAME
YOUR MOTHER*

today's behavior because it isn't meeting today's needs - you are no longer yesterday's child.

My own feeling is that the moderns ignore the fact that if an adult did not get his basic needs met and the proper "parenting" accomplished as a child, they are still not met today, and the phony relationships forced upon us when we were children (because we had no defense against them) often still persist in exactly the say way today, as adults.

Thus two conclusions stand out clearly. Even though we are adults, we often get locked into deceptive and destructive relationships with our parents that carry over into our adult lives and deeply affect the way we relate to our spouse and children.

Secondly, very few therapists seem to recognize a potentially powerful ally we might term "psychosomatic health". If our parents (inspite of deep love and good intentions) do, in fact, have the power to cause all types of psychological crippling effects on us, can they not also have the equally powerful and significant impact of psychological cure? No two people in the world have more potential for good and bad in the lives of each one of us than our parents. Let's turn on the "Parent Power" to heal the sick and crippling aspects of our personalities, and find a new kind of love, rather than a justification for hate.

Blame is not the issue. Few parents wake up saying, "Today, I am going to destroy my child." Their motivation may be good and they really do want to be effective parents, but sometimes they just don't know what the needs of the children are...or how to meet them. At various times, parents may have a good effect on their children or a bad one, but always an effect. The better the parents understand this cause and effect relationship, the better they can be in rearing healthy children and improving the relationship.

In order to be a healthy adult, you need to go back to the child and the relationship with your parents to know what your legitimate rights and needs are and take them seriously now. Then and only then, can you respond to the needs of others and successfully approach being in a parent role yourself.

For most of you reading this, I would guess that the relationship with your parents could best be described as "phony". For example, if you were asked to be honest and real with your parents, perhaps your answer would be something like this, "If I told my parents how I really felt, they would: a) have a heart attack, b) disown me, c) knock me clear across the room, d) never understand, e) bug me about it the rest of my life, etc., etc." If so, you fit the qualification for a phony relationship. In other words, both of you are cooperating in a conspiracy to pretend that the relationship is healthy, when in fact it isn't. Carrying on this pretense to protect yourself and your parents doesn't really meet anyone's needs. Because of this, you eventually begin to look around for help. Eventually you read a book or article, get into a psychology class, or go to therapy, and begin to realize that the relationship truly is phony.

The first real reaction to this revelation is inevitably anger; to the extent someone takes away your freedom, you will hate them. A phony relationship with your parents takes away your freedom to be yourself, and this leads to intense anger or hatred. The purpose of this chapter is to take you from the initial phony relationship - through the anger response - to the ultimate of a love relationship with your parents, which will truly win you back your freedom, to possibly finish some incomplete bonding of the child within you, indulge in the unconditional, authentic love, or just add to your adult support system of people who care about you and what happens to you.

*LOSS OF FREEDOM
EQUALS ANGER*

*ANGER IS
MOTIVATION TO
REGAIN FREEDOM*

*BITTER IS ADDING
UP THE COST.*

Two Types Of Anger

Before you can really deal with the phony-to-anger-to-love process, there is a need to clarify two different types of anger. Most of us are very afraid of anger and have a tendency to see it as only destructive and bad. It must be realized that there is destructive anger and there is constructive anger.

Destructive anger is punitive - it punishes others for whatever they have done to you or whatever you have **imagined** they have done to you. It is defensive in that it protects you from being hurt further. It attacks the other's character as the best means of punishing them or paying them back for hurting you. It covers up the real feelings which lie underneath: of hurt, embarrassment, and vulnerability. Destructive anger always starts with a "you" statement and assumes the worst motivations. "You deliberately hurt, attack, embarrass, or humiliate me because you don't like me and have malicious and vicious intent." "You see me as impugning your motives and attacking your character." "I certainly shall not give the impression that I am hurt or vulnerable or really care."

Constructive anger does exactly the opposite. It may be just as angry, loud or noisy; but it reveals feelings rather than covering them up. "I am angry with you because of what you did." It does not punish the other or defend against the other or attack the other, but clarifies and tries to tell how you feel and why. In the long run, it draws people together.

Constructive anger can be just as hurting and upsetting, but it talks about "me" and my feelings rather than "you" and your badness. "I feel hurt, embarrassed, or whatever as a result of your actions." Constructive anger can be expressed without creating an all-out battle.

Phil and Elaine had made a private agreement between themselves that they would never embarrass each other, or have arguments in public or in front of their friends. One night at a party, Elaine did something that embarrassed Phil very deeply, which he felt made him look like a fool. His destructive impulse was to lash back at Elaine in public and to embarrass her as badly as she had embarrassed him. Phil did not do this since he felt it would have made both of them look very bad. He did not know for certain if his wife had intentionally tried to embarrass him. He could have taken Elaine aside and talked to her privately in another room but he decided to wait until they got home. Phil struggled with himself the rest of the evening trying to decide whether or not she had acted deliberately to hurt him. Almost as soon as they walked through the door of their home, he asked her very simply and in a rather pleasant but hurt voice, "Are you aware of how I felt when you did...(this particular act)?"

The look on Elaine's face answered for her. She had no idea how her action appeared to him and had no intention of hurting him. Hearing his feelings expressed, she realized how he had interpreted her behavior and simply apologized. The constructive anger Phil expressed avoided a fight.

The destructive anger reaction would have assumed that Elaine had deliberately tried to embarrass and hurt Phil. He would have lashed out because of that assumption, attacking her character and "putting her in her place". Her reaction would have been equally defensive, and even if she knew she had not intended to hurt him, she would have had to defend herself against his stupid attack. She would have wound up really trying to hurt and punish him for his accusation.

By asking Elaine about her motivations and intentions, Phil made no assumption or accusation and gave her an opportunity to tell him exactly what she was feeling and what she was trying to say to him. Elaine might have said that she was angry with him at the time of the party. This would have given them an opportunity to deal with this in a reasonable way. As it was, she had no intention of hurting him and said so.

Destructive anger occurs between parent and child when each offended party assumes that the other is doing malicious things because of hate and both are trying to destroy each other. There is no alternative but to defend one's self at all costs. To the contrary, there is no harm or destructiveness in anger that confronts with the intent of healing a relationship and bringing love out of the chaos.

There are two very important factors to consider when analyzing this use of anger and what children need from their parents through this anger: 1) every child needs to know that he cannot destroy his parents; and 2) every child needs to know that his parents cannot destroy him. "Destroy" may sound like a strong word but many people literally experience a fearful "power of life and death" type relationship with their parents, and act as though one side or the other could literally be destroyed emotionally. "I won't be able to live without this relationship." Thus, the basic reason parents and children do not confront each other with their needs is because they are either afraid of destroying or being destroyed. If they destroy the other, they cannot live with the guilt and if they are destroyed, they cannot live with the pain. Of course, there is the reality that people do kill other people. That's not the focus here. The point is, that emotionally, you do not have the power of life and death over your parents; by the same token, they do not have the power of life and death over you. You can only be responsible for your own actions and have no control or responsibility over someone else's reaction, even if that reaction is to have a heart attack or to commit suicide. This may seem like a cold attitude, but it is not intended to be, and hopefully it will become more clear as we go along.

If I am afraid that my parents will be destroyed by my needs, I certainly do not want to risk the guilt of presenting my needs to them. By the same token, if I am afraid that their rejection of me can destroy me emotionally, I cannot risk that rejection with any type of confrontation of my needs and feelings. A child has a responsibility and obligation to himself and to his parents to first of all know what his needs are, and secondly, to present these needs to his parents.

"IF ONLY THEY COULD BOTTLE IT"

Revelation and Change

Every child has two things he needs from his parents: 1) Unconditional Love, "I love you because you exist and need no other reason to love you. There is nothing you can say or do that could cause me to stop loving you. I may not agree with all your values or ideas, or of your actions, but I love you and nothing can change that." And, 2) **you need your parents to reveal themselves to you**. You need to know who they are and why they are, above all else. You are the child, growing and changing, and the need for your parents to treat you differently as you mature, to agree with your values is vital. Since you can't see them as changing, there appears to be no hope for the relationship. Change is not the issue - revelation is. If you understand why your parents do the things **they** do, and feel the way **they** feel, it will help **you** relate differently to them and feel differently about them, and vice versa.

When a child feels unconditionally loved and knows that nothing can change that, when his parents tell him how they feel and why, he then goes very quickly to a third stage. He can now reveal himself to the parents so they understand why he is like he is. This point cannot be stressed enough...the real importance of parents and children revealing themselves to one another. Over and over again, in my office, I see proof that the breakdown in a relationship is due to bad communication of why we do the things we do. You may already know or think you know why, but for some reason, hearing them admit their fears and anxieties out loud makes a world of difference.

A beautiful eighteen year old student brought her parents in for an interview because she was afraid her father was physically going to beat her. He was a large man, well over six feet tall and weighted two hundred eighty pounds. She saw him as rather rigid. When he would tell her to do something, she would ask him, "Why?" At this, he would fly into a rage and become enormously angry and demand that she do it. If she continued to ask, "Why?" he would threaten to drive her into the wall with his fist, and she believed him.

The mother, father and daughter all came into the office for an interview and the recurring theme from the father was, "Tell my daughter not to ask me why!" From the daughter it was, "Get my father to explain to me why!" After an hour and a half of this hassling, the father was asked very directly what he was feeling in his body when his daughter looked him in the eye and said, "Why?" He became very thoughtful and took the question quite seriously. After a short period of time, he smiled and said, "Fear." That's the feeling. Fear. I'm afraid of her. I guess I'm just afraid of being wrong. My mother doesn't respect my judgement, and my wife certainly doesn't and when this eighteen year old kid comes along and tells me that she doesn't respect my judgement either, that's the last straw!"

The father was smiling and rather relaxed. In revealing his feelings to his daughter, he had learned something about himself that he didn't know. His daughter's reaction was spontaneous and surprised. She hadn't known this. The father was asked what would happen if the next time they had a confrontation or he told her to do something and she questioned "Why?" (and if he felt the anger rising within him), he would just say to his daughter, "There it is again. I feel afraid and very angry, I can feel myself wanting to attack you because I'm afraid you'll be right and I'll be wrong." What would your daughter do? Do you think she would react any differently than she does now? The father just smiled and nodded, "I think it would change every-thing."

Twenty year old Paul brought his father for a confrontation in a therapy session one day because he wanted to "tell him off". In the course of the confrontation, Paul was very angry and pointed out a particular problem that happened over and over again when he was a child. "When I would do something wrong, mother would never spank me, but warn me that Dad would take care of that when he got home. Then, you would come home and beat me up terribly. I never felt that this was fair since Mother would make you do her "dirty work" for her. I would go to my room and cry and about thirty minutes later you would come in on your hands and knees and apologize for what you had done. I always felt this was inconsistent. If you're going to spank me, why should you apologize - and if you're going to apologize and you know you are wrong, then stop beating me so badly. I always saw you as weak and phony."

The father began to cry as the boy talked. He said very softly to his son, "I know I have a terrible temper just like my father. When I was a little boy, the same thing would happen to me. My father would come home from work, take me to my room, and beat me up. I never knew why and he would never tell me what I had done wrong. I would become so frustrated and angry at my father for never telling me what I had done, that I always vowed if I ever had a son and had to spank him like my father spanked me, at least he was gonna' know why. When I came to your room thirty minutes later, it was not to apologize but to explain to you what you had done wrong and what I expected of you in the future - so you wouldn't do it again and I wouldn't have to spank you again. I do know that my anger was unreasonable and much too violent and I'm sorry about that."

Paul sat there rather stunned. All of his life he had seen his father was weak and phony and apologetic when he actually was trying to explain to his son how he felt and what he needed from him so that the son would be able to respond properly. Nothing had changed about the past except that now the son understood the father's feelings and motivations. Instead of feeling resentful and angry toward his father, he was saying, "Wow, my father really loves me."

Additionally, once the child knows what the parents are really feeling, change often does take place. If I react in a less defensive and less offensive manner to my parents, they are going to treat me differently. If I am more direct and honest with them regarding my feelings, they are going to be more direct and honest with me.

It would be an ideal situation if all parents knew their child's needs, anticipated them, and took care of them without the child having to present them at all. This just isn't the case. Children as individuals are different and parents are human and not always proficient at mind reading. There is no way a parent can meet a child's needs unless he knows what those needs are. At best, a parent can only guess at what the child is feeling.

A child has the responsibility to present his needs to the parents. To the extent he withholds this (for any reason), he is rejecting his parents by robbing them of the opportunity to "parent" him. I'll talk later about types of confrontation and methods of approaching your parents with these needs. Everyone is different and everyone will view this in a different fashion. The point is that each person must acknowledge to himself that he needs unconditional love and that he needs to know his parents. That's meeting your responsibility to yourself and also to your parents as a good child.

Parents Have Two Choices

In return, the parents have two choices: 1) they can accept your needs and meet them; or 2) they can reject your needs for whatever reason. This is reality and we have to accept that. Not all parents seem to be capable or willing to meet the needs of their children, but most will come through. They may not do it in the exact fashion desired, and may never be the perfect parents that you are looking for, but they can still meet your needs. Realistically speaking, because of their own sickness or problems, there are always parents who can't or won't. We read constantly in the newspaper about parents who beat, or desert, or even kill their children. Others are so defensive or sick that they blame everything on the child and cannot accept any responsibility for whatever problems may exist. The fear of your parents saying "No" is probably much more real than the possibility of them actually saying "No" - but it is nevertheless a distinct possibility and one that we have to face and deal with in advance.

If your parents accept your needs and give you the unconditional love and the revealing of themselves that you ask for, life takes on new meaning. It is very easy to go from phony, to anger, to love, and have a new love-relationship with your parents if this is their reaction. How could you do anything but love parents who are giving you this kind of feeling, acceptance, and understanding? I deeply feel that this will change every other meaningful relationship in a person's life - particularly those relationships with a spouse or child.

But what if the parents reject? Now what happens to the child? Is he destroyed?

Your mental health and emotional well-being do not depend on your parents or anyone else! What your parents do with your needs can either make it easier or harder for you to meet your needs, but it is not final.

You Have Two Choices

If your parents reject you, then you have two choices: 1) You can also reject your child needs; or 2) You can accept your own child needs as legitimate.

When the parent rejects the child, the appropriate reaction is hurt. Because nobody wants to feel hurt; the reaction is natural to compensate by rejection. "I don't need them, they're no good. I'm a big boy now, I can live without them. Who needs it!" When this happens, you are not only rejecting the parents, but your own needs as well. You are agreeing with your parents and, in essence, saying, "I do not need parents. I am an orphan who can live without them." This is a lie! Are needs legitimate only if they are met? Of course not!

If you are thirsty and need a drink of water, that is a legitimate need whether there is water readily available or none within a hundred miles. Your thirst is either legitimate or it is not legitimate, and has nothing to do with the availability of water. As a child, your needs for unconditional love and for parents to reveal themselves are legitimate whether they are met or not.

To deny your own need is to be an emotional cripple. The tendency follows - and this is the tragedy of it all - that when, as a parent yourself, your child comes to you and says, "Hey, Dad, I need you," your reaction will most likely be, "Go away you little creep, if I don't need parents, you don't either." Or if society has made you feel guilty enough not to be willing to admit this publicly, then you may try to overcompensate and smother the child with love. This reaction tends to create resentment, and actual jealousy, since the child is demanding and receiving something you didn't get from your own parents. Both extremes are wrong, and certainly not authentically meeting the needs of either you, the parent, or the child.

As the rejected child, you do have another option available, a different perspective to deal with the situation. Even though your parents have rejected your needs, you still accept these needs as legitimate and right. In this case, the child simply says, "I need a mother and a father. I need a mother's and father's unconditional love and emotional support and affection. I need to know my parents so that I can better discover who I am and what my own needs and values and desires are. I do not have this." The result is intense pain, grief, and mourning, a total acknowledgement and acceptance of the loss.

Perhaps this would be easier to understand in terms of a death. If as a child, your parents are taken away from you by a car accident or illness, you know what is legitimate to do. You go to a funeral and grieve and cry because you have been deprived of the love and presence of your parents. This grieving may last for a few days or a few months, but you cry it out and let yourself feel the deep sense of loss and deprivation. After a period of time, the grief passes and life continues. You don't ever lose the sorrow completely, and from time to time may remember your parents, you may cry and deeply miss them, and feel very badly about your loss. But, the grief seems to diminish. As a matter of fact, you may even enjoy the sorrowful memories of them; you may even enjoy remembering the sweetness of the times you did share with them.

If your parents reject you, this, in reality, is an emotional death. They have refused to meet your needs, but your needs live on. You must allow yourself to feel over-

*CHILDREN — GOD'S WAY OF PUNISHING
YOU FOR ENJOYING TOO MUCH SEX*

whelmed with the grief, the pain and the sorrow of what has happened to you. It is difficult to explain totally why or how this happens, but through this grieving, a healing takes place. By accepting the legitimacy of your own needs, and the acknowledgement that your needs were not met, you have, in effect, given yourself unconditional love. It frees you from having the negative influences of your mother and father, to continue, and you will no longer punish your children, or your spouse, for whatever grievances you may have had with your parents. You legitimately grieved and it's a finished issue. There is no need to perpetuate the pain.

Now, when your child comes to you and says, "Hey, I need you," your reaction will be, "Yes, I know what your needs are because I know what my needs were (as a child). Mine weren't met, but I certainly want to meet yours." The resentment is gone because you never denied the reality of your own needs as a child, and therefore, have no need to deny those of your child.

The Healing Power Of Confrontation

Confrontation is the missing link in most therapies that deals with parental relationships. It may seem like a very cruel, painful and hard thing to go through, and many times it is. It has to be made perfectly clear that the child is in no way rejecting his parents. He is accepting the reality that his parents have rejected him. In Biblical terms, he has asked them for good food and "...they have given him a stone." He is rejecting the bad food they gave him in the name of love. I believe very strongly that this is what Erich Fromm meant when he said in the *Art of Loving* that a mature person becomes his own mother and father in a very real sense, able to give himself unconditional love and acceptance.

A young man who had endured this tragic experience of being rejected by his mother was once asked by a friend, "And what have you done for a mother since?" Approximately four years had passed and this question had never been asked before, and the young man was taken aback. After considerable thought, he smiled and had his answer. He told his friend, "All my life I thought I had a pretty good relationship with my mother. All my life, also, I had collected mothers everywhere I went. It brought me a great sense of satisfaction to know that older women enjoyed mothering me, and making over me. With every girl I dated, it seemed I had a better relationship with her mother.

Then I went to therapy and found out that my relationship with my own mother was tinged with negative possessiveness. In the process of my therapy I tried working this out with her, but Mother became scared and defensive, and literally ran away. I cried and grieved over the loss and in a short time "healed up!" He then smiled broadly. "Come to think of it, it was at that point that I stopped collecting mothers...I haven't needed one. I have been 'mothered' at times by my children, my wife and my friends. But since that time, I have never needed 'mother'."

This man's needs were met by his own acknowledgement that they were legitimate. He did not deny his needs or "blame" his mother, simply felt the pain of loss until it healed up. He will no longer need to punish his wife or friends for not giving him unconditional love constantly, and he'll have less need to play the role of the deprived child who tries to force everyone around him to constantly mother him.

At this point, whenever lecturing or sharing this subject with others, there is an inevitable reaction: "What right have I got to do this to my parents?" To do what to your parents? All you ever asked for was love. How can you deny your parents the opportunity of being your parents? If you do not come to them with your needs, and then your needs are not met, your parents can rightfully say to you "We never had a chance to be your parents, because you denied us this."

When I was a child, I had both hay fever and asthma, and as a result, was always rather skinny and weak. Mother was constantly trying to build me up with milk shakes and as many milk products as she could pour down me to gain weight. In the process of trying to discover the allergic cause, a doctor told Mother I was allergic to cow's milk. Mother had been "poisoning" her child all those years. Obviously, if I had died, Mother would not have been tried for murder. She did not intend to poison me but in fact, was trying to do what was best for me. By loading me up with this milk, the very thing that was causing the allergic reaction, she was, in effect poisoning me. As soon as she found out, she stopped. To further illustrate this point, let's pretend that Mother never finds out about the milk and continues to pour quarts of cow's milk into her son until the day he leaves home as an adult.

I go on to get married and have a family of my own. A doctor discovers the allergy to cow's milk, and advises a switch to goat's milk, which is healthier for asthmatics and does not cause an allergic reaction. The advice is taken, I switch to goat's milk, gain weight, and am in better health than ever, with no more allergic reaction. I now have a child myself, who perhaps has the same weaknesses. Rather than risk any chances with cow's milk, the child is raised on goat's milk also.

After a few years of living away from home, I visit Mother and take the family along. I cannot wait to share the good news with Mother and rush into the house expectantly, "Mother, wait till you hear the good news! My doctor told me I was allergic to cow's milk and you've been poisoning me all these years," I say with a laugh. "Look at me now. I've been drinking goat's milk, gained all this weight. I've color in my face and I feel great. Our son has been raised on it too, and look at him." I expect Mother to be thrilled at what has happened to me.

Instead her reaction is, "What do doctors know? I'm your mother. I know what's best for my child. Nobody can tell me that you're allergic to cow's milk. Goat's milk is for goats. When you come to my house, you drink cow's milk and your children drink cow's milk." (Or, chicken soup, or whatever it happens to be, the "Jewish momma" comes in all flavors.)

"Wait a minute, Mother. I don't think you understand. The doctor said I'm allergic to cow's milk. It poisons my system. Since I stopped drinking it and have been drinking goat's milk instead, I am healthy!"

Mother refuses to understand and demands that as long as I am visiting in her home, out of courtesy to her values and beliefs, I must drink cow's milk and my children must drink cow's milk or they'll have to leave.

What would you do? I have a few people who respond, "She's an old woman, your mother, so why not humor her and drink a glass of milk. You'll get over it, and you don't visit your mother very often."

What would you do? It seems rather obvious that very few would stay and drink cow's milk. You have come to Mother to share your new discovery and new health, and she has rejected your needs. You have asked for good food and she has given you bad food in the name of love, not only risking your own health, but the health of your child as well.

Of course, most of us would leave. It is easy to see that we would take a stand on something as concrete as whether or not we are going to risk drinking cow's milk and endanger our health.

How much more important is our emotional well-being? We come to our parents and ask them for emotional "good food". If they give it to us, we are emotionally well fed, and nurtured. If they give us "bad food", we have an obligation to ourselves and to our parents to reject it. We do not do our parents any favors by accepting this "bad food" and pretending that it is good. By calling it "bad food", which it is, we are giving them an opportunity to not only correct their mistake, but to profit from it.

I want to emphasize that the child does not reject the parents when he rejects the bad food. He is simply refusing the food as bad and refusing to pretend that it is good. He walks away from the parental home grieved and sad, and deeply hurt that he is being misunderstood and rejected. He loves his parents and knows on a deep level that they love him. The problem is not whether they love, but whether or not they can express this love in a way that will meet his needs. Also, the parents are not getting their needs met either, since by offering the food (be it good or bad) they expect a response of love from the child, but instead, get rejection.

In one of my marriage and family classes there were two nineteen year old girls who were daughter and daughter-in-law to the same woman. Each had a daughter about six months of age. When we were discussing parent-child relationships, both of them complained about "Mother" in the same way. She bugged them about everything they did as mothers. They could do nothing right in the area of dressing the child, disciplining the child, washing the child, or anything for that matter. They were both very angry and upset with her and resented being around her at all. Neither had done anything about it because they thought it would hurt her feelings. Instead, they stayed away. In order to protect her feelings, they rejected her and kept away as much as possible, depriving her of her grandchildren.

Were they really doing her a favor? The honest, direct method might be least hurtful and present the best opportunity for working out a relationship. All they have to do is tell her how they feel. Tell her that they feel she has no confidence in them, that she constantly treats them as little children who don't know what they're doing. Explain that they feel no emotional support or caring from her, even though they are aware that she is trying to help. Her attitude constantly gives them the feeling of being rejected and put-down. Certainly this confrontation will hurt her feelings and will be difficult for the girls, but it will provide an opportunity for all of them to change and work it out to mutual satisfaction. Just quietly and slowly withdrawing from her, and depriving her of their love and presence, as well as the affection and love of her grandchildren, won't really do anyone any good. Revealing one's needs in such a confrontation can open up new and joyous relationships.

Chapter 8

Nurturing the Deprived Child Heals the Angry Adult

Sickness is misused health...

Won't is misused Will...

Hate is misused Power...

Premature death is misused Life...

What happens when our child needs are not met growing up? No one is fully evolved as a child nor fully deprived, thus we can say, **to the extent** one's basic needs were not met as a child, he will continue attempts to meet them at the adult level through romantic relationships, competition in the world of work, striving for fame and public adoration, and often through trying to mold his own children. This striving for growth needs to be met will be influenced by and motives contaminated by the unmet need for approval and love.

It is sometimes very difficult to determine - even within one's self at times - what the true motivation is. The accomplishment or act itself does not necessarily reveal the motive.

For example, even the most actualized person needs the validation of others. This is a healthy need; if no one believed in your value except you and your parents, you would soon be overwhelmed with doubt and insecurity. It feels good to have validation from romantic love, friends, peers, and associates that you are well thought of, highly regarded, and respected. This strengthens one's own self concept and validates one's own self-worth.

The contrast to this is the person who wants more than validation of what he already knows and believes (leaving room for normal self-doubt) and instead asks the world to give him the self worth he doesn't have. "Convince me I'm good and loveable so that I can believe it." This might even work if the person could receive it. The rest of us could then act as substitute parents and give an unconditional positive regard that could be used to establish a new self concept. The problem is that most of these people caught up in this extreme need won't believe or accept what is given. Like bottomless pits, they are continually unfilled and never satisfied. They have insatiable thirsts and will not let you quench them. Eventually they tire people out and are left alone with their "payoff" - "I was right, no one loves me."

Healing Feelings Of The Past

There are five steps to heal the past feelings of a deprived child:

1. **You can accept the reality of what is. "My needs were not entirely met as a child and it's difficult for me to believe in or accept the love of others, and that's where I find myself now.**

For some people, this is the hardest step of all. To admit the truth about yourself is to judge harshly that I may be sick, bad, degenerate, worthless, and unacceptable. Judgement is not the issue here. Until you honestly look at and evaluate your present circumstances, it is almost impossible to change them. Once you grasp this concept and admit fears, faults, inadequacies, and needs without feeling judged by yourself or others, a great relaxation, healing, and even change takes place. You lose the need to defend against this awareness, can now listen to criticism without fear of being destroyed by it, can see and learn from your mistakes, and actually like yourself as a result. Once it is understood that defensive behavior is for the purpose of protection and not because you are a bad person, the need to protect yourself lessens and the defensive behavior begins to change.

2. **You can actually go back to your parents and get the unconditional love you need, or at least reassure yourself it is really
   there. The need to be loved as a birthright is powerful and carries over into all your relationships.**

3. **In dealing with this need for self-worth, I have used guided daydreams or hypnosis to enable a client to confront his parents,
   even parents who are deceased, unavailable due to distance, or
   are just too defensive to approach. In therapy, the client becomes
   as a child in an actual situation from the past.**

As the therapist, I often suggest that the client is a child in his own bedroom and very upset. Invariably, an actual prior event will be seen. We can "bring into the room" the parent the client wants to confront and have the child say what he is really feeling. It is now safe to take risks that could not be taken by the young child in reality. Interestingly enough, the feelings and fears of the young child are being experienced and strong support is usually needed on the he part of the therapist to encourage the child to state his feelings. Sometimes the child just can't do it. Then it is suggested that the adult client walk into the room and confront the parent in defense of the child. This will generally create enough courage for the child to say what needs to be said to the parent.

A Guided Daydream Encounter

Here is an example:

Therapist: Visualize yourself as a small child in your room. You are very upset. Tell me what you see.

Client: I used to sleep with my brother in the same room. I'm six years old, sitting on the bed, upset. I never cried as a child. I'm upset because Father punished me and I had decided not to cry because the punishment was unfair. He wouldn't stop spanking me till I cried, so I did;

didn't want to give him the satisfaction, and I'm mad at myself that I did.

Therapist: Why did he punish you?

Client: I called one of his friends "fat." I didn't mean to be disrespectful. Dad took off his belt and hit me in front of everyone.

Therapist: Dad is now coming back into the room to talk to you about it.

Client: He wouldn't do that. It was casual and fun for him; he wasn't even mad. He went to bed.

Therapist: Go to his room and tell him how you feel.

Client: (To the Father). The spanking was unfair. I didn't mean to say it.

Therapist: Be the six year old and tell him.

Client: I can't do it as a six year old.

Therapist: Then have the adult you go into his room and say it.

Client: You didn't do right when you spanked him. He's a person too. (To Therapist). No one ever talked to him that way.

Therapist: How is he responding?

Client: He is quiet and seems to be hurt. I feel pity for the child (client begins to cry).

Therapist: Pick up the little boy.

Client: (sobbing heavily) It hurts. It's embarrassing to cry. I'm embarrassed; people will find out I'm such a softy and will think less of me. Father would!

Therapist: How do you feel when other men cry?

Client: That's O.K. They are lucky that they can cry.

Therapist: Can you allow your sons to cry?

Client: Yes, I encourage them to and comfort them, but I punish myself. God, I'd love to quit that.

Several things happened in this session. The client relived an unpleasant experience that really happened to him as a child. He found he still could not confront Father as a child, even though it was a "daydream" and not real Father. However, the adult did have the courage to confront Father and there was a new reaction. Father became quiet and hurt; there was no prior experience to predict this happening. Then he found deep feelings of sorrow and hurt for the little boy, but it was very difficult for the adult client to cry without feelings of guilt and embarrassment. It was a real breakthrough of emotion for the client to cry as an adult man in the presence of another adult (the therapist), even though others who had this privilege were considered "lucky" by him.

Often, the parent starts out very defensive and angry, and then breaks down and admits his own fears and needs. When the therapist can provide emotional support and a direct, firm method of approach for the client, the "parent" in the daydream is able to respond with true feelings.

I am sharing some rather extreme situations with extreme fathers to show how effective this technique can be under almost impossible situations. For most people the parents are not that angry and hostile in their approach to life, and the experience is less severe.

Guided Imagery Confrontation

The following is an even more difficult father-son situation. The son had absolutely no possibility of dealing with an unreasonable father in real life, and now as an adult, is so angry with Father, he is afraid of his own potential violence.

Therapist: You are a small child in your bedroom. What do you see?

Client: (describes the room in detail) I'm five or six years old, standing. I feel estranged; don't feel a part of the room. Not a pleasant feeling.

Therapist: Your Father is coming into the room and is very angry with you.

Client: I feel stark terror; I see blood and guts piled up deep in the room, like he's already killed me. He killed me and left - he's gone.

Therapist: Become the blood and guts.

Client: I feel totally rejected - more than a punishment - my person has been destroyed. I'm all alone, no help.

Therapist: Call out for help.

Client: Mom comes in the doorway. She tells me I shouldn't have done what I did.

Therapist: Tell her you're dead.

Client: She says, "I can't help that."

Therapist: Ask for her help.

Client: She says she can't. She finally sees the blood and guts; she screams at Dad. She's mad at him now. She is holding me and rocking me back and forth. She's protecting me from him. I feel safe - protected more than loved. Dad is looking at me and making me feel horrible that I can't take my own punishment. He feels punishment is forever. Father says getting nourishment from Mother is wrong.

Therapist: Ask him why he is so angry with you.

Client: He doesn't want me around. I know why. He's had enough unpleasantness and doesn't want more from me at home. He doesn't like coming home anyway.

Therapist: Tell him that.

Client: Dad is startled.

Therapist: What else would you like to tell him?

Client: All you do is take; push people around, bully people and have no feelings yourself. (He's angry.) All the things I say just make me hurt.

Therapist: Share the hurt with your Father.

Client: That makes him feel bad. He didn't know I felt that way. He's trying to deny it. I've beat him down to the floor.

Therapist: Tell him you understand his feelings; you know he's part of you and is very frightened but you love him and see through his anger to the fear.

Client: He stood up. That's what he wanted to hear. (To Father) Why were you afraid of me? (Father: Because you were a little kid - part of me.)

Therapist:	Become the adult you.
Client:	I'm hugging him. He feels rigid and uncomfortable.
Therapist:	Tell him to relax.
Client:	He's crying and relaxing. I understand. I feel strong. I feel like his parent and "all together." Mother is standing there. She feels amazement. The blood and guts are all gone.
Therapist:	Put the child there.
Client:	I picked him up and am hugging him.
Therapist:	Reassure him there is nothing to fear anymore.
Client:	I feel a lot of pain. The child wants to go to sleep now. I feel so sorry for the little guy. He's asleep in my arms (client is crying softly).

To those who have not experienced it, this scene may sound somewhat strange and unreal, but it is a deeply moving and life transforming experience for the client. I have witnessed time and time again that the client's "integrity" is in touch with and understands the parents' "integrity", beneath the defense mechanisms, and is able to communicate on that level. We have had clients who never did have a need to "confront" their real parents after doing so in a daydream. They understood the parents so well it was as though they had already had an actual confrontation. Therefore, their feelings for the parent changed in a positive way and love was now possible instead of defensiveness, rebellion or phoniness. As a result, the parents also changed and the child did experience direct love.

The real principle here is understanding the true motive that underlies the behavior. When you understand that your parents did unloving things to you (sometimes even to the point of being vicious and cruel) because of their own fear, feelings of inadequacy, and defensiveness, your insight can lead the way to compassion. They behaved that way out of their own self ignorance, not because they hated you or you were unlovable. And when the parent can admit this, beautiful changes take place on a deep, feeling level. These are literally changes from the inside out, not just intellectual decisions to "act" differently.

4. **Another very effective tool to improve feelings of self love and self worth, is what I call "re-parenting". It is a process also expe-**

rienced in the relaxed state of a guided daydream, and can be repeated at will by the client. You could experience it right now.

Re-Parenting The Crying Child

The client is asked to relax himself in a chair, close his eyes and visualize himself as a child crying in his room, very upset. This time we are not confronting the parent. Once the scene is being experienced (and the child's feelings generally come very quickly to the surface, even to the point of instant tears), we ask that the adult client walk into the room.

Therapist   What do you see?

Client: The child is sitting on the bed crying. His Dad just spanked him for something he didn't do and he's very hurt.

Therapist: Does he see you?

Client: Yes, he seems pleased I'm here. (Tears)

Therapist: What would you like to do?

Client: I just picked him up and am rocking him on the bed and holding him in my arms. We're both crying now and I'm telling him not to cry.

Therapist: But he's hurt. He needs to cry. Just reassure him of your love.

Client: Yes, I am. It is O.K. to cry, damn it! All my life I've been told not to cry. I'm holding him very tight and he feels very safe. He's glad I'm here with him and says no one understands.

Therapist: But you do, don't you? No one understands the thoughts and feelings of that child like you do.

Client: Yes.

Therapist: Tell the child he will never again be alone. You can't protect him from pain, but you can give him love and comfort so he won't be alone.

Client: He wants to know where I've been and I told him I didn't know I could come and comfort him like this. But from now on I'll come often and we'll have fun together.

I ask the client to "visit" with the child for five minutes or so every day till the next appointment. This is one of the most exciting happenings in many of my clients' therapy. They usually come back excited, relaxed and with deep feelings of inner love and peace.

It is the child in us that feels unloved, unworthy, abandoned or whatever. The tendency is for the adult in us to go on treating the child in us like our parents did, either out of habit or subconscious belief that the parents were right. Once this pattern is broken and you are given permission to love, appreciate, and enjoy that little person, both the child and the adult benefit. The adult enjoys the good parenting he is giving and the child enjoys the unconditional love.

Revisiting Childhood

Here is an example of an adult female client visiting with her small child-self.

Therapist: See yourself as a small child in your bedroom, crying.

Client: I see a five or six year old little kid, kneeling by the bed. Her fists are all balled up. Mother is mad at her. I'm not sure why. She is crying but trying not to.

Therapist: The adult you is now standing in the doorway watching her. What do you see?

Client: I'd like to go over and hug her. I want to tell her she doesn't have to cry. Now we are sitting on the bed together and I'm reaching out to her. She wants to be held and hugged. It feels so warm and loving. I want to take away her hurt and let her know everything will be O.K.

Therapist: Let her know you love her and care about her regardless of what happens to her.

Client: This makes her calm. She isn't as tense. Her hands are relaxed. She feels comforted.

Therapist: Become the five year old. How do you feel?

Client: I feel good and safe. I believe the adult loves me. I love her, too. She's a friend; she's going to be there when I need her. (She's now crying softly.)

Therapist:	Draw strength from the adult you. What is the adult feeling?
Client:	Warm, tender feelings. I like the feeling of comforting her.
Therapist:	Can you see the "specialness" in the child?
Client:	Yes, she has a bright quality about her - alive and alert and happy most of the time. She bubbles over, her eyes sparkle; she's bright, really going to grow up to be something.
Therapist:	Tell her you are available at any time and you love her.
Client:	I have!

This young woman had some very positive feelings about her "child" but needed to re-experience and remind herself. She was going through a separation at the time and had a very poor self-image, as well as a weight problem. In the next few weeks, there was a definite change in her self-concept and she became much more assertive regarding her needs.

The following older man saw himself as a very ugly and undesirable child and was struggling to overcome this poor self concept when he visualized this re-parenting daydream.

Client:	I see a seven year old with glasses - homely, funny looking little squirt.
Therapist:	What does he feel about himself?
Client:	Kids call him Percy and "sissy". He's picking flowers in the back yard.
Therapist:	Let the adult you go into the yard with him.
Client:	Such a smart little guy and sensitive; too much feeling for his own good.
Therapist:	Give him some love.
Client: (Child:	I put him on my shoulders. He likes it. I tell him I love him. Do you really mean it? That's what Mom and Dad say but they have to say it. I can't believe it.)
Client:	It's not like Mom and Dad. No obligation. Mine is very objective. I love you because you're you.

(Child:	Gee, where have you been?)
Client:	This has been so hard to think about - I've turned you off.
Therapist:	Tell him you're sorry you did that.
Client:	I'd like to be your buddy. You don't have to be a whiz kid for me, winning scholarships and all that. You're O.K. the way you are. I'll come often now. You make me feel good. I'll be me and you be you. We can be real with each other.

Occasionally, you will find clients who cannot love the child. They have adopted the parents' point of view so strongly that they feel guilty and sneaky loving the child. It's like going behind the parents' back and disobeying the edict to not love the child. Often they don't believe the child deserves to be loved, but instead, feels the child should be strong that there is no place for crying, or feeling the pain, or admitting weakness. This is very sad and very difficult to deal with. The therapist strives to present the child's birthright of love and attempts to provide a safe enough environment for the client to experience this love. If, even after the client has been given the "permission" to love, he finds it difficult or impossible to respond positively to the small child of the past, I see this as a very serious symptom that says the ability to love others as an adult may be seriously impaired. This condition would be especially damaging to the marital relationship and the ability to love as a parent to children.

The Needs For Approval

Tere is a mid-thirties, divorced, highly successful business woman from the east coast, where her family still lives. The first time she got a job as Vice President for a large corporation with a good salary and benefits, her father's response on the phone, when she called to share her excitement, was, "I don't believe it, no one gives a vice presidency and that kind of money to an unproven woman!" It took a long time to convince him this wasn't a job "in name only" with some fly-by-night company with big titles and no future. Three years later when she took an even better position in the same industry, there was just a long silence this time on the phone; and then "congratulations!"

Tere's angry reaction was easy to understand. "My father is a chauvinist who is only moderately successful in a slow-moving career. He is jealous and upset that I've done it better and faster. He loves my aggressive, male, successful side, and brags that

I got it from him, but really, he can't handle it. He loves my soft, feminine, loving side and responds with warm affection, but he dismisses women as weak, stupid and inadequate. I can't win. He's hard of hearing, too, so I have to yell to be heard and then he berates me for yelling!"

"I married a man just like my father. We were happy. I was a school teacher and sharing in the family income, but when I moved into the business world and became more successful, while he was losing ground, he turned bitter, violent, and mean. Finally he left me for another woman. I would have done anything to save the marriage. Divorce was not acceptable in my family...or to me."

"All my life I have chased after the approval of men to feel good about myself. My father and my husband wouldn't give it to me, and for that matter, no one else has either."

In a hypnosis session, Tere's heart became very heavy and in pain. The message was that this hurt is very old and not connected to recent events. "The hurt belongs to the heart and the fear is Tere's." Because of the previous hurt and pain, Tere is frightened and putting herself in a position of being hurt again and again.

We went back to this original hurt and found herself at home at the age of six. "I don't want to leave - my life will change. We moved the next year and my emotions shut down at that point. I could give you facts and events, but I won't experience them. At age six, it didn't matter, no one would listen to me anyway."

Looking back, she became aware that she lost some sense of security, and that major, negative changes occurred in her life when they moved at age seven. She anticipated this at six! All children fear change and resist moves. Their security is often more tied to a physical home and environment than to people, even their parents. The key is that she felt helpless to have an input. "They never listened to me or believed me."

Tere suddenly turned quiet. "I won't let the hurt come to the surface to be healed."

"What do you suggest?" I asked.

"Getting out of the office. I'm scared."

In the process of the hypnosis, Tere's heart with its pain, had become symbolized as a beautiful, young deer. I suggested she allow the deer and myself to comfort and protect her while she allowed herself to simply experience the fear.

Much of therapy, and particularly hypnosis or imagery, is simply providing a safe, non-judgmental environment where the client can experience pain, fear, anger, and whatever is normally too stressful to experience alone. Since they feel they can't survive the experience emotionally, they tend to deny, distort, or repress it. At that point, it continues to function, but more outside the conscious control of the client.

The client becomes a victim of this own inner self. Bringing negativity to conscious awareness and providing a safe place to do this begins a healing process. Because it was experienced and they did survive it, the feeling becomes less frightening. Seen at a conscious level with the help of a therapist, they can be comforted, in the midst of pain and torment, and not feel ALONE. Often, that is enough. "I'm not being criticized or condemned for my feelings - I'm being comforted and loved." The next step is to see clearly what the pain is trying to tell them and receive greater understanding of self. Finally, they are able to make better choices after seeing all the options more clearly.

When it was suggested that Tere simply feel the fear, her response was, "I'm not afraid of my physical safety. The worst thing is that I'll be left alone and won't know how to take care of myself." This is the six year old talking. She then went through several experiences of feeling abandoned. Her dad took a job in another state for a time and was only home on weekends. When Tere was three and one-half years old and her sister was born, her mother went to the hospital for two weeks and Tere stayed with the grandparents and "I shut down." No one told her why. She didn't get to share in the happiness and anticipation of a new child. There was no explanation of mother's disappearance or suggestion as to when she would return. "They didn't think at three and one-half, I'd understand."

"Real feelings of abandonment. Alan (her husband) left me. My heart not as heavy as it felt before. I know it all. The rest of my life taught me to understand. I broke my arm and no one believed me. I fell off some monkey bars at a park. My parents wrapped it. Days later, found out it was broken - teach her but don't believe her. Listen to me - I know I'm right in the divorce. All this self doubt but I know that I knew. They still do it to me."

You can see how the issues of the six year old have become the angry struggles of the adult.

"I have to make them believe I'm right. Otherwise, I doubt myself and don't feel O.K. That is the issue!"

At this point, I asked the deer for a suggestion as to how we could heal this problem.

"Brain says shut down - deer says NO."

I suggested that she see the deer and I holding and comforting her. She cried for a long time. "No judgement from the deer, no right or wrong, just unconditional love." Remember, the deer is her own heart. This is one of the most important sources of love and comfort.

The next week, Tere returned more peaceful and calm. She had been doing affirmations to strengthen these new feelings. One of them was "I do not need the approval of men for my own self esteem!"

She found it in a book and liked it but felt some discomfort with it. Think of the contradiction in a negative affirmation. Does the mind really hear the words DO NOT or does it reinforce that I DO need the approval of a man for my own self-esteem?

It was suggested she turn this into a positive affirmation:

I need my own approval for my own self-esteem!

Say that over slowly five or six times. Feel it build within you. Feel the excitement, joy and pleasure it generates. Feelings of power and authority well up in your chest.

I need my own approval for my own self-esteem!

A negative affirmation is tinged with hostility and resentment. "They COULD have believed in me - they SHOULD have believed in me. I deserved to be taken seriously. They cheated me. They are stupid."

All those statements, as a matter of fact, are true. A child's original self-esteem comes from the reflected appraisals of the significant (and sometimes not so significant) others in his life. "If they think I'm smart, pretty, good, talented, and acceptable, then I can believe that, too. After all, they are older and God-like in their wisdom, and told me so just yesterday! If they think I'm dumb, ugly, bad, untalented, and not acceptable, it will be very hard for me to believe otherwise."

How many times have we said those words to our children?

Children are psychic computers and they program in the words they hear. Obviously, many of those messages are contradictory.

"Yes, I told you you were bad yesterday, but a week ago I said you were good."

Children seem to be born with different levels of ego strength. Some overcome amazing handicaps with ease and others crumble under little pressure. As parents, our job is to learn to "read" our children's responses and be appropriate in the way we relate feelings to them.

WHEN YOU HAVE YOUR OWN APPROVAL, YOU HAVE NOTHING LEFT TO PROVE.

AN EXCESSIVE NEED TO "PROVE" SOMETHING (TO SELF OR TO OTHERS) MEANS A LACK OF SELF APPROVAL.

5. **The fifth step is one we use daily without being entirely aware of it. We use social relationships - bosses or friends - to work through many of our parental conflicts.**

A five year old, who has had a hostile and rejecting mother, may find his first warm and loving mother image in a grandmotherly kindergarten teacher who cares very deeply for him. In order to find their good images, young people turn to and identify with aunts or uncles, scoutmasters, pastors or youth leaders, sports heros or musicians.

Larry is a client whose experience demonstrates this in another way. A few years ago, Larry was in his mid-thirties with a wife and several children. He held a rather average job as a salesman and deliveryman for a small company where he worked for approximately four years, along with five or six other salesmen-deliverymen. Larry's very sadistic father had died approximately ten years previous. It seems little coincidence that his boss was also a rather cruel, sarcastic man. Larry saw his boss as one who picked on him continually and always took advantage of him. It appeared that the man never took similar advantage of the other drivers. Larry fumed about this for years, but put up with it for fear of losing his job, which he needed to support his family, and because he was not too sure he could get another job.

This situation came up one night in a couples' group he was attending. Larry was really able to get in touch with his needs as the group encouraged him not to put up with this nonsense. They urged him to confront his boss with his real feelings. After one particularly productive group session, Larry went home determined to confront his boss the next morning. He went to work with this on his mind and simply waited for the boss to give him an opening, which he knew would come very quickly. No more than fifteen or twenty minutes after he had arrived at work, the opportunity presented itself. When the boss started his tirade, Larry immediately began to feel his anger. After a very brief time, he stopped the boss by saying that he had taken all the nonsense that he was going to take from him and was tired of being treated in this despicable manner. He was a human being, intended to be treated as such, and was no longer going to put up with the inhuman treatment he was getting. He was not going to be taken advantage of any more. He was not going to do all the extra things that were never appreciated. He wanted the same type of treatment the other men were getting and he wanted it now or, "You can take your job, and I'll tell you what you can do with it!"

At this point, Larry stepped back waiting to be fired. He had already made up his mind that the boss in no way would accept this type of answer and that he would be fired. He had just decided that his integrity was more important than the job and it was worth being fired for, as he needed the respect of his wife, children, and himself more than the needed the job.

Surprisingly enough, his boss also took a step backward and a deep breath. He profusely apologized to Larry, saying that he was totally unaware of treating him in this fashion. He confided that he had always liked Larry better than the other drivers and actually had teased him and been sarcastic with him because he liked him best of all and thought that Larry knew that. He assured him that his behavior would change and that he would never take advantage of him. Over the next several months, they became almost like father and son, and a short time later, Larry received a generous raise in salary. Needless to say, he kicked himself for waiting for years before taking his needs seriously and expressing himself.

Everyone likes stories with happy endings, but what would have happened if Larry had been fired? Because he had been so cut-off from his own feelings, he had no way of predicting the outcome; and the percentage was on the side of his being fired. Would he then have been wrong for having taken his needs seriously?

Larry received his bad father-image from a hostile real father. It was validated by having a hostile real boss, who symbolically represented this bad image. By telling the boss exactly how he felt, Larry was able to improve his relationship with his boss and therefore change his bad-father image. In reality, there was little chance that the boss would fire him, because Larry had already stated his terms for keeping the job. In other words, if the behavior did not improve, he was going to quit, if the boss rejected these terms and let him quit or fired him, it would have been O.K. too, because Larry had been a good father to himself and kept his integrity. If you can't change the situation to meet your needs, you meet them by removing yourself from the situation so that you can no longer be burned by it. The bad father cannot hurt him if the bad father no longer has authority or control over his life.

Although we can do our best to improve any relationship, when the other person does not cooperate with us, we have no other alternative but to cut off the relationship so that the person no longer has the power to upset or hurt us. If we can successfully deal with our problems on an image level in this manner, we find our need for violent solutions disappear.

Part 2

Healing and Revealing Communication: the Sharing of Self

In previous chapters we have stressed the need to know the self: stop, look and listen - accept, evaluate and understand. Now comes the second, more crucial part: Once tuned into the self of the moment - both positive and negative, in transition or in concrete, what now?

Do I share with others, how much do I share with others, at what point do I violate the space of others?

KNOWING the self is a great first step. SHARING the self in an appropriate manner, with the best odds of a desirable response is a step up in difficulty.

I have a right to all my feelings. How about the right to share them? What happens if I DO - or DON'T?

What good does it do to possess something - be it money, education, knowledge or talent - if it is not experienced or shared? A diamond locked in a vault or music locked in the imagination of the composer is of limited value and becomes wasted treasure. But, sharing the self is not easy. Part of my responsibility to self and the world I live in is to **BE** and express THAT ULTIMATE SELF, as much of and as close to as I am capable of doing.

I not only have a RIGHT to that but an OBLIGATION as well. I owe that to myself and to my world. It is the one debt to life we are all capable of repaying.

In the next three chapters, we will concentrate on that psychological stereotype or cliche called "communication skills".

First, we will deal with the withholding of self - also known as CRAZYMAKING.

Secondly, we'll discuss the abusiveness of self: THE DESTRUCTIVE or ABUSE USE OF ANGER.

Finally, we'll discuss AUTHENTICITY: THE AFFIRMATION OF SELF.

"TOO BAD GEORGE DIDN'T COME TONIGHT —
EVERYONE HAS SO MUCH TO SAY ABOUT HIM."

Chapter 9

Crazymaking: the Withholding of Self

What does it mean to be crazy? None of us like the feeling or suggestion of being crazy - out of touch with reality. We would certainly reject the idea of our being a crazymaker - one who acts in such a way to make others feel or look crazy. But many of us do this routinely, often in the name of love, sometimes for simple self-preservation!

To withhold pertinent information about ourselves, to lie or cover up feelings in an effort to protect ourselves or a relationship, to force people into mind-reading, guessing games in order to please us are just some of the ways we become crazymakers.

While some of us find it almost impossible not to express feelings, even when the consequences are harmful to ourselves and our loved ones, there are others who find it equally painful and discomforting to express anger, hurt, fear or any intense emotion. It's too naked, vulnerable and dangerous to put themselves on the line, presenting the other person with material that could later be used against them, and risking the reality of rejection - all because their feelings and needs were unacceptable. Interestingly enough, many of these people are, therefore, experienced as and labeled by others as unfeeling, cold, unaffectionate and emotionless. Part of the game, then, becomes a challenge to get them to feel, experience, be alive, even if we must hurt them to do it. Otherwise, we have no idea how they feel about us or if we have impact on their lives.

We laugh about the engineer stereotype who fits this pattern, a person more comfortable with machines and projects than people. The truth being they may not be comfortable with the people because they are too emotional, too volatile, and too vulnerable to allow their emotions to come to the surface. Some carry these emotions quite close to the surface and are in a constant inner sense of turmoil and unrest.

If you find it difficult to share portions of yourself, there are probably very real and legitimate reasons or blocks that stand in the way. Revealing and understanding these blocks will eliminate some of the need for them, and allow some tentative risk taking toward openess and new intimacy. Others have become so practiced at this way of life, their emotions are buried deeply and not easily reached. For those, some deep, life-shaking trauma (like the possibility of a divorce) is needed to plumb the depths beneath which these emotions have been buried.

You will note that most of these feelings center around anger and negativity. It is generally easier to express positive feelings than negative ones. We question our right to disagree, to be upset, to say no or to express what we want or need. This fear of being misunderstood or rejected makes us angry at ourselves for being afraid and angry at the other person for putting us in this jeopardy position.

Blocks to Expressing Self
Block #1: Lack of Knowledge or Information

Some people don't know they have the right to get angry or fight back. They've never been given permission and don't know how to give it to themselves. They can give dozens of reasons, excuses, whatever, to justify the other person's hurtfulness and the fact that they should not be hurt or angry in return.

"She didn't mean it."

"He had a good reason to be hurtful."

"They were drunk."

"I want to be seen as an understanding person."

"He's too old; he wouldn't understand."

Just knowing that anger, for instance, has the potential for positive benefits can bring improvement to a relationship. This simple matter of education can open an entirely new experience with a minimum of time and effort.

The person, however, who is so out of touch with feelings that there is no conscious awareness of being hurt or angry, needs an extended period, usually with professional help, of asking the question "What am I feeling right now?" until the response is automatic. Discover your feelings, explore them without judgement and share them with others.

Block #2: the "You Owe Me" Syndrome -
Or - The Overwhelming Power of Guilt

"How can I possibly disagree with her when she's done so much for me and sacrificed so much for me all my life?"

It must be Mother. Who else is so pure and unselfish? And reminded you of it just yesterday?

"He's such a nice guy - I come out the heavy - or look like a fool."

Could that be dear old Dad?

"I must be terribly ungrateful and selfish to be mad at him/her. He's so good to me, and I don't seem to appreciate it."

Where do these feelings of guilt come from? Much of the time they are programmed into our subconscious by the incessant grocery list recited by our parents over and over all our lives.

Debt comes from obligation; they often want us to feel obligated so we can more easily be controlled and manipulated to love them or at least do their bidding. If this sounds like the beginning of a blanket condemnation of parents, and wholesale blaming to get neurotic adult children off the hook, it is not meant to be. Where the shoe fits, I hope to add enough pinch of pain to help both sides break a destructive pattern, and find a new and more exciting way to relate - with love - not with guilt and obligation.

There is neurotic guilt and there is normal guilt - a world of difference not always easily discerned, even within ourselves. Normal guilt comes when the person has violated his own integrity, broken his own values and deliberately struck out to injure or destroy another (either from fear, vindictiveness or whatever). Not to have guilt under these circumstances would be pathological (what we call a sociopath or psychopath - persons without social or personal conscience.) Neurotic guilt can be defined as that which is inappropriate to the situation. This occurs when a person is conditioned and trained to feel guilt under certain circumstances because of someone else's value systems, even when they know they've done the right thing at the right time.

Bob invites his parents over for Sunday dinner to celebrate Dad's birthday. A last minute opportunity arises for Bob to take an all-expenses paid trip to Hawaii that weekend and he postpones the birthday dinner. Both parents are deeply hurt and feel rejected and Bob feels guilty. Why? He was programmed to believe that if someone gets hurt because of something he does, he's responsible, regardless of his motives or the circumstances. That's neurotic guilt and should be rejected as such. Whether or not we "hurt someone" depends on our motivation and reasons. "Getting hurt" depends on your interpretation of the reasons and motives, plus secondary needs for control and power.

"If I hurt you, I'm sorry I hurt you! If you felt hurt as a result of my taking my needs seriously and acting in a manner I felt best served my interests (after taking your needs and feelings into due consideration), then I'm sorry you got hurt. But I didn't mean to hurt you." Motive makes the difference.

Why do parents give their children love? Is it an overflow of expression that comes naturally from a confirmation of self love, couple love and unconditional positive regard for these individuals to whom they gave birth? Or is it for the purpose of being loved by the children? Some people give an abundance of "love" that is designed primarily as a means of obligation, control and with the expectation of getting even more love in return. That is exploitation.

One of the most potent examples of this kind of parent-child conflict and confrontation was seen in the classic movie, **Guess Who's Coming to Dinner**, where Sidney Portier portrayed a black man planning to marry a white woman. There was a very emotional scene between Sidney and his parents. His father listed all the sacrifices they had made over the years to see to it their son had all the advantages they never had and would not face the handicaps they had to face. In a very dramatic conclusion, the father blurted out that they did not want their son to "pay them back" by marrying a white woman. The father was demanding obedience to this request on the basis of "You Owe Us!"

The equally impassioned response (paraphrased here) was, "I don't owe you anything. Either you gave it freely out of love or the whole relationship was a hoax. There are no strings on love. I owe my son - my children - what I was given freely, but I don't owe for love."

We don't totally agree a child owes nothing to his parents, but the principle is correct, love has no price tag and obligations are not love.

What then, do we owe our parents? The same we owe ourselves and the rest of the world, to be the "best me possible", to love as we are loved, to give generously and openly of ourselves. If our methods of doing this and our values of "best" differ from those of our parents, the result may make both of us sad at the differences. The parents certainly have the right to disagree with us, however, ideally, they will have enough faith in us to believe we are honestly being the "best me" possible, and go on loving us unconditionally, regardless of their reactions to our behavior.

Carl Rogers, the highly respected creator of Client-Centered therapy, once remarked that the most difficult personal task he faced was allowing his wife, children and co-workers to have beliefs, values and ideas different than his own, without interpreting it as a personal rejection of himself and his beliefs. Therein lies the issue. Parents usually over-react because they take these differences personally. They see such differences as a rejection of themselves, the parents, rather than as an honest expression of the beliefs and values of the child.

Guilt also plays a part in this since most of us as children find it difficult to admit hateful or angry feelings to our parents, or to anyone we love for that matter. Gratitude and anger can easily co-exist, love and hate are not necessarily opposites (indifference would be the opposite of love). We are often angry because we love them, because they are important to us, because they have the most power to hurt us.

Even the most exploitive parent may not be totally insincere in his giftgiving, but the gift may have a double edge, "How can you be mad at me or disagree with me when I'm so good to you?" The parent would not understand or accept the child's message of "I'm not mad at you because of the goodness, but because of something you did that hurt me."

In the extreme, the "over-giver" parent, or spouse, may have a strong need to be loved and appreciated to compensate and overcome his fear that he's not lovable. His behavior says, "if I don't give, I won't be loved. No one could love me for just being me. The relationship will end. You will leave me if I don't continue to please." This kind of love is contaminated by fear of abandonment.

Another variation of the above is the "martyr syndrome". "He's so weak he can't handle my feelings, especially negative ones." If the parents or spouse can get you to believe that they are too weak to be confronted, they have accomplished total control over the relationship. You have been rendered helpless, left to deal with your feelings alone, as you can, however you can. Beware of the weak, helpless martyrs of life - they never lose!

For the person trying to relate to a martyr or who finds himself being exploited, he is consistently defining his own responses and sense of worth around another person's reactions and values, rather than his own. He tries to "guess" what is expected of him and what will bring the most favorable response, thereby surrendering his power to the other. He is forced to assume that the other is "correct" in their responses and always knows best. It doesn't really matter that's right or best, as long as he gets the favorable response he wants or avoids the unpleasant one he doesn't want. "Peace at any cost" is generally more expense than any of us can afford.

Beware, this is different than being "sensitive" to another's emotional state. I do not advocate reckless selfishness, or taking what you want regardless of how it affects others. Doing what is truly the "best for me" in any particular situation (which I strongly advocate) has to take into prior consideration all those who are important to you and will subsequently be affected by your decisions. Even though it is unrealistic to assume your feelings and needs will always be in complete harmony and agreement, taking the other person into consideration when making your decision will generally produce a compromise to meet your needs at little (or less) cost to others. Considering someone is different than being controlled by someone. Do what's best for you. It's the best you have to work with.

Block #3: A Strong Moral Judgement That Only Sees Anger As A Negative Force And Therefore Not To Be Expressed

This type of attitude and value system is often developed through two quite contrasting backgrounds: A violent home, where screaming and hitting are commonplace and terrifying, or a cold, unfeeling home, where anger is not tolerated or openly displayed.

If a person has had no prior experience with a healthy expression of anger, where people confront each other directly and intently, resolving the situation with feelings of closeness and love, it is difficult for him to imagine that it can and does take place. ANGER, IN AND OF ITSELF, HAS NO MORAL VALUE, THE MOTIVE AND EXPRESSION DETERMINE WHETHER IT IS DESTRUCTIVE OR CONSTRUCTIVE. In a violent home, children cannot handle violence if these motives are destructive. They do not understand the limits and have no natural defense of their own. This includes both verbal and physical violence; to watch it or receive it can be traumatic in devastating fashion.

Children need to experience and share intense feelings, to disagree, express anger. And they need to experience these feelings and know that no one will get hurt, that people will still love each other, that nothing of the good will be lost, no harm, no foul. The child must also be given the right to his feelings of anger, as well as protection from his own tendency to violence.

Modeling behavior for the child, the explanation of limits (what is accepted behavior and what is not), and firm consistency of discipline coupled with love, affection and freedom to grow and experiment, are all necessary ingredients in teaching a child to deal with emotions.

"I don't throw tantrums, and you can't."

"I'm not rude, and you are not to be rude."

"I don't break things, and you can't."

"I don't call names, and you can't."

"I don't hit, and you can't hit."

Spanking, by the way, is not hitting. It is a punishment designed to fit the crime (not an angry release of tension for the parent using the child as a scapegoat).

The more outlets for anger afforded the child, the better. If he is not allowed to cry, talk back, disagree or express displeasure, what will he do with the anger? "The same thing I had to do as a kid. Hold it in or get my head knocked off." Yes, and how loved did that make you feel? Give the child some outlets that are acceptable, or he'll find his own that are not acceptable, eventually. You can count on it!

"You can yell, cuss, disagree, beat up your punching bag, tell me you hate me, tell me what you'd like to do if you could!" Whatever the parent can tolerate in his own comfort zone. "You cannot, however, do anything that would be hurtful to me, to you or to the relationship between us." A good line to draw.

But what about violence through intimidation, insults, character assassination and humiliation, with no recourse for the child? Two male students now in their twenties related to a marriage and family life class the details of being reared in that type of home, one by a step-father and the other by his natural father.

Both went away to the service and grew into powerful men. One came home and provoked a situation where he physically beat up his father. The other came home and the step-father woke up at 2:00 A.M. with the step-son holding a large knife to his throat. There were no words, no movement, no exchange for the next three to four hours. then, tired of the game and feeling he had made his point, the son left and never saw the step-father again.

You might feel like, "Wow, what satisfaction they both must have felt to get even in ways most of us could never do." To the contrary, neither one expressed much satisfaction or seemed to feel that good about it. The experience was rougher on them than the fathers. Both sought therapy for these and other problems. Perhaps a more helpful method would have been direct verbal confrontation, where the person, now an adult, could verbally express what the child was not allowed to.

Block #4: The Need To Impress
Others And Fool Oneself - The Perfectionist Syndrome

"I don't want others to see me out of control."

"I don't want to look and feel foolish."

"You win if I let you upset me."

The idealized self goes further and deeper. "I must act the way a perfect person should act, regardless of how I feel or I destroy my image of myself." This need for perfection is a tough act to overcome. These perfect responses are learned in childhood, practiced in the teens, and perfected in later years. Only positive feelings are accepted without guilt. A strong, rigid, religious upbringing where "niceness" is constantly demanded may reinforce this to an extreme.

An Army chaplain once commented to me that "Ministers are the world's angriest men, because they are not allowed to feel or express anger." Perhaps this is the reason they ride herd on "principles" and hate "sin" with such a passion. It's their only legitimate outlet!

For years the culture has conditioned women to believe it is unfeminine to express anger. In some settings it is actually considered attractive for a man to be crude, violent, vulgar and hostile but for a woman, no! Actually, a "nice guy" has the same problem. Don't blow your image by expressing angry feelings. It is overdue for the double standard to fall. BE WHAT YOU ARE, EXPRESS WHAT YOU FEEL, NOT IMPULSIVELY OR OUT OF CONTEXT, BUT APPROPRIATELY, ACCORDING TO YOUR INTEGRITY.

Block #5: Fear Of "Going Crazy" Or Out Of Control

There are people who have suppressed their feelings for so long, it has left them feeling like a string of firecrackers, once they start blowing, they might not be able to stop. Add to this a history of violence, maybe they actually did hurt someone badly or went temporarily out of control and the problem is multiplied. This is a real danger and cannot be minimized. There are scores of people fitting this description, who are potentially dangerous. Some are almost milktoast in appearance to compensate for this fear, others give off volcanic rumblings from time to time that warn you not to tread too closely.

What steps can be taken? Here are several things to consider:

a. Respect the fear and the violence. It is not therapeutic or cathartic for people to get hurt.

    As a therapist, I look first for the origins of anger. Who are you really mad at, and why? Prior events that traumatized you and brought on these feelings of hate, must be brought to awareness, re-experienced, understood and faced. Then they can be released.

b. Violence comes from suppression, not expression. To hold feelings inside builds a pressure that eventually requires release. You must find a constructive way to be heard. A violent person (or one who tends to violence and violent feelings) does not expect to be heard and has already programmed himself so that he will not be heard. The history is that he probably hasn't been, so the expectancy is certainly based on prior reality.

    Many children learn early in life that their parents don't listen to them or take them seriously. Because of this emotional set, however, they are often not aware when they are heard. The expectancy is so conditioned that whenever a new confrontation takes place, an automatic defense system goes into effect and there is an inability to wait, listen or react appropriately to any new, individual situation. They immediately perceive a threat and react rashly to protect themselves.

c. As I discussed previously, one method of providing a safe environment for experiencing trauma, anger and fear is through guided daydreams. In this relaxed state, it is possible to experience rage, to maim, to kill, or go berserk or out of control without danger to self or others because it is all in fantasy. Also, there is a "guide" or therapist to protect, reassure and comfort the client through the experience so that he is not alone.

Perhaps it is difficult to understand how fantasy can be so effective. It is not the same as an idle daydream where you imagine beating up someone you dislike and feeling better for a few minutes. A guided daydream reaches into the subconscious and allows the client to deeply and meaningfully "live and experience" these emotions, not just think about them. Most people eventually get to the "monster within them" and learn to love and tame it, rather than destroy it. Accepting the shadow or negative side of themselves as a legitimate need that is just being poorly expressed helps to be less angry at others.

d. How can you protect yourself from these angry outbursts? Until you have some measure of physical control, you will have to avoid situations that trigger the reaction. Walk away from potential violence. Many a husband has done just that but the wife doesn't perceive it that way. All she knows is that he walked away from her and discounted or rejected her feelings. She generally provokes more to get a response, creating more potential danger. If the husband could tell his wife that he does want to find a way to listen and to respond, but he must walk away to avoid violence, he'd probably get a better reaction.

Find a substitute release. One man's solution was to roll his window up in the car, turn on the radio and yell, curse and swear! Physical release is also helpful. Pound a pillow, or the bed, imagine you are hitting the person you hate at that moment. It may sound childish and you may feel foolish at first, but it works! One therapist I know recommends that all his clients buy or create their own punching bag (out of burlap bag and old clothes and rags), hang it in the garage and have a 15 minute "hostility workout" twice a day, once before going to work and then again after coming home. What is accomplished is a release of tension and toxic buildup in the muscles, and a subsequent energy and emotional release as well. Since anger transforms itself to tension in the muscles and nervous systems, a weekly visit to a chiropractor can often accomplish the same thing, particularly for those who do not exercise. A 10 to 15 minute treatment can totally relax the body, and break down the tension. A regular exercise program that includes sports, (tennis, golf, handball, softball, etc.), jogging, or working out can also help keep the tension released and give you an emotional release for anger as well.

e. Learn to take your needs seriously. Anger buildup is often the result of an inability to say "yes" to yourself or "no" to others. You have the right and obligation to do what's best for you, without explanation or justification. I am not talking about extreme selfishness that does not take others into consideration, but the everyday choices to do something because you want to, without feeling it will automatically take something away from your loved ones, or say "no" for the same general reason. If you can't do this without feeling guilt, then the resentment begins to build, and you justify it with anger.

f. Don't push yourself. Take your time. You are struggling with an extreme and potentially explosive problem. Be patient. Ask your family for patience, understanding and help. If they see you are trying to find new solutions with the goal of getting closer to them, patience comes more easily. If they see your request for patience as just another method of buying time and keeping them at a distance, they will be resentful. You must learn to share your struggles and growth so they can feel a part of it and have something to work with and hope for.

g. Learn to accept and develop all your emotions. Violent people are generally afraid of all emotions and experience them all as anger. Emotions such as tenderness, warmth, vulnerability, fear or anxiety are the most frightening because they make the person feel weak and unable to protect himself. Anger therefore, becomes a fortress of protection that is needed to survive.

Whether aware of it or not, these emotions are there and available to you. Gradually allow each a place in your area of experience, like easing yourself into a hot jacuzzi or the cold ocean. Take a small step, relax, experience, and then take another. As you live through these experiences, you will become less frightened and slowly you will be comfortable with many intense emotions, both pleasant and unpleasant.

Block #6: Fear Of Getting Hurt - Retaliation

When you're a 98-pound weakling in a world of giants, this is very real. In an interview for Playboy magazine, Robert Blake (Baretta, of television fame) was quoted as saying, "Yea, though I walk through the valley of the shadow of death, I will fear no evil, for I'm the meanest S.O.B. of them all." That may be a great credo to live by if you're Robert Blake, but most of us can't pass the physical.

When you've gone through life being intimidated by bullies, you learn indirect methods of maintaining your sanity and expressing your hostility. Retaliation can take many forms:

a. Silence or withdrawal. The dirtiest of all in some respects, since there is no defence against silence. It is a total denial of the other's personhood; a crazy-maker in that it leaves the other person trying to guess what's going on inside you.

b. Physical violence toward a smaller person: A scapegoat you can beat up on.

c. Acting out behavior: Vindictive, getting even, flirting, stealing, sexual acting-out, etc. Safer than direct conflict and effective in bringing pain to the other person.

d. The close-off: Ending the relationship, or constantly threatening to do so. This is particularly effective with a dependent, frightened spouse, until they get tired of it and call your bluff. Then the bluffer falls apart and reveals his dependency and fear.

e. Ridicule. Striking out at the person's self esteem.

All of these were discussed earlier but are repeated here in the context of fear of direct violence and anger.

Block #7: The Final Block - The Hidden Agenda

This is more a mechanism of control than a block. I am capable of anger but choose not to express it, because if I do...

"There won't be any sex tonight."

"It will ruin the concert, vacation, party or trip..."

"My spouse won't listen anyway."

"It won't do any good so why bother to experience the stress and pain," or

"Look how great I am. I should have been angry and I wasn't."

There's nothing wrong with picking your issues ("Is it worth it?"), the time and the place ("Being appropriate"). Having an intense fight in public might not be appropriate. What's important is your real motive. Is your motive that of being appropriate, or is it one of avoidance, because you don't expect the expression of your feelings to bring a positive result?

How Do We Remove The Blocks?

Here are eight suggestions for releasing blocks and opening yourself to intimacy and love:

1. Explore the blocks: Where did they originate? What feelings are being experienced? What are you really afraid of? What is the worst thing that could happen? Could you handle it? What are the basic issues? There must be no judgment of your feelings at this point or you can't be free to explore them. Remember, you are looking for personal information and understanding.

2. Listen to the blocks: They are trying to give you messages about yourself. Just as thirst, fever and pain give you messages of truth from within your body that must be responded to, so are the blocks to feelings. For every block there are multiple reasons, information, examples of who you are and how you became that way, as well as new options for change.

3. Validate your feelings: Own them and admit them as your own. Give yourself permission to experience even the most irresponsible or undesirable feelings, without judgement. Don't scare them off.

4. Be aware of the cost: What do these blocks protect you from? What do they keep and prevent you from? They protect you from immediate pain and discomfort. They also prevent you from achieving intimacy, happiness, better sex, a successful marriage, a good self-image, as well as physical and emotional well-being. Is it worth that cost to achieve the temporary relief, to momentarily relieve your anxiety.

5. Experiment and learn new ways to express your feelings: Discover the feeling underlying the anger, your real need. Anger is almost always a secondary and protective reaction, rather than a primary feeling. It is a reaction to feelings of hurt, embarrassment, humiliation or fear.

    Now, respond to your own needs directly. Once aware of the true primary feeling, express it in a straightforward, honest manner. Anger is generally indirect, like a game of charades. "I'll act out my feelings and you guess what they are?" That is bad enough, but it gets worse when the wrong clues are given. "I am angry and yelling at you because I want you to love me," may be the truth, but it will rarely get the results you want. Showing how hurt you are for not being loved might be more effective.

6. Take the risk and discover that you can handle pain. You are not going to be overwhelmed by the first sign of discomfort and anxiety. Stand your ground, experience your strength, prove you can take it without being destroyed.

7. Explore alternatives: Remember you can walk away. If you have tried to be reasonable and honest, but your partner insists on attacking and insulting you viciously, you can always choose to leave the situation. You aren't obligated to be anyone's scapegoat. You can reject the insults. Just because someone deliberately sets out to hurt you, doesn't mean you have to accept the hurt. You don't have to believe the insults and you don't even have to believe your partner actually means them. All you really know is, at the moment, your partner is angry and wants to hurt you.

   You can express yourself firmly. Regardless of your partner's attitude, approach or motives, you can be what you choose to be in any situation. Express who you are, how you feel, how you are being affected by this conversation and relationship, and how you wish to change it. You are only responsible for you.

   You can ask for what you want and not settle for less. "But he won't give it. It won't do any good." That's beside the point. Take responsibility for meeting your own needs, with or without the cooperation of others. When we express ourselves without defensiveness or attacking others, we are generally heard and responded to. Even if we aren't, we still feel good about ourselves and will set out to find another way of getting our needs met.

8. Be willing to let go - release control.

   Give what you are...

   Say what you feel...

   Respond to what you receive...

   Then, let the situation be. Accept the reality of the results. Know when to stop pushing, trying or controlling. "This is who I am. I can do no other." There is no argument against integrity.

Hopefully, this chapter has clarified and more fully identified the many reasons we apply for withholding of self. As you more clearly understand your motives, you can "catch yourself in the act" of defeating the purpose in getting your needs met. Being able to identify the angry or hurt feelings is a major step toward minimizing destructive tendencies, and opening new areas of the positive use of self. There are methods of expressing self which minimize pain and draw people closer together, rather than pushing them further apart. As a result, both partners have a better opportunity to get their needs met, to have their feelings heard, and to know they are cared about and loved.

"WELL, I FINNALY TOLD MY BOSS WHAT I THOUGHT OF HIM TODAY."

Chapter 10

The Destructive or Abusive Use of Self (Anger)

Some people have little difficult in expressing the self. We call them aggressive, pushy, self-centered, abusive, and angry. They easily, or at least quickly, demand everything their way and for their own benefit, much to the dismay of others. Therapy is often criticized for turning people from "nice, easy-going doormats" into these selfish, uncaring egotists.

Neither extreme sounds appropriate or turns out to be a true expression of self. Anger CAN BE a true expression of appropriate feelings or the exact opposite, depending entirely upon how it is expressed. Most of us, however, resent anger - our own and that of others - but find it an effective tool in the defense of self. Anger **is** there to protect us and as long as we restrict its expression to a recitation of our own feelings and needs and why we feel that way, it can be quite effective.

In a very true sense, destructive anger is really a distortion of anger, not a real and direct expression of self, and has two basic purposes in a relationship, to control and to create distance. If you stop and consider your own anger and the motives involved, you can recognize your own need for control and distance in any specific situation. You are trying to control: 1) your self image ("I don't want to appear as weak, vulnerable, hurt, embarrassed, etc."); 2) the other person ("If I can control their

Distortion of Anger: To Control & Create distance

behavior, I am safe from whatever they are doing or may do that frightens me"); and 3) what happens, the eventual outcome of your disagreement ("If I get my own way, I win, or I keep from losing").

In the process of this self protection, of course, you distance each other and hence feel safer for the moment, at least. Because the closeness and intimacy of the relationship itself often creates a factor of fear, you may even create an incident in order to provide distance. Also, the fear of a fight or of rejection or losing whatever, may have created the need for distance and for time to recover.

Many people need, desire and desperately strive for intimacy and love, yet are at the same time terribly afraid of the closeness and find it difficult to sustain for any appreciable length of time. Rather than admit this paradox to themselves and try to work through to a solution, they often subconsciously create an "excuse" for a right to justify the distancing and thereby avoid the real problem: I need to be close, but I am afraid of being close.

The following is a list of ten ways we use anger to distort, control and distance. There are undoubtedly others you can add to the list and many of these have overlapping qualities.

How Relationships Become Derailed: The Abuses of Anger

1. "It's All Your fault" - The Blamer

These are the "right-wrong", "good-bad" and "win-lose" people. Probably the most difficult couple to work with in therapy, and I've had my share. There is absolutely no contact in the exchange and it is definitely used for the purpose of creating more distance. Nothing works better for this purpose. Neither partner will take responsibility for his own actions nor those of the other.

"My actions and your actions are all your fault. I would always act in a proper manner if not for you. You set me up. I have to defend myself. You're wrong and you never will admit it. You will never see my point of view. You don't listen."

This is in reality a survival defense. Both parties have to win to survive. Losing is death, admitting you are wrong, stupid and a total failure. Because of the seriousness of the consequences, neither party will ever concede, so it's usually a stand-off in each individual situation, although each will claim "you hurt me more than I hurt you."

A noted athlete in counseling with his wife admitted his whole theory of competition, relationships and life is to "avoid losing". Here is a man who drives himself incessantly, has an extremely destructive temper, excels even beyond his ability, and rarely loses. But he's not a "winner". Every victory is just one more day of avoiding the inevitable loss. He cannot really savor the satisfaction of victory, and hundreds of victories do not improve his self image or self esteem. A loss (of a game or argument) simply reveals to the rest of the world what he feels every day, "I'm a loser, a failure, a person of little worth." That's too high a price to pay, so he "wins".

The blamer never reveals his own feelings or what's going on inside. He talks about you - your motives, your feelings, your badness - but never about his hurt.

The real issue breaks down to this. Susan says, "You hurt me." It would be nice if the statement came out so direct and so matter of fact, but usually the message is buried in accusing, demoralizing of the other's motives and lack of character. The underlying issue is: "You hurt me." Sam responds: "I am not a bad guy." This is also disguised beneath hostile attacks and lethal accusations. Since neither one has heard or understood the other's message, they continue to debate two different subjects with no possible solution. Sam hears Susan tell him that he is a bad guy, has always been a bad guy, and always will be. Furthermore, everything he does will be influenced by that fact. Perhaps Susan is saying that because it is safer to talk about Sam's badness than to admit Susan's hurt. Regardless of how she expresses it, the bottom line remains, "You hurt me" or at least, "I got hurt in that exchange." She is fighting to have him apologize and be sorry that she got hurt. Only then would Susan feel loved and cared about.

But if Sam apologizes and expresses genuine sorrow that she was hurt, in his mind, he is admitting that he is a bad guy, he was wrong, she is right. "She wins, I lose, and she'll never forget it." So, Sam must talk her out of that need. "You shouldn't feel that way because..." If this sounds foreign to you, you're not a blamer, and perhaps it is impossible for you to believe people can take situational feelings to such a life and death extreme, but they can and do.

How do you break this pattern? First, by revealing what the real issues are: Susan is hurt and Sam doesn't want to be thought of as a bad guy. Once this is expressed and made clear, Sam is free to respond to Susan's hurt "I'm sorry you feel that way. I didn't mean to hurt you." and Susan loses her need to attack Sam since he has responded to her feelings rather than to her words.

When we are no longer adversaries, defending and attacking characters, we can sit down to discuss and solve "our mutual problems". We are trying to understand and change behavior that bothers us and at the same time doing so in such a way that both can feel listened to, understood and loved. When you feel your "life" is at stake, it is impossible to listen to or care about anyone else. The solution sounds easy, and it is. The difficult part is getting a frightened person to listen long enough to hear the solution.

2. "Why Did You Do That?" - The Questioner

Interestingly enough, this person asks questions that cannot really be answered. He is not looking for information and understanding, but actually putting you down in a subtle, indirect fashion.

George spills his drink all over the dinner and onto Mary's dress and she screams at him, "Why did you do that?" It is difficult to put a question mark there because it is more of an accusation than a question. What she is saying is: "Why are you so stupid?" "Why are you consistently clumsy?" "Why are you thoughtless?" The insinuation is that George is deliberately choosing to be hostile and hurtful and did it because he wanted to. "Why did you want to spill your drink on me at this moment in time?" That is a difficult question to answer but the laughable part is that we try. George can't come up with an answer that will satisfy Mary. "I don't know if I was born that way, or if it took years of practice." So, instead, he blames it on her to get himself off the hook. "You confused me." "You asked for the butter and I was trying to pass it." "If you weren't always yelling at the kids, I could relax at the dinner table." "You never liked that dress anyway."

Interrogators are dishonest because no answer will satisfy them. They love to debate facts, demand justifications, explanations and reasons which are never good enough or acceptable.

They never have to reveal their own feelings and they totally control the conversation by placing others on the defensive. The solution: Don't try to give an intelligent answer to a stupid question. Deal with the issue, not the question. George could simply say:

"I'm sorry I spilled my drink on your dress."

"I know my clumsiness upsets you. I wish I had better control of it."

"You really see me as a hostile person who manages to work you over, don't you?"

"Are you saying I did it deliberately?"

Any of the above responses deals more closely with what really happened and what her reaction implies. What if she stays on the attack? George needs to stay with the issue and to refuse to be dragged into a name-calling contest.

Another example that may more closely fit with some of you is the Mother who inquires of her adult children...

"Why don't you love me?"

There is only one answer that seems to immediately fly back - "But I **do** love you, Mother."

Of course Mother doesn't accept this answer and the next 90 minutes are devoted to your trying to convince Mother you do. She won't be convinced but for an hour and a half she had your undivided squirming attention and the time of her life.

There **is** a better answer. "What do I do that makes you **feel** unloved?" We don't respond with that question for a very obvious reason - SHE'LL TELL US. Mother will pull out her grocery list of complaints we've heard a million times before and beat us into guilt with it.

DO IT ANYWAY. Then you have many choices of response. Start with the truth. If you know you are not ACTING IN A WAY THAT MOTHER WANTS YOU TO don't deny it!

"You never call." "Yes I do!"

"You never come over." "Yes I do!"

What is the truth? If you don't call, come over, run errands, clean your room or pay attention to Mother as much as she wants you to - ADMIT THAT!

"No I don't do _____ **as much as you'd like me to**, I'm aware of that."

"WHY NOT?"

Tell the truth of your feelings.

"I don't feel any amount of time would be enough to satisfy you."

"I have other obligations. I'm sorry you feel neglected and unloved."

"The reason I don't call or come over is because you are never glad to hear from me, but just criticize me for not doing it more often."

"It's difficult to enjoy you when you complain all the time."

"Why do **you** feel I don't do what you want?" She might even reveal why **she** suspects you are angry with her.

"What do you really want to know? I'm not sure I understand the question. Are you saying the only way to show my love is to always be there for you?"

Since the questioner is couching an accusation in the confusion of an unanswerable question, there is a lack of honesty in the approach. It is our responsibility then to search out the honest feelings. Don't guess - make the person spell out true feelings and accusations.

"Are you implying such and such?"

You can be angry - upset or irritated with someone and still love them.

"Why don't you love me?" can be answered, "I am angry with you or acting the way I do because... That has nothing to do with whether or not I love you. I am sure you are feeling the coldness or distance between us and you are correct. I am sorry if that makes you feel unloved."

You are responding to Mother's TRUE FEELINGS of hurt, but not apologizing for being a hateful or unloving child. "I'm sorry you feel unloved" is not a confession that I don't love you, but a response to your feelings.

3. "I'm Only Trying To Help!" - The Critic

If you criticize from a place of love and caring, people generally will not be deeply hurt. Criticism is the most hurtful when coming from one who is threatened and has his ego at stake. It is also the most hurtful to this person. People who criticize can rarely take criticism. They subconsciously know what an effective weapon of control criticism is because of the devastating effect it has on them. Since the best defense is a good offense, they go for the punch with a killer instinct. Often, they are not aware of this double standard.

In a therapy session that included a married daughter and her parents, the mother consistently started sentences with the intimidating phrase - "You already know...

...I love you"

...that's immoral."

...You shouldn't have done that."

When the therapist pointed out to the mother that those statements were judgmental and critical, she became flustered and upset. "I don't mean to be critical and make her feel stupid. She has to understand that it is a habit of mine. That's just the way I talk." Before the sentence was hardly finished, her tone of voice and mannerism turned abruptly from embarrassed apology to anger and bitterness. "My husband always says that to me - 'you already know' - and I always feel he is calling me stupid and I deeply resent it. I have tried for years to get him to stop that, but he doesn't care about my feelings at all."

Until it was pointed out by the therapist, the mother never got the connection between what her husband said to her and what she said to her daughter. It never occurred to her that the daughter felt stupid, or that she was calling her daughter stupid, or how her husband could be so dumb as to not recognize the wife's feelings. The hostility in the husband toward the wife, whether he would admit that or not, was being expressed also by mother to daughter.

Criticism and anger are best expressed directly and openly, not with indirectness, sarcasm and ridicule which later can be denied. "I disagree with your decision or values" is easier to respond to than "You are stupid to act that way." You have a right to disagree but no right to judge someone stupid or wrong for having an opinion different than yours.

There is a place for warm, gentle humor - a kidding of the human condition - "Yes, I notice your clumsiness and forgetfulness and it is mildly irritating, but if I can kid you about it, I can live with it most of the time."

4. "When I Get Through With You..." - The Vicious

This can be defined as a "deliberate attempt to hurt someone in an area in which you know they are vulnerable". It is designed primarily to achieve distance and it works. Viciousness creates deep feelings of being wounded and hurt. Adjectives provide good weapons here. Calling someone a "creep" hurts, but a "fat" or "ugly" or "bucktoothed" creep personalizes it and hurts even more.

Surprisingly, the vicious attack often occurs after a long period of warmth, closeness and intimacy. This makes it more effective because of the element of surprise and the lack of warning. It is used as a homeostatic process for those who cannot sustain long periods of intimacy. They need to balance with space because the closeness can no longer be tolerated, but they do not know how to simply ask for it. Therefore, the distance must be justified by hard feelings, and a vicious interchange accomplishes that.

Needy people, who go for "instant intimacy" often find themselves using viciousness to provide relief from an overwhelming romantic episode. They do not "ebb and flow" with a relationship and are so dependent they cling 24 hours a day until they reach a saturation point. Since they do not understand the concepts of space and privacy in a relationship, and are afraid of being misunderstood or rejected if they asked for it, they find the only solution is in a fight.

Awareness of the problem within yourself or your partner is a good first step to change this type of behavior. Total possessiveness is the most obvious sign of insecurity and dependency. All of us need to develop our own sense of inner peace and security through time alone and inner awareness. Togetherness is more nourishing and appreciated when there is space and time apart to rest.

5. "I Don't Get Mad, I Get Even" - The Avenger

Tit for tat, getting even, king of the mountain, got'cha last, up the ante, and escalation are various ways of describing this process of destructive anger which can also be vicious if necessary, to accomplish the goals.

"You hurt me, so I'll hurt you worse, and show you I don't care." This is the most common excuse for sexual acting out, alcohol or drug abuse.

"My spouse and I had a big fight so I went out and got drunk, or laid, or whatever."

Sometimes we want them to know we got even, often however, we do not. It is sometimes satisfaction enough that we did it, if they find out, now we are open to receive retaliation.

6. "The End Justifies The Means" - the Manipulator

This is winning by intimidation, being angry for the purpose of producing an effect, not because you feel it. A very manipulative method in dealing with those who are afraid of yelling and fighting. Raise your voice and get your way quickly and without bloodshed, also without sharing your real feelings.

The "I want what I want when I want it" mentality is often expressed as loud and intimidating, but is just noise. Noise without feeling, just volume, contrived. Constructive anger, in contrast, is not noise, it has feeling behind it. Although we call it anger, a temper tantrum is totally self-indulgent and has no contact with the other person. It is a catharsis, a blaming with no vulnerability. Actually the person is having a good time!

Those who resist any new approach to intimacy with the reaction "What's the use of trying, it won't work?" only see anger as manipulation, not as a true expression of self. "No matter what I do or how I behave, I can't manipulate you to give me what I want. If I can't get what I want, why waste my time expressing myself?" This person is only concerned with results (controlling the other) rather than integrity (expressing the self). A healthy person says what he feels and behaves constructively because it meets his own needs, and it makes him feel good about himself. The success of this venture lies in his own behavior (for which he alone is responsible) rather than the responses (for which he is not).

Interestingly, when you feel a need to "protect" the relationship by being less than candid and manipulating in an indirect fashion, the results are usually negative. When you get angry enough that you "don't care" about the reaction and you feel an obligation to express your true feelings and let the chips fly even if it costs you the relationship, you usually get heard, and get the results you wanted. I'm not saying "don't care" about the other person, or aggressively see how destructive you can be, but "don't care" about controlling the results.

7. "Who Me?" - The Innocent

This is one of the most frustrating and effective means of destructive behavior simply because even the perpetrator himself is able to stay deceived. This varies from cunningly planned, covert activity to totally subconscious reaction. The passive-aggressive person frequently denies the intent behind the act and seems totally innocent of wrong doing. This behavior is characterized by what the people "omit" or "forget" rather than what they do, and generally infuriates the victim, who is then made to feel petty for complaining.

Symptoms are: forgetting, accidently breaking things, always being late, "nice guy syndrome", innocent questions, not understanding, complimenting beyond reality.

You are ready to do the dishes and realize you are out of soap. Your boyfriend offers to turn off his favorite TV program to go to the store. You are thrilled and ask if he will also bring back three other items. "Of course." Fifteen minutes later he returns with three items - he forgot the soap. You are furious and he can't understand why. "I offered, I turned off the TV, I got three things, so I forgot - my intent was good." You are angry because it happens all the time, not just in isolated situations.

PASSIVE - AGGRESSIVE:
WHEN YOU CARE ENOUGH - NOT TO GET CAUGHT

The truth is that he unconsciously withholds because he can't say "no" or feels inadequate in expressing feelings and is therefore resentful. He "wins" by withholding on an unconscious level.

The real reasons for the act are kept out of awareness and denied. The key is not in what they give, but what they withhold in the process of giving.

8. "Give It To Me Now!" - The Violent Abuser

Violence is a direct result of suppressing assertion. Assertion is comfortably taking your needs seriously - in a direct manner. Violence is assertion gone sour. When a person does not feel the right to take his needs seriously, when he holds them inside, tension builds until he blows. Building assertion avoids violence.

A large, powerful and angry husband once asked in a couples' group what he could do with his anger. "You won't let me hit her anymore, so I try repressing it. Then it builds for several weeks until I blow up and scream and holler and that's not acceptable either. What can I do?" He had no concept of quietly, firmly and expectantly asserting his needs and feelings and being heard!

CATHARSIS:

THE ABILITY TO
RELEASE TENSION

AND OFFEND
PEOPLE AT THE
SAME TIME

Violence is a method of contact and homeostasis, though not a very satisfying one. Sadism is the flip side of helplessness. sadists were usually the object of sadism as children. All child abusers were abused. To be a sadist requires a helpless object. Since you were once the victim, you choose now to be the winner for a change. Punitiveness comes from a need to control others. In the case of parents, we can see this as a very clear need. It comes from a fear of not having control. We are not talking about appropriate punishment for the child.

When a person experiences inner chaos, he feels a powerful need to control his environment, often through fear and punishment. When there is inner peace and tranquility, he can tolerate fewer controls and more chaos in the outer environment.

Punitiveness generally produces three reactions in the recipient: 1) It creates resentment and hostility. 2) It does not work, except temporarily. 3) It blocks generosity. Obligation and fear will produce the minimum response one can get away with to avoid further punishment, no more, no less. When punishment is removed, people are much more generous by free choice.

We often hear the expressions "get off it" and "release it". What it boils down to is we can't let a situation go because our ego is involved, and we put ourselves in a win or lose, life or death situation. The child (or spouse) picks up the challenge and now he can't let go either. It is not a matter of no longer caring what the other does, but of letting go of the manipulation and power struggle. Tell the other person how you feel and what you need and expect. You are leaving him an implied choice of consent and acknowledging you can't totally dominate his life. When respected in this manner, the person usually gives you the behavior you wanted.

The most common example is getting a teenager to clean his/her room. "Clean your room or I'll knock your head off." If the teen believes the threat, he will get the room just clean enough to avoid the head being knocked off - no more - no less. Each new day will require a new threat.

"I am very angry or upset about your filthy room" is a statement of your feelings with an *implied* threat. What action I will take if this continues is not addressed, so there is some anxiety about possible consequences.

There is also implied choice to clean the room or not. "If you want me to stop being angry and be nicer to you, you'll clean the room. If you don't care you won't." Everyone wants to feel they have a choice.

Aggressive behavior that intrudes into another person's psychic space is characterized by a negative, selfish, uncaring attitude, the opposite of assertion. Aggression produced by needy, desperate people "taking" what they really don't deserve, or could get any other way. It is assaultive violating behavior, justified by the extent of the need.

"I was angry."

"I was drunk."

"I was hungry."

Or, blaming you -

"You shouldn't have done that."

"You dared me."

"You made me mad."

Some people feel assertion is no match for aggression because assertion is bound by the rules of courtesy and appropriateness, while aggression is not. We admit there is no changing another person who refuses to be reasonable; however, each owes it to himself to assertively stand his ground, share his feelings and meet his own needs, regardless of the irresponsible behavior of others.

9. "Sock It To Me" - The Victim

Surprising to some, being a victim is also an expression of anger. This too comes from the inability to take one's needs seriously, just as aggression is. Anyone can fall occasional victim to a circumstance in life, but if a pattern exists whereby you find yourself continually abused - either physically or emotionally - taken advantage of, used or hurt and no steps are ever taken to protect self or rectify the situation, then you are a true victim.

Perhaps you feel deserving of the beating because you see yourself as a "bad" person, or it relieves guilt for your behavior or justifies the inner hatred you feel but never express. No one can have true self esteem and remain a victim. Rights must be asserted and feelings expressed. If the other person is violent and won't "let" you, then your responsibility is to leave that relationship and take control of your own life and destiny.

Much has been written in feminine literature that women need to find their rage to break out of abusive relationships with men. I agree. It is rarely pointed out, however, that much of that rage (in all of us when we feel like a victim) is rage at the self for being weak, frightened, dependent and unable to protect ourselves. Turn that rage into power that says I can and will protect myself from abusive and hurtful people and situations. The victim gives self no "rights" or sense of personal authority.

10. "Let's Laugh At Him" - The Joker Is Wild

This is the practical joker, the Don Rickles or Joan Rivers type of person. Great sense of humor, makes everyone laugh especially those who are the butt of the joke. All the better to cover up the hurt.

Sarcasm is almost always a cover for hostility, a method of indirectly releasing anger and feeling superior. It is backed by a strong sense of denial. If you complain or get offended, "you have no sense of humor" or "I was just kidding." Oh, yeah!

Sarcasm is a release valve to keep from blowing up. Take away a person's sarcasm and pure anger generally follows. Since ridicule is used a lot to keep children in line, most of us feel like children again when we receive it. It is very difficult to penetrate the defense mechanism of the person with this behavior trait, making it doubly hard to deal with the real issues and feelings involved. The victim is made to feel foolish for being so "sensitive" and easily hurt.

How many of these ten points can you identify with? When was the last time you used such behavior? Can you see new possibilities for changing that in the future?

Integrity is

Giving what you are
Saying what you feel
Responding to what you receive
Letting go of the results

Chapter 11

Authenticity: the Affirmation of Self

What does it mean to be authentic? To be genuine, authoritative (a good authority), trustworthy, reliable, real, honest. Also in agreement with fact or actuality, something that really IS what it is represented to be, emphasizing freedom from admixture, adulteration or sham (genuine silk, genuine grief). Bona fide is properly used when a question of good faith is involved; meritable implies correspondence with the truth and connotes absolute affirmation. The opposite is spurious, counterfeit or sham.

Who would not want to declare self as authentic and genuine? Yet to be such requires at least two principles: To know who you are and to appropriately express who you are. Very few of us qualify in this respect. Furthermore, most people are generally reared in a manner that literally fights against these principles, given one of two messages by their parents as children growing up: "Don't be angry - be afraid"; or "Don't be afraid - be angry." Rarely will you find a home where both of these emotions are openly accepted. Most of us can readily identify which family message we received.

Books on assertiveness and "creative aggression" or intimidating others succeed mainly because we are not comfortable with our anger and have spent years developing a casual "Joe Cool" approach to life to avoid angry confrontations. Some of us are afraid of our own anger (loss of control under stress), fearful of thereby physically hurting someone or "looking like a fool". Others are afraid of receiving the anger of someone else (being hurt physically or emotionally). In spite of these fears and all our best intentions, most of us manage to experience and express anger with relative ease and consistency, often at the expense of relationships and people we highly regard. "You only hurt the one you love, the one you feel safest to explode all over." Along with this, society has usually taken a dim view of people who take their own needs seriously in too strenuous a manner. Often, due to our fear of anger (our own and that of others) sometimes because we are reluctant to "rock the boat" of mediocre co-existence; perhaps due to a desire not to look selfish or self absorbed; we ignore, overlook, give up, deny and otherwise refute our own basic, day to day needs and feelings. This is being IN-AUTHENTIC - THE DENIAL OF SELF.

This leads to frustration, resentment, misunderstanding, bitterness and hurt that has to come to the surface and be released somehow and/or it turns to physical and emotional illness if not properly released. So, as stated above, it usually winds up hurting the ones we least want to hurt - ourselves and our loved ones.

We have already discussed at length some of the reasons people withhold their feelings and the painful and destructive results of crazy-making, as well as the awful turmoil it brings to the individuals involved. Withholding and denial of feelings can lead to ulcers, nervous breakdown, heart attack, stroke and (some researchers feel) even cancer for the withholder.

Then we discussed the destructive misuse of anger and its subsequent hurtful consequences, both to the giver and receiver of the abuse. So, then what we are to do with our intense, personal, negative and often overwhelming angers, fears and needs?

Do we dare express them?

Do we have a right to express them?

Is there an appropriate way?

Is it possible to get positive results that actually improve relationships, clarify situations and promote harmony rather than destroy it?

Is it possible to do this and feel good about yourself?

Is it possible to do this without looking selfish and uncaring or foolish and unfeeling to others?

I want to serve self (BE AUTHENTIC) in a way that meets my own needs, responds to my own integrity, keeps my body healthy and well, and increases my feelings of self worth, while at the same time, makes me "look good" in the community, with no negative fallout or sense of loss to the significant others with whom I relate on a continual basis. Moreover, I want my service of self to actually enhance communication, smooth out the exchange of information, increase the free flow of love and finish with a situation which clearly evidences to the world that what is best for me is also best for the important others in my life and we are uplifted by this exchange.

CAN IT BE DONE? SOUNDS IDEALISTIC AND IMPOSSIBLE.

In the words of our current American hero, Rocky Balboa, "GO FOR IT!"

I believe in the full range of emotions - ANGER, LOVE, LOYALTY, RAGE, DISGUST, AMBITION, INTENSE FEELINGS, EVEN VOLATILE, FEARFUL AND PARANOID ONES.

They all need to be fully experienced and properly expressed or addressed by each of us. There are acceptable and successful ways of doing this as well as unacceptable and unsuccessful ways.

TO DO IT SUCCESSFULLY IS TO BE AUTHENTIC.

TO REFUSE IS TO BE A SHAM.

To withhold these intense feelings (especially anger, springing from unresolved pain) is to withhold great sections of self from a relationship and that prevents love from being expressed as well. How can you freely love someone who can't or won't relate to your anger? Anger and love are not mutually exclusive but passionate expressions of self.

This chapter is entitled: AUTHENTICITY: THE AFFIRMATION OF SELF. To be authentic is to know oneself and ASSERT oneself. What does it mean to assert? To join to, state positively, declare, affirm, insist on one's rights, thrust oneself forward, state positively with great confidence.

Synonyms that elaborate the meaning:

TO DECLARE - assert openly, often in the face of opposition
(declared their independence)

AFFIRM - implies deep conviction in one's statement and the unlikelihood of denial by another

AVER - connotes implicit confidence in the truth of one's statement from one's own knowledge of the matter.

ASSERTION IS RESPONDING TO AND TAKING CARE OF ONE'S NEEDS IN A DIRECT AND APPROPRIATE MANNER. It's counterpart, aggression, is attacking the other person in a hostile manner. To be assertive is to confidently, firmly, appropriately and directly state your feelings, needs, convictions and attitudes to another human being. At the same time, it includes respect for the other person's feelings. When we assert ourselves, we necessarily consider the feelings of others. When we are aggressive, we do not. Assertion is "putting yourself on the line", describing and relating your experience in the relationship, how you are being affected.

ANGER AS ASSERTION IS PASSING INFORMATION FOR THE PRIMARY PURPOSE OF BEING BETTER UNDERSTOOD, RATHER THAN JUST TO CHANGE BEHAVIOR. It is not designed to be intimidating or controlling, but is very effective in achieving the desired results simply because of the methods used.

Being assertive, you use "I" statements of feelings, rather than "you" statements of accusation. You do not intrude into the space of others or question their motives, integrity or heritage. Responding to this attitude, others are not as apt to be defensive, are much more likely to hear what you have to say, and therefore, be more free to respond to your desires.

A very mild example may demonstrate this more clearly. Charles was playing solitaire when his son, Eric, who was quite young and just learning the game himself, joined him.

Since Daddy was playing, Eric also wanted to play and they set up on opposite sides of a rather narrow counter. As the games progressed, Eric slowly moved deeper across the counter taking up more room and moving into Dad's space. It became somewhat upsetting and the temptation was to treat Eric with irritation. "Don't do it", "You're in my way", or "It irritates me when you don't give me enough room." All of these statements are "you" statements tinged with blame and rejection.

To deliberately test whether a youngster could respond to simple assertiveness (and to feel better about himself), Daddy simply said to Eric in a tone of information only (no hostility or irritation), "That's my space." Eric's reply was immediate - "Oh", and he moved the cards. He did not feel the need to apologize or feel guilty and simply moved the cards without being directly asked to. Of course, he invaded the same space at least six or seven times in an hour, and each time, it was handled exactly the same way with the same results. Some of you may wonder why it happened so many times and whether Eric was testing Daddy. That's possible, and it is also possible that he became so involved in the game he didn't notice. The point is Daddy got what he needed each time he asserted his space and did not have to get angry to achieve it. With anger he might have cut it off sooner but it would have put a damper on their fun. Eric felt related to as a reasonable, responsive person and he reacted that way; he moved the cards.

Now, let's look at twelve points that focus on what this assertion really is and demonstrate how assertion can affect our lives and the lives of those we relate to. What are we really asserting and why is it important to do so? In some respects this could be referred to as the healthy expression of anger because we are usually talking about intense, personal, important feelings, not just day to mundane day experiences.

These are integrity issues, value belief systems, defending one's honor and "not to be taken lightly" issues.

What are the reasons and rights for these expressions and the methods that bring results? Many of these points will naturally overlap but experienced as a whole, tend to demonstrate what BASIC communication skills at their very best can accomplish in these intense situations.

THE AFFIRMATION OF SELF IS:

1. A FEELING

Feelings are not subject to moral judgement. They just ARE, they EXIST. Anger, for instance, does not need to be explained, justified or defended any more than love does. If you want to see real anger, by the way, just tell someone, "You shouldn't feel that way BECAUSE..." "Don't tell me how I **should** feel (the Gospel according to you). This is how I DO FEEL (the truth according to ME). Feelings are always truth but not always accurate. Sometimes they are based on faulty perceptions, paranoia, defensiveness, distortion or denial, but they always truthfully tell us about whatever causes them.

Feelings are inner messages trying to get out in the same way fever is a message from the body that is currently fighting off disease or germs. The job of the intellect is to properly listen to those feelings, correctly identify and decode the messages and then decide an appropriate way of either responding to them or expressing them to others.

We don't have to like them, we can't always control them, but just be aware of them, understand where they come from and the messages they are trying to bring to us.

We ARE responsible for and in charge of our ACTIONS. Actions might be defined as the outward expression of our feelings.

YOU CAN GO TO JAIL FOR WHAT YOU ARE DOING - NOT FOR WHAT YOU ARE FEELING.

Strong words, by the way, are the poetry of feelings. Anger is a strong and intense emotion and it is incongruent to express strong emotions with mild words. Even those who do not believe in "four letter words", cursing or whatever you chose to call it, find themselves creating a substitute language of acceptably strong words: such as "darn" for "damn", "doggone" for "God damn", "heck" for "Hell".

The other side of the coin, however, is that strong words are virtually useless if they prevent you from being "heard". You may have to clean up your act in order to get someone's attention. This is a point that needs to be understood when generations clash and obscene words are used to shock one's elders. If we already know certain words offend the persons we are trying to relate to, the use of those words might be the very source of losing any opportunity for success. Remember, words can be offensive, so don't get hung up in words at the expense of being heard.

2. A SOURCE OF DISCOVERY ABOUT SELF

Listening to oneself, to those inner thoughts and feelings, knowing what upsets you, can tell you a lot about yourself. In what areas are you sensitive, have strong moral convictions, are easily threatened, petty, judgmental, caring, defensive or intolerant?

This is an opportunity for discovering strengths and weaknesses, values and convictions, by simply learning to listen to your own feelings and reactions. Give yourself permission to experience and own it all, the good and the bad. You have all the choices necessary to decide how to act on these feelings, the key is to first be aware of them and what they mean to you. In this way, you can take full responsibility for what hurts you, and why, and be able to do something constructive with that information.

3. A GIFT

What more loving and intimate gift can be shared than one's intense and straight-forward feelings? Why give just a small part of yourself? Give the entire gamut of your emotions and reactions, share who you are in the moment, give a gift that says "you are that important to me." "If I don't hear your anger (hurt), I can't trust your love."

The excuse I most often hear is that "my relationship with (Mother, Father, spouse or friend) is too IMPORTANT TO LOSE. Therefore I can't take the risk of being honest (angry) because I could lose the person and I couldn't handle that loss." Unfortunately, it isn't that simple. Withholding your anger "to keep peace" only brings temporary aspirin-like relief. The issue that caused the anger (the way the person is treating you) is not resolved and since you haven't brought the issue to their attention, there is no reason to change and the hurt continues. You get more and more angry inside due to their "refusals to care enough to change" when they haven't been told.

The hurt client often responds - "he knows or **should** know what he's doing - how can he **not** know what he's doing to me?" Because he is NOT seeing the situation from your point of view, because he is NOT a mind reader, because you think you are spilling emotional blood and you are not, or perhaps he doesn't HAVE to change because you don't insist. So why bother? It is not the other person's responsibility to read your mind and guess what you need. It is your responsibility to give the gift of your honest and open feelings - including negative ones. It is the other's responsibility to **respond.** Tell this significant person of your fear of hurting him, of being misunderstood or rejected. Then say, "You are too important for me to withhold these feelings. I don't want any unresolved hurt or anger festering between us and causing damage to the relationship. If I hold it inside, the feelings come out as sullenness, withdrawal of love, or eventual explosion. I don't want that to happen to us. Here's a gift of my feelings."

It is a gift in process, one that is never complete. The packaging varies from support to confrontation to caring - and it's a genuine way of expressing love.

4. NOURISHING TO SELF

The primary purpose of expressing authenticity is to take care of one's self, protection by being clear and open, not by blocking or creating distance. If you can't protect or express yourself when necessary (or you fear you cannot), then great blocks of energy must be constantly withheld to afford this protection and build a fortress against potential attack. Sullenness, resentment and withdrawal are all great energy drains to the system, as well as is the need to be constantly alert to attack from all sides.

The powerful man, well trained in self-defense, who knows he can defend himself, will often walk away from a fight and have no reason to participate, nothing to prove. The one who is constantly provoking fights or at least can't walk away from one, is usually a person still trying to prove to himself and to the world how tough he is. He doesn't really believe in his strength, so he has to constantly reassure himself of its presence.

When you know there is natural anger and strength available to protect you on call, then the body can relax. Energy can be directed to productive channels and there is a tremendous experience of vitality and aliveness. It is good for the body to release feelings rather than sit on them. Most, if not all, psychosomatic illnesses come from repressing feelings. We have shown examples of this in other portions of the book.

Destructive use of anger could cause as much damage to the body and nervous system as repression, creating more anxiety and turmoil than it resolves. "The angrier you get - the angrier you get." The expression of or acting out of anger for the purpose of revenge, one-upsmanship or winning, without any subsequent resolution of feelings is destructive to both parties and the relationship. The person doing it may feel in control or vindicated, but still has difficulty releasing the anger itself. Unfinished anger comes home to roost in the henhouse of the angry person.

The constructive expression of self is a catharsis, a release of tension and a cleansing of poison from the system. Saying directly to the person involved with a firm and clear vision of "I am angry with you because..." that describes what went on between us, how it affected me and why I feel the way I do, cleans out the toxic resentments. Each person taking responsibility for his own feelings and actions - no good or bad guys - just an honest exchange of feelings. These added benefits of positive response, can help greatly to bring about healing.

5. MULTI-LAYER

Top Layer	-	**Anger**
Middle Layer	-	**Hurt**
Lower Layer	-	**Blocked tenderness, Caring and a Hope for Something Better**

Between each of these layers could be filters of fear as well. There is Love-Hate in all intense, intimate relationships. To keep the relationship alive and vital, it must be brought to the surface and dealt with.

Hate or anger first blocks off the hurt that needs to be expressed so you can be more deeply understood. If you refuse to share this second layer of hurt or if the other person refuses to acknowledge and care about your hurt, then the real block takes place. Then the deep, tender, loving feelings are effectively blocked off and cannot be expressed. It is very difficult, virtually impossible, to love someone who won't let you be angry with them, who forces you to cut off those intense feelings, or who discounts your hurt feelings as childish, inappropriate, or not important.

That is why sex is one of the first things to go when anger appears. How can you express tenderness and love when you are still angry and hurt? For those who report that the only thing going for the relationship is great sex, sex evidently symbolizes to them something other than tenderness, love and respect. Perhaps it is their method of expressing hostility and conquest, while for others, it may be a security blanket to relieve anxiety.

However, anger can be a real turn-on, not because it is hurtful, but because you become vulnerable, open, totally who you are at that moment. Anger may trigger true contact at its very best, with a response that is natural and immediate. To the contrary, anger unexpressed is a major block to both loving and sexual feelings.

6. RESPONSE

Intense emotions are always reaction rather than initiating action. They respond to what someone has given to you and to your own internalizing of that gift. Often, it is a response to hurt, jealousy, disappointment, fear, or loss. One feels safer and less vulnerable responding with anger than expressing any of the above. The fact that you broke a dish is not so important, unless it symbolized that "their" things were not important to you and somehow that gets interpreted as an example of how you misuse the relationship and reject their love.

This is usually a mixed bag of tricks, however. Part of you wants to be angry and express it (getting even with the other person for hurting you) and part does not want the hassle involved. Perhaps you would like to just "hit and run" - express it and be done with it. Sharing feelings is a door opener to even more important feelings and fears, so that if you attack first, you have opened yourself to a heavier counter-attack and more hurt, with more escalation. You want to run away; not only from the immediate angry reaction (if it would stop there, great!) but the escalation that follows. That can be simply an escalation of "I got you last" or painfully, into deeper levels of who you are and what you really feel about the other person.

7. A RISK

WE have no control and actually must relinquish any control over the outcome of our sharing our feelings, or else it is manipulation. "This is me because I need to be me, not because I have to have any prescribed result."

In my counseling practice, I often speak of an "emotional divorce" and how every bad marriage needs one. What that amounts to is the willingness to risk a divorce in the process of changing yourself and your relationship. You and your growth have to be more important than the continuation of the marriage.

When you "protect" the marriage by not rocking the boat or doing anything that could upset your spouse enough to leave, you are, in effect, stifling it to death - foregoing any opportunity for constructive growth and learning. This generally happens when one or both of the marriage partners are insecure and terrified of being alone. The prospect of having to face the challenges of single life, without the financial or emotional security of a spouse is just too overwhelming. For those who can take the risk, all the odds increase in their favor. For them there is a better chance for the marriage not only to survive, but to grow into something unique and special. Also, their individual growth will do the same and each feeds good nourishment to the other.

I recently received a warm Christmas card from a former client with the concluding sentence, "I would love to see you again but it would only make things worse." Joanne was originally introduced to me as part of her son's therapy. He was going through a bad marriage and saw his mother as an "angry, controlling bitch." In the mother-son context, with a reasonable son who wanted to love her, she was able to change, be more honest and open and less angry and vindictive.

She continued in therapy for herself but her husband was passive, sullen and withdrawn. She admitted she did not love him and never had, but was in her 60's now and too scared to divorce. Coming to therapy made her aware of her needs. She acted on them to a point, but could go no further so quit therapy rather than risk divorce.

I have had quite a few clients that felt "divorce was not an option" due to financial fear, religious belief or could not get past the stigma of failure or being alone. If divorce is not an option, neither is marriage. You haven't chosen to stay married you are stuck. Once the other person figures that out, they really feel free to beat you up.

For those who do not take the risk, the best they can look forward to is a deteriorating version of what they have now, an illusion of security contaminated by continual mistrust, resentment and concealed hostility that erupts from time to time and could impulsively push either or both into a readiness for divorce anyway, without ever having had the true opportunity for growth.

While anger keeps coming up in various settings, the message remains the same - Let go of control, what will be, will be. Let go of the outcome. It is not your responsibility. Let go of your "image". Let people see the real you. They might surprise you and like it.

Everyone is really put on notice to be responsive to and responsible for their own feelings when one person takes charge of his life. "I'm putting out myself and inviting you to do the same, assuming you can and will." There is no hidden agenda for us to protect each other's feelings and play "nice guy" to avoid controversy or pain. This is a compliment to all involved. You are strong, you are capable, and you can speak your need, you won't crumble under stress. "I can afford to be myself with you, you really are a peer, an equal in every way."

8. BUILDING COMMITMENT

The big issue with commitment is that people will never believe in your verbalized commitment to them, until they see concrete evidence that you are totally committed to and capable of loving and take care of **yourself.**

Authenticity says: "I take care of me! I am affirming my commitment to me!" The reaction: "Gee, I want a person like that on my side. Here is someone you can count on when you are in need."

The paradox of commitment is shown by two clients in Palm Springs, a mother, Mary, and her sixteen year old son, Woody. Woody was angry, rebellious, heavily into drugs and totally incorrigible, but seemed to enjoy the idea of counseling and readily agreed to be involved. As time progressed, it because obvious that Mary feared Woody for several reasons. He had previously tried to commit suicide and would often use this as a threat to get what he wanted, or to get her off his back. He was occasionally violent and she was physically afraid of him. She felt guilty and partly responsible for his condition and felt she had no "right" to express her anger. Whenever she got angry, he would get worse. And finally, she was trying to make up to Woody for his father's rejection of him.

The therapist continually encouraged Mary to recognize that Woody would not change until he had to. Limits had to be set and enforced, feelings of anger and hurt must be expressed. She resisted all of this pressure saying that if any bad (worse) happened to Woody, she could not forgive herself. She just could not risk alienating him further and causing a total collapse in the relationship or, worse yet, death. One day Mary called hysterically to say she had taken the advice, that there had been a violent confrontation and Woody left. She would never see him again, he was probably already dead and it was all her fault. She related the following story:

Mary decided to take her needs seriously as suggested, but Woody took it lightly and ridiculed her. When he tired of that game, he told her to shut up because he was tired of listening. He went to his room and locked the door, lying on his bed and beginning to play his guitar. Mary pounded on the door, screaming in a very real anger, "I'm not through with you yet." He cursed her and continued to play. There was a long silence and Woody was relaxing in the belief he had won an easy one when there was a sudden loud noise. Five foot, 100 pound Mary had taken a long run down the hallway and had broken the door open with her shoulder, sending it crashing against the wall. Now she was moving toward the bed with hands upraised, yelling, "I said, I'm not through with you yet." Within seconds, Woody had burst off the bed, knocked Mary out of his path, jumped on his motorcycle and was long gone. Mary was sure that this final blow would push Woody to suicide, and she was plagued by guilt.

Mary was reassured she had done the right thing by taking her needs seriously and that Woody was going to have to be responsible for his own life. She could not keep him alive. Since Woody was due in group the next day, she was asked to relax and play a waiting game, give Woody a chance to respond. Sure enough, Woody attended the group the following night. He arrived ten minutes late and carefully looked the room over for his mother before he came in, expecting her to be there to kill him. He related the same basic story as Mary had and put the entire group into absolute laughter. The punch line came at the end. "My mother broke down that door (awe in his voice). My mother really loves me. She was going to kill me! My mother really loves me. That was the first time in sixteen years I knew my mother loved me."

It may be difficult to get the connection between a mother's anger that is strong enough to kill, and experiencing love from that situation, but it is real. Woody had first of all interpreted her passive leniency and lack of discipline as not loving or caring about him or what happened to him. Next, he had absolutely no respect for her as a person because he had watched his father take advantage of her, and now he continued the game as well. Finally, if she cared so little for herself, she surely could not love anyone else. If he couldn't make her mad, he couldn't be very important to her. All that changed with one broken door! The message was multi-leveled. "You've pushed me around long enough. I'm committed to MY survival. If anyone is going to die in the family, it will be you, not me. I love you too much to let you destroy me or to cooperate in your destruction of yourself. You can destroy yourself if you choose, but not with my help."

Woody got the message. I got them together the next day and reconciliation was begun.

9. SITUATIONAL RATHER THAN CHRONIC

Chronic anger is rarely appropriate to the situation, either in intensity or reality. The angry person is, in fact, not responding to the situation, but using it as a trigger that sets off a far deeper and more intense emotion from within. Then it is usually expressed as an over-reaction.

Chronic anger is identified with a prior pattern of events, causing an over-reaction. It's swatting a fly with a baseball bat, over-kill.

Marge, in good humor, mildly put down her husband, John, for a corny joke he told at a party. Since John's parents ridiculed him as stupid all his life, he now hears Marge doing the same thing. He reacts with violent rage that shocks and embarrasses everyone. Ninety percent of his anger is directed at the parents and was totally inappropriate to the situation. When chronic anger has been properly dealt with (by going to the original source and facing it), one is released to situational anger which is more appropriate to the situation and is no longer tied to the past.

Unresolved parental conflict can cause many marital and parent-child difficulties. We tend to use our spouse and children as the scapegoats for our past, demanding from them the unconditional love we never received from our parents, and inflicting on them the anger we could never resolve with our parents. Compounding this, we tend to marry someone like the parent we "haven't finished with" because we subconsciously desire to improve that relationship.

Situational anger is only a reaction to that situation and is appropriate in intensity and feeling to the immediate moment. Once expressed or responded to, that anger is gone. There is no more reason for it.

"It irritates me when you kill my spontaneous feelings by calling my humor corny."

Or in John's case, sensing and feeling the warmth in Marge's kidding, and therefore, not being irritated because he feels loved anyway.

10. CONFRONTATION AND BUILDING A FOUNDATION

Confrontation is used as a bridge in the relationship providing an arc of communication. It is reaching out, instead of waiting to be reached for. It is a message of trust and support for the other person as well.

"It is O.K. for me to take my needs seriously and confront you with my feelings. I trust that I won't do it destructively or with vindictiveness. I trust you are strong enough to handle my feelings and care enough to want to. I support our relationship with this sharing of myself. It is too important not to share. I'm thereby creating an opportunity to share and relate, offering - yes, expecting - the same in return."

The larger the base of trust, confidence and knowledge, the more anger and confrontation or intensity can be sustained. There must be some awareness of who you are and if you can be trusted. "Are you setting me up for a fall?" We build this solid base by expressing feelings and getting feedback. Intensity needs a solid base to come back to or it can be destructive. Going out too far on a limb requires the firm foundation of a solid tree. the foundation is the relationship.

11. A RHYTHM PROCESS

Each of us seems to be born with a rhythm that is natural and comfortable to ourselves, but so many environmental factors have distorted this rhythm that we find it difficult to always identify.

Learning a new skill may help you identify your rhythm process. Is it fast, slow, start-stop, an hour and then a break, all day or whatever? If you can be aware enough to pick up the maximum speed and pace that is successful for you, without pushing your limits, or being lazy, and then fit in the pattern of learning as well, you will maximize your abilities and success possibilities.

Incompatible rhythms are often seen as power struggles. "if you don't keep my pace, do it my way (which is more efficient, of course) and have my energy level, it is an affront to me and a deliberate irritation."

This may sound like a minor issue, but is one of the most subtle but common complaints I hear from couples, who almost always take it personally and feel their spouse is acting that way to annoy them. Are you aware of your own "best times" and personal rhythms?

Examples are numerous. One person needs ten hours sleep and the other five. One wakes up at 6 a.m. spouting, "Good morning, God." The other falls out of bed 9:30 a.m., groaning, "Good God, it's morning."

At midnight, however, the latter is just getting a second wind, and wants to dance all night, while the early morning spouse went to sleep in the middle of the movie.

One races across a parking lot while the other falls behind mumbling about not being loved or noticed. There are different ways of doing dishes, making beds, or raising kids, and separate tolerance levels to noise and stress. In all this, there is always a right way to do things (mine) and a wrong way (yours). Sounds petty and it is, but once taken personally, the issues run deep and hurt even more deeply.

Once we have recognized a rhythm pattern that is comfortable for me and different for you, it is easier to tolerate the differences. When you keep demanding a person change and do something your way, and they don't, it is easy to interpret that response as a passive-aggressive way of telling you to get lost. Both parties need to see differences for what they are. After that we will be free to solve our mutual problems the best way we can, without the added tension of questioning our partner's motives. It is possible that the differences in temperament, athletic ability, rhythm and interests create too large a gap to overcome. Even then, a divorce will be much less emotional or ugly since we now understand the differences are not hostile and deliberate or anyone's "fault".

12. HEALING

Healing is also a rhythm process. How long does it take you to heal? The experience ends at the point that you can re-engage and relate again. Healing is the final piece in any angry confrontation. You can't be close again until healing takes place. When you go against your natural rhythm, your body rebels. On the other hand, some people enjoy open wounds. They refuse to heal in order to maintain guilt and continue to blame the other. We have, however, an obligation to be true to ourselves and not to manipulate others, or let others manipulate us.

The ultimate healing experience comes from truly being and experiencing self in all authenticity, being and expressing who I am and what I feel to you in a non-defensive, non-attacking, simple, sharing of information for the purpose of clarity and understanding, providing both of us the safe environment of love and caring that truly is best for the situation and the people involved. What could be more healing - both physically and emotionally?

AUTHENTICITY HEALS ME AS I EXPRESS IT.

AUTHENTICITY HEALS YOU AS YOU UNDERSTAND AND RESPOND TO IT.

AUTHENTICITY HEALS US AS IT CLEANS OUT THE TOXIC RESENTMENTS BE-TWEEN US.

When the true motivation is to reveal myself in a vulnerable way, reaching out to you, authenticity becomes the contact that promotes healing, through intimacy and caring.

The Avoidant

I need to be touched, for I'm lonely
    The body cries out for relief.
I desperately put out the signals
    Please find me and bind up my grief.

You touch me, anxiety lessens
    We kiss and it's food for the soul.
We love and eternity beckens
    What once was a part, is a whole.

But solutions just bring other problems
    Sustaining emotions I can't.
The closeness becomes claustrophobic
    I've got to get out and I'm trapped.

I must push you away, I can't stand it
    There must be relief from my fear.
You've swallowed me up in your passion
    My thinking is not very clear.

So you pull back in utter confusion
    You were sought, and responded in kind.
What happened, that made me reject you?
    This is my great double-bind.

I need to be loved and have closeness
    To shut out the sorrow and pain,
that loneliness brings in the darkness
    With the fear you will not love again.

So I crave it, and seek it, and find it
    My vessel so empty and bare.
But it fills to quick overflowing,
    I cannot sustain when I fear.

When I have fulfilled my desires
    I feel eaten alive by my prey.
So I turn and I run and confuse you
    As you hold me and beg me to stay.

So I weave us a pattern of heartbreak
    While struggling and reaching for hope.
Ever briefly I find my fulfillment
    Of needs so conflicting in scope.

Chapter 12

Compatibility

Will we ever find the solution to the man-woman dilemma? FACT: Men and women NEED each other, SEEK each other out, FEEL INCOMPLETE without each other. JUDGE themselves and their attractiveness or self worth on the basis of their success in this search - game. Society has always held this out to all of us as the ultimate success: TO LIVE HAPPILY EVER AFTER with the one you love.

Then why is it so difficult? Almost everyone gets their shot at it (some several times) but very few seem to reach the goal. Is there such a thing as male-female compatibility? Are we so different in species, nature or nurture that there is no real hope? Is it only the differences that attract and compel us (and at the same time REPEL us)?

Compatible: Webster defines it as "capable of being together harmoniously or getting along well together; in agreement, congruous." (Corresponding to what is right, proper or resolvable; fitting; suitable; appropriate.)

What makes one couple capable of living together harmoniously and another one not? What are the factors or ingredients that fill in the blanks of definition and provide a formula for success that can be understood, copied and applied to one's life?

Three areas seem all important to me: values, interests and personality traits. This is closely followed by a fourth factor: communication skills. Without the skills to truly communicate how we feel and who we are to ourselves and others, how can we hope to know if the other three factors exist or not?

List your own VALUES:

1. Religious beliefs

2. Morals

3. Career goals

4. Life style

5. Beliefs about family

6. Sexual values

List your own INTERESTS:

1. Music

2. Sports

3. Hobbies

4. Theater

5. Entertainment

What's the difference between the lists? Values can be described as WHAT YOU ARE. Interests as WHAT YOU DO. It's easy to see that interests can be more easily compromised, modified or even given up without great loss of self. Values cannot not. Values do change or modify over time. As our perceptions mature and our circumstances change, we often find ourselves valuing very differently at various states of life, but these come slowly with time and sometimes with much stress or pain.

A third factor was personality traits.

Are you extrovert or introvert, coming from sensation or intuition, thinking or feeling, perceiving or judging? (To borrow from Kersey-Bates.)

Some personality types obviously blend well with one person and not with another. Some attract for healthy reasons, others for neurotic ones.

Freud believed men tended to marry their mothers and women their fathers. For that to be true, there must be a corresponding truth: men tend to be like their fathers and girls like their mothers. In Freud's time and space those stereotypes tended to exist so he was probably mostly correct in describing what he saw.

I would like to propose Leviton's five hypotheses, for today.

A. PEOPLE TEND TO BE MORE LIKE ONE PARENT THAN ANOTHER.

B. PEOPLE TEND TO LIKE (be closest to, fondest of, admire more) THE PARENT THEY ARE MOST LIKE IN TEMPERAMENT AND PERSONALITY TRAITS.

C. PEOPLE TEND TO MARRY (date, be attracted to) THE PARENT THEY ARE THE **LEAST** LIKE AND HAVE THE MOST UNFINISHED BUSINESS WITH (hard to get close to, angry at, feel rejected by).

D. THE UNHEALTHIER YOU ARE (neurotic, defensive or extreme) THE MORE YOU TEND TO MARRY YOUR OPPOSITE.

E. THE HEALTHIER YOU ARE (well balanced, middle of the road, open and growing) THE MORE YOU TEND TO MARRY YOURSELF.

So how did you measure up?

A. Are you most like your mother or father? In my college classes and public lectures, it tends to come out 50-50 for both sexes. In this non-stereotypical society we take on personality traits (or are born with traits) of either and it is more easily expressed and recognized than before. A few people report an equal sharing of traits, or of **not** being like either parent, but most tend to favor one parent.

B. Most people report LIKING and being closest to the parent they see themselves as the most like in personality and characteristics or values. It is just easier to identify with, understand and enjoy this person. If you find yourself in the opposite situation; you do NOT like the parent you are most like - YOU ARE IN TROUBLE! That means you do not like yourself to a strong degree.

C. Why do we find ourselves attracted to someone romantically who tends to be more like a parent we like the least, can't get close to, or even feel unfinished with? That is a great part of the attraction - the unfinished business. It provides additional opportunities to finish the job, prove I'm O.K., get the approval I couldn't get before, prove the parent wrong, etc., etc., etc.

D. Since I am saying most people tend to marry their least likeable parent (or opposite), I am saying that most people are not especially healthy. This is a relative statement and calls for a great deal of qualification. Looking at our mathematical bell-shaped curve, we come up with our 2 1/2% each A and F

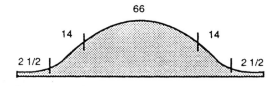

people, 14% each B and D people, and 66% C or average people. Even lumping A's and B's into one category, we are only talking about 16 1/2% reasonably well-adjusted people in the world - or if you will - the top 16 1/2% of all of us - regardless of definition of health.

E. The healthier one is the more well balanced, well adjusted, psychologically sound and close to center (not out on extremes). **That** person is attracted to one more like himself. He likes what he is and wants to share those qualities in a spouse.

To further pursue these premises for yourself, take this brief test.

I have provided you with a checklist of common personality traits listed under the headings of mother, father, me, spouse, spouse's mother, spouse's father. Check off all the words - even list them in priority order, 1 to 10, that most fit each persona. Do it with a minimum of thought, on an emotional level, otherwise we tend to rationalize, excuse or feel guilty about our answers. Remember, most of us have desirable and undesirable traits and contradictory ones. Spouse is defined as the person you are now in a relationship with or a pattern description of the kind of person you usually date or mate with. (Use Worksheet "A" at the back of the book.)

	Mother	Father	Me	Spouse	Spouse's Mother	Spouse's Father
Warm	☐	☐	☐	☐	☐	☐
Cold	☐	☐	☐	☐	☐	☐
Touching	☐	☐	☐	☐	☐	☐
Distant	☐	☐	☐	☐	☐	☐
Angry	☐	☐	☐	☐	☐	☐
Loving	☐	☐	☐	☐	☐	☐
Critical	☐	☐	☐	☐	☐	☐
Supportive	☐	☐	☐	☐	☐	☐
Bright	☐	☐	☐	☐	☐	☐
Dumb	☐	☐	☐	☐	☐	☐
Alcoholic	☐	☐	☐	☐	☐	☐
Conservative	☐	☐	☐	☐	☐	☐
Liberal	☐	☐	☐	☐	☐	☐
Dominant	☐	☐	☐	☐	☐	☐
Submissive	☐	☐	☐	☐	☐	☐
Aggressive	☐	☐	☐	☐	☐	☐
Passive	☐	☐	☐	☐	☐	☐
Stubborn	☐	☐	☐	☐	☐	☐
Lenient	☐	☐	☐	☐	☐	☐
Generous	☐	☐	☐	☐	☐	☐
Stingy	☐	☐	☐	☐	☐	☐
_____	☐	☐	☐	☐	☐	☐
_____	☐	☐	☐	☐	☐	☐
_____	☐	☐	☐	☐	☐	☐

Fill in your adjectives not previously listed.

Now check with your priority list and see which parent you come closest to. Were you surprised? Some people report they are most like mother and then check the list and come out most like father or vice versa. When that is true, it's usually because of **negative** traits that we don't want to admit to.

Now check your priority list for spouse. Which of your parents is Spouse the most like? If Spouse is closest to the parent you like and admire and you are too, that is a good sign. If Spouse is like the one you **least** like, that is a negative warning sign.

We are not always aware of this. A few years ago, a female client came in and complained for a session about her over dominant, angry spouse that could never be pleased and was always critical of her. The next week, she described her mother in the same terms. When I asked why she married her mother, she laughed that they were not at all alike in personality. When I pointed out that both treated her the same, she was shocked at the new revelation. She had never made the connection. There is no clear-cut, easy way to establish this. Each one has to evaluate for yourself. Picture a teeter-totter as life.

X _____ △ _____ X

The further out to the left extreme one is, the more he is attracted to someone on the opposite extreme to provide balance. The more extreme one is, the more one sided or out of balance, so he needs the opposite or missing part of himself and seeks it in a mate. These could be called INCOMPATIBLE OPPOSITES or NON-COMPLEMENTARY and help explain why opposites attract. If two extrovert clowns marry, they drive each other crazy competing and demanding center stage and wanting an audience that isn't there. If two quiet introverts marry **NOTHING** happens. They stare into space or TV in total boredom. The clown needs an audience. The audience needs entertainment. A perfect fit you say and it seems so.

BUT each is interpreting what is seen in a somewhat deceptive manner. He tends to see her quiet shyness as confidence, inner peace and strength. She sees him as dominant, confident and successful. Both are wrong. She is quiet to cover up her fear and insecurity and he is loud for the same reasons. The very traits that attracted each, now make it difficult, if not impossible, to identify with or understand the thinking processes of the other.

He complains, "Don't you ever have an opinion about anything? I make all of the decisions, do all the entertaining, take all the responsibility."

She retorts, "If you'd keep your mouth shut for five minutes, perhaps someone could get a word in the conversation." Both are correct about the other and lying about themselves - they wouldn't change anyway.

OPPOSITES ATTRACT

... *PAIN*
    MISUNDERSTANDING
    CONTEMPT
    CONFUSION

COMPLEMENTARY   OPPOSITES

——————————— X ——————△——————— X ———————————

Healthier people do not live in extremes. They tend to be more complete and balanced within themselves - able to see both sides of an issue, to be quiet or loud, aggressive or submissive, whatever seems to be more appropriate to the circumstances, rather than a "one note song" that is stuck to it's own nature regardless of the stimulus or environment.

Such a person can only be happy with someone equally balanced and appropriate as himself. There is nothing that is missing to search out, he just wants to share what he is.

This could be referred to as Complementary Opposites. Enough differences to be interesting and stimulating - enough similarities that they understand each other and enjoy the same tastes and activities.

Astrology is a fun illustration of this: Four general categories of FIRE, AIR, WATER and EARTH. Fire and air are complementary opposites as are water and earth. Fire warms and expands air; air feeds fire. Earth and water provide boundaries, substance and life for each other and could not exist without the other. Earth and water tend to "put out" or smother fire and air. That makes them non-complementary opposites.

Same signs have all the good things in common to strengthen them but the negatives could become exaggerated. Two fire signs would enjoy a high degree of equal energy and could be happy to find someone to "keep up with me." But their competitive natures could drive them apart. Two earth signs could enjoy resting and investing together but criticize each other to death.

You don't have to believe in astrology, by the way, to understand how it illustrates the point of complementary and non-complementary opposites.

Now that you have a more clear picture of which parent has influenced you most or you are the most like in personality traits, values and approach to life, ask yourself how that feels and what you have learned about self.

The more positives you see in yourself and the parent, the better your situation. The more negative, the more dangerous - or need for correction.

Now that we have discussed some underlying factors of compatibility, how do we apply these principles to better understanding our individual relationships? Are the differences now being experienced in your relationship temporary or hardcore, neurotic or poor communication, solvable or grounds for divorce?

It could be argued that all couples are compatible or they wouldn't be together to begin with. But as we have already discussed, some pairings are based on deficiency needs and neurotic tendencies. That is a scary thought to those dedicated to saving all marriages at any cost because the "institution of marriage is sacred."

The "institution" or concept we call marriage may very well be a sacred, spiritual and idealized symbol of life functioning at its finest, but that can hardly be said of most individual marriages out there in the **REAL** world. **People** are sacred - not institutions or ideas or laws. What is truly best for the people involved is the most spiritual approach we can take. Settling for a marriage that is destructive at its worst and blah at its best is nothing even sane, let alone sacred or desirable.

What is compatible enough? How much do we need to share in common to truly be happy? Are some values or interests more important than others? What happens to the areas we do not share in common?

These are all individual issues with no set of prescribed answers to fit all. Obviously, no one partner can meet all the needs of another, but it makes sense that the more we have in common (and the more important the issues that we share) the better chance for the relationship and the people as well, to flourish.

Which issues have the greatest point value in measuring and predicting marital success? The ones closest to INTEGRITY and VALUES. While interests can be modified or expanded and tastes can be stimulated and changed, life styles and integrity values are more representative of the person himself. Exceptions abound to any rule of thumb, but some principles of personality stack the odds. Areas that generally don't change much over a lifetime or are deeply symbolic of who the person really is, would be religious faith or preference, conservative or liberal orientation to life, extrovert or introvert, musical or artistic tastes, sense of humor and orientation toward family life as well as sexual desires and attitudes.

The more each partner demands the spouse supply all one's needs, the more contact points are necessary and the greater the demand, the strain, on the relationship. To the extent each partner freely gives and takes freedom to fulfill his/her own needs and to share contact points with friends and relatives, the more growth is possible. Again, it depends on the integrity level of the need. For most of us it is far easier to watch our loved one play tennis, cards, or attend the theater with a friend, than for them to have a sexual relationship with that same friend. However, some people cannot allow their spouses casual friendship even with members of the same sex, let alone the opposite sex, because they are too frightened of any competition. This is very confining to a relationship and the individuals in it.

Do you have enough of the essentials? Can you tolerate the differences between you? When a loved one has a major difference of opinion or value from yours, do you tend to take that as a personal affront? What will you do with your needs that do not match?

These are vital concerns for your growth and future happiness. These questions are generally ignored when one is more interested in getting married than in being happy, when relief from loneliness takes priority over the exhilaration of anticipated growth, when needs surpass thoughtful preparation and when it is more important to have anyone, rather than patiently wait for a certain special someone.

So many people marry for fearful and neurotic reasons that we shouldn't be surprised at the divorce rate or the need for rehabilitation and reconstruction of marriages to help them survive.

People often tend to see only a need to improve the relationship but not the people in the relationship or at least "not me, just my spouse." Personal growth heals relationships faster than vice versa, although with some folks, they happen simultaneously.

The following is a series of thirteen very simple but basic questions to ask yourself about any romantic relationship. These are not profound or all-inclusive, but do

The Anxious

I act like I act cause it feels good
    I do what I do 'cause I want.
I say what I say to relieve me
    From pressures I don't comprehend.

Don't ask me to change for that scares me
    Don't ask me to stop, I just can't
Not to fight back would leave me defeated
    To lose is the worst of all fates.

Self-destructive I cannot relate to
    Who says what I do brings me pain?
"The future be damned" is my motto
    My goal is immediate gain.

If my logic confuses your thinking
    If deprevation's the name of your game
Then you must be depressed and letharic
    Drugged to the concept of pain.

To be anxious is life's motivation
    Don't change me, I have to control
Don't tell me my actions offend you
    More guilt only makes me act worse.

contain common elements of success or failure that seem to effect most couples in their pursuit of the "happily ever after".

1. Are we both far enough along in our separate searches for personal identity that we can bring out the best in each other, or are we still locked into the negative attractions of unfinished business?

> *So you're headin' down the trail*
> *And the road is rough and steep*
>
> *And you stub your toe too often*
> *Never look before you leap*
>
> *You will find no consolation*
> *From the likes of me, my friend*
>
> *For life serves us from the platter*
> *We ourselves create and blend*

This refers to the individuals who subconsciously marry the parent they most dislike in an attempt at reconciliation, or are looking for the missing element in themselves. Many of us fully expect marriage itself or our spouse to give us this identity. Marriage is certainly a dominant factor toward maturation - some call it "shock therapy" - but the more healthy and complete you are before marriage, the better chance of positive growth and success IN marriage. One clue of a reasonably healthy person is "one who can comfortably live with his faults and tolerate the faults of others without undue strain, resentment or judgement".

2. Am I comfortable around this person?

That is, can I be my real self, or do I feel a need to work hard to impress the other or live up to unrealistic expectations? If you don't feel worthy of the other or constantly find yourself "being phony" or hiding parts of yourself that might not be accepted, you are being grossly unfair to yourself and prospective partner. No one can live under the constant pressure of pretense.

One of the most fraudulent situations abounding in marriage is for one or both partners to maintain this phony front right through the nuptials. Once married, each now feels safe or free enough to show the "real" self, the hidden parts, they were afraid to show before.

ANYTHING YOU PLAN TO DO OR BE AFTER MARRIAGE, NEEDS TO BE HON-
ESTLY SHARED BEFORE. OTHERWISE, IT IS FRAUD.

3. Can I permit the other to be freely himself?

This is the other side of the authencity coin. If you can't wait to change this person, rescue him or correct some bad habits - forget it and find someone else. If your lover is too good to pass up but definitely requires an overhaul, DO IT BEFORE MARRIAGE. If you both survive and still want to marry, you'll probably make it. A good relationship helps both parties grow and mature but some people have a need to rescue.

That generally means you have a "need to be needed" and receive your sense of importance and self worth from being the hero. If you succeed, and the other matures, he no longer needs you and the basis of the relationship is no longer valid. You'll have to find someone else to rescue in order to feel important. If you don't succeed, the constant failure disrupts the marriage for both. Become a social worker. There will be enough successes and failures to keep you happy and motivated.

4. Have we been acquainted long enough to know how well we agree on im-
    portant matters?

Or are we two desperate, needy people rebounding from past hurt or greedily grabbing at our one chance for love? Instant love is always suspect. It DOES happen and it FEELS great, but no matter how open, honest and intimate one is, a certain amount of time is required to experience the totality of each individual. That first rush of love is like a drug high. Enjoy it but don't become so intoxicated you forget to experience each other at more realistic levels.

Total agreement is not always necessary or even desirable, but the ability to "see through the eyes of the other", experience empathy through identification and understanding of the other's perception is essential to intimacy. The INABILITY to see reality from the other's point of reference prohibits the passing of any meaningful information between you, so that positions become polarized and behavior is inter-preted as deliberately punitive or hurtful.

5. How many interests do we share in common?

Do we both enjoy the same kind of music, people, books, activities and recreations? Is one of us bored by many of the things that please the other? (Sports on television, card games with friends.) Does one like to travel and go out a lot while the other is a homebody? Does one like the classics and opera, while the other craves country music and "Good 'Ole Boy" movies? Do we see humor in the same situations? Is one serious and intense about something that seems humorous to the other?

Interests may seem shallow and less important than values but many interests are very symptomatic of a person's entire personality and not to be taken lightly. Telling one what kind of music you enjoy might be enough to provide a rather complete personality profile.

Interests are what we do for fun and relaxation. Unfortunately, most people work to support themselves and don't necessarily enjoy it. Interests then can bring that added dimension that brings relief from tedium and added meaning to life. Not to share common interests is not to have a common language.

6. Are our backgrounds similar enough so that we can understand each other readily in marriage?

Race, religion, family background, economic background, geographic differences (small town vs. large city approach to life), cultural differences. We are products of the manners and lifestyles of our past - do they blend well with each other, or contribute to new growth? Are they irritants to be overcome? (A man or woman from a wealthy background, extravagant beyond current assets, married to a fiscal conservative.) One divorced and with children - the other not previously married. These are all potential problem areas.

The key word here is UNDERSTAND. It is not enough to see what you do or be aware we are different. How is that perceived? Why do you do what you do - what is the meaning or value that underscores the attitude and behavior? The more I understand you the less I take our differences personally as an affront to my beliefs.

The less I understand the motives and feelings, the more I see you as "stupid" or "wrong".

7. How do my family and friends react to him/her? Does he embarrass me around them? Is it because I am overly sensitive or is it that he really doesn't fit with the other people I love and care for?

This may seem irrelevant to many people who see themselves as madly in love and unneedful of the rest of the world, and tend to close themselves in a love cocoon all of their own. The truth may well be that you are very much like those in your family and if they don't like him, it may be in the very near future that you won't either. Perhaps your judgement is clouded by other factors, and you are unable to see the total picture. Also, while you may feel little need for family ties and relationships in the first bloom of love, as time goes on you will want and need to be close to your family and relatives and for your loved one to be accepted and appreciated by them as well.

If it becomes necessary to choose between them and "giving up" your family, it is common later on to "blame" and "resent" your spouse for this loss rather than to accept personal responsibility for your own choice. It may well be that your family was wrong and the healthy choice was to walk away from their rejection of you. This requires ultimate maturity in the choosing and care to accept one's own decision, rather than blame others for your disappointment later on.

8. What about the family of the one I love?

Are they a happy, well-adjusted family? If he comes from an unhappy family, how has it marred his personality?

This is a good spot to complete our parental checklist from the beginning of the chapter. We will now add two more columns entitled:

SPOUSE'S MOTHER   SPOUSE'S FATHER

MOTHER, FATHER, ME, SPOUSE, SPOUSE'S MOTHER, SPOUSE'S FATHER

Which of **his** parents is he the most like? Does he like (get along with, admire) or dislike (have problems with) the parent he most resembles? Which one are **YOU** the most like? If it's the negative parent, you have an important warning sign and some indication how he will tend to treat you after marriage.

If you are not sure...slow down...take the time to find out.

9. How well do we agree on the roles of men and women? You might ask a second version: on the roles of husband and wife.

A WIFE IS NO LONGER A GADGET YOU SCREW ON YOUR BED AND IT DOES YOUR HOUSEWORK FOR YOU.

In this changing culture, we are experiencing a wide variety of values regarding role expectation. Many people, for instance, verbalize and act out total equality and liberation between men and women in all areas: work, money, household responsibilities, freedom to experience friends of both sexes, no real restrictions. They carry these values through courtship and even living together, only to retreat to chauvinistic or traditional roles once married. "I couldn't say no or stop you before but NOW you are my wife or husband and wifes and/or husbands DO certain things or DON'T DO certain things that are O.K. for unmarrieds."

If you agree on role model it is less important what you believe. However, people tend to change as society changes. A liberated or equality point of view is less likely to change with time and partners tend to be more tolerant of growth or new ideas. The more rigidly traditional one is the less tolerant of change or differences between them.

10. How much do we confide in each other?

People who confide in each other are establishing better patterns for their future happiness. There is no other way to resolve conflicts and establish mutual avenues of direction that to openly discuss everything and anything. Elsewhere we discuss the need for mutual revelation: that love is based greatly on knowing each other deeply and intimately.

People who tend to be private and resist this kind of sharing as an invasion of themselves usually fear exposure as a "bad" person. "The more you know me the less you will like me." Usually the opposite is true and without knowing there is no real loving.

11. Can we quarrel constructively?

A constructive quarrel is one where the issues are resolved or at least both learn and grow from the disagreements. If both of you agree on everything, one of you is unnecessary. If both feel heard, listened to and cared about - your feelings and point of view treated with respect - agreement is often less important. A few quarrels may occur in all relationships. A nonconstructive one is where both take turns hurting each other and issues are left hanging and unresolved, only to pop up again as ammunition for continued hurt. Many quarrels or a consistent pattern of unresolved quarrels during courtship might mean a serious communication problem in marriage. If you can't work through disagreements on "good behavior" (during courtship) it probably will not be easier when the mask is off (during marriage).

12. Do I respect my partner's judgement? Are there many occasions when I perceive him/her to be opinionated, judgemental, impulsive, indecisive, or not too bright?

It is very difficult, if not impossible to have a warm close relationship with someone you feel is stupid, has poor judgement or makes decisions and displays behavior you can't admire.

All of us need to BE admired and reflected in the love and respect of our partner. Loss of this creates anger and resentment. Also, to not feel this respect for our partner brings to question our own judgement to fall in love with someone not worthy of it. Both of us lose both ways.

13. How AUTHENTIC are we being with ourselves and each other?

True love and intimacy are based on genuine openness and caring, on honest sharing of feelings in a way that supports and complements both parties involved.

Withholding true feelings and needs - even for "good" reasons is usually disruptful and dishonest. We rationalize that we don't want to hurt the feelings of the one we love, or don't feel they can handle our anger, or we don't have the "right" to complain or criticize, or we feel petty. There is the added fear of rejection or retaliation so we "cover up", deny, that anything is wrong or simply withhold information.

Being authentic is telling the truth about how we feel on important issues for the purpose of clarity, understanding and improvement - NOT for control or to inflict judgement or pain.

Not to do that tends to build resentment and anger within us because there is no chance for change or improvement. (We still blame the other for not reading our minds and changing even without our input.) It also is "crazymaking" to our partner. He "feels" something is wrong but you continue to deny it. These conflicting messages make him feel "crazy".

We earlier stated:

People who are integrated, tend to marry themselves. That is precisely what is meant by the statement that the liberated or actualized person will not, and cannot, be happy with less than himself.

There will be many contact points of mutual interest, concern and values. Attitudes and approaches to life are more important than facts of individual taste, but even these will greatly match or at least be appreciated. The differences will not rest in the areas of integrity but will be easily compromised or tolerated. This latter comes from the freedom of privacy and individual pursuits as well as shared ones.

When two persons are not possessively or fearfully locked into a couple-front, they can resolve many momentary variances in needs by allowing each to seek out his or her own pleasures, alone or with a friend. If one wants to watch football and the other prefers a movie, it helps to have two television sets. If everything has to be compromised by both doing one person's thing, there is a lot more chance for feeling misunderstood or rejected. Even people with exact likes don't always share the same timing..."I may love to dine out, but not tonight."

On the other side of the "Great Divide", there is enough love and consuming desire to be together, coupled with a deep sense of fulfillment and satisfaction from being together, so they rarely allow too much space between them.

The differences between them serve as stimulation to growth, new opportunity for learning, relief from boredom and a balanced perspective.

No one has to be perfect and balance is not static or rigidly encased. To know that you have come far enough in life to really experience enough self-love and appreciation to truly be married to "oneself" and enjoy it, you've come a long way, baby.

When the true motivation is to
reveal myself in a vulnerable way,
reaching out to you,
Truth becomes the contact that
promotes healing, through intimacy and caring.

Chapter 13

No Demand Revealing - No Solution Response

Society seems to delight in a variety of extreme positions -

Conservative - Liberal
Right - Left
Chauvinism - Feminism
Heredity - Environment
Authoritarian - Permissiveness
Violence - Passivity

One section of psychology advocates that there are no absolutes while another discusses archetypes and universal symbols.

The danger of espousing any position on any subject is that it is impossible to do so and at the same time cover all the exceptions to the rule or acknowledge that there are other significant positions that might work as well or better under varying conditions.

Child rearing is a great example of this problem. How many approaches fight for recognition? How many times have we modified what society says is the correct and proper way? To spank or not to spank, reason, manipulate, yell, call for "time out", make rules, remove rules, take responsibility, use natural consequences?

They all work! They all fail!

The more rigid you are in your approach the less successful you are apt to be - the more flexible - the more successful. Using the same successful tool over and over dilutes its effectiveness. Having a variety of choices available to you as a parent puts you in the position of choice based on the present circumstances, combined with where you happen to be emotionally and your own intuitive sense of what's best RIGHT NOW.

Perhaps therein lies the problem. No one wishes to REALLY take responsibility for his or her own feelings, wishes, choices, intuitive sense of right and wrong - so we fall back on rules, regulations and cultural belief systems.

Tell me what to do and I'll do it! I want to be right, correct, successful. The more desperate the need, the more extreme the position taken.

If there is truth contained in all extremes then all extremes must be included in the TRUTH.

This then is a plea for sanity - a balance of polarities, a happy medium, a middle ground that ebbs and flows with life as it happens.

Some people see compromise and negotiation as only successful if "no one is happy" from the results. Others feel it should be bland and boring with no opinion and a "don't care" attitude. I like the win-win approach. There is something here for all of us. When one stops being demanding, defensive and combative and shares true needs, real feelings and authentic reactions, something good emerges for all involved.

NO DEMAND REVEALING
NO SOLUTION RESPONSE

Let's break that down.

DEMAND: to ask for boldly or urgently, to ask for as a right or with authority, to require or need. Implies a calling for as owing or necessary, connoting a peremptory exercise of authority or imperative need.

REVEAL: to make known something hidden or secret, disclose, divulge, expose to view, show, exhibit, display.

SOLUTION: the act, method or process of solving a problem. An exploration, clarification or answer.

RESPONSE: something said or done in answer to something else. Reply or reaction.

When two non-integrated, rather dependent and needy people get together or meet for the first time, they immediately set out to impress each other and put their best foot forward. The legitimate explanation for that is: 1. we prefer talking about the best parts of ourselves; 2. let's not overwhelm and scare off this person with a list of my faults and negatives; 3. it's none of their business anyway.

The less legitimate implication is that there are a lot of parts of me you wouldn't like and/or would reject me for. I know this because I reject me for these.

Another hidden implication of our sharing the best - even an exaggerated version - to impress the other is a hidden DEMAND for a particular response.

"I WANT YOU TO LIKE ME, GO TO BED WITH ME, MAKE ME FEEL IMPORTANT, FALL IN LOVE WITH ME, ETC., ETC."

We are revealing what we want to reveal for the express purpose of achieving a desired response, leaving out any pertinent information that might deny us what we want.

If a salesman sells us a piece of property by deftly avoiding negative information that could influence the value, we call this unethical or criminal behavior, but we do it on a personal level constantly as a matter of course.

When we add revealing to demand, it takes on deeper significance. If I am to reveal, expose or display parts of myself (even the good ones) to you, that costs me a certain price of anxiety and vulnerability. You had better pay for that and make it worth my while by giving me a required response (that will make me happy that I shared) even if I don't tell you clearly what that expectation may be.

DEMAND EXPECTATION is the norm of relationships.

SILENT, DEMAND EXPECTATIONS - CONFUSED, GUESSWORK RESPONSE

If I dare to share - reveal part of myself - you'd better give me what I want in return or else, even if I don't know what I want or can't tell you what I want.

How about the RECEIVER in this situation? You have come with your demand and your revelation of self, what am I, the receiver, to do with that?

Obviously, you expect, and I want to give, a response - an answer, reply or reaction. What kind of response?

The most common response seems to be to offer a solution - the process of solving a problem or clarifying an answer.

That generally starts with judgement. You are right or wrong in what you have revealed and here is WHY you are right or wrong.

That segues nicely into advice. What you ought to do, feel, say or act is the following - "it's always worked for me".

We started this example with two insecure people trying to impress each other. This generally brings some success in beginning a relationship, dates, sex and intimacy (not necessarily in that order).

The more we try to maintain and expand this relationship while continuing to minimize the negatives, the heavier the demands and expectations without subsequent information to back it up.

The more important you become to me, the more I expect from you in reading my mind, wanting what I want, understanding my thinking and feeling. BUT without my giving you more than just bits and pieces of information you need to be successful at that.

When two relatively independent, secure, self-sufficient and actualizing people meet they automatically begin the process of expressing and sharing WHO THEY ARE, and HOW THEY FEEL. The implication is that "I want you to see, know and experience all of me because the more you know the more you will like - because I know me and I like me."

They also don't have a need to overwhelm with information in the first five minutes but share as appropriate without concern about the consequences. Even their own faults they can have a sense of humor about and don't experience as devastating, so can share those also with an expectancy of acceptance.

Underlining all this is an inner security and peace that says, "I can share myself, with a minimum of concern because it's O.K. regardless of the results. Even if you DON'T like me, I'm not devastated or my ego wiped out. I was being me and hopefully you were being you and it didn't fit. All people don't have to fit and we don't have to waste time trying to be something we're not and no one has to be bad, wrong or at fault. I am loved and loveable the way I am, and you are too, so we don't need every person in the world to verify that. If I am phony and you like me, what did you like? If I am phony and you don't like me, what did you NOT like?

If I am real and I am liked or disliked, it's all out front and O.K.

Most of us "guess" what the other would be impressed by or expects and then try to act out that expectation. When your actions are based MORE or PRIMARILY on the expectations (known or guessed) of the other person and less on the genuineness of who you are and how you feel, you are being to that degree phony or dishonest.

When your actions are based primarily or more on genuine feelings and who you really are, you are being genuine, authentic, honest, real.

I do not wish to imply the feelings or expectations of others are not important or should not be considered. I want to understand, explore and respond to your feelings at all times, while being true to my own as well. I can acknowledge and fully appreciate your position without agreeing to it or pretending to share in it.

Remember, there are two distinct issues: **YOUR** AUTHENTICITY AND **MINE**; **YOUR** RIGHTS, FEELINGS, BELIEFS AND DIGNITY...AND **MINE**.

Neither one of us have preference over the other BUT I am primarily responsible for how I express myself and you are primarily responsible for you.

Responsible is a complex term. As used here it implies being responsive to the needs of the moment. I can only be responsible FOR myself. I own, take responsibility for, pay consequences for my thoughts, feelings, behavior and attitudes. No one else can do that.

I can only be responsible TO you. When you put out your thoughts, feelings, behavior and attitudes to me, it is then my job to "be responsive to" those in the most appropriate way I am capable of acting.

Appropriateness is quite a variable and is difficult to agree on, depending on one's perceptions of all the circumstances and uniqueness of the situation.

Meeting my own needs cannot be separated from meeting and/or responding to the needs of the significant others in my various circumstances.

People with "tunnel vision" often have extreme difficulty seeing situations from the other person's point of view. It's as though they have such little faith in their own position, that it is too scary to explore the other's position for fear it might be more correct than mine, or I might have to give them what they want anyway. It becomes "my feelings, right or wrong".

The more you understand the other person's feelings and beliefs - even if they are distorted or wrong - the more you can understand why he acts the way he does and not take it so personally or "against you". In guided imagery, we often ask the client to "become" someone else - your parent or spouse - or even "become" a symbol, a tree or animal. In this manner, you practice getting inside another frame of reference, seeing the world from another place, identifying with something outside oneself. Those that learn to do this become more objective, less judgmental and less defensive of others. Those who "can't" do it find it almost impossible to give up their defensive posture.

The issue should be THE SEARCH FOR TRUTH regardless of where I find it.

All of us seem more interested in searching out truth that supports our belief systems and justifies our behavior. Anything that questions that tends to be discarded or avoided.

Most of us are convinced and act from the base of our inner feelings as though there are certain terrible, despicable, ugly truths about ourselves that would destroy us if acknowledged, seen or accepted. Truth is Truth. Denying, distorting, repressing or lying about it changes nothing. The ability to look at life AS IT IS no matter how disastrous that may be, and accept all that it implies, is a healing experience. I have clients who cannot accept the death of a parent, the loss of an arm, the reality of divorce, etc. The longer and stronger the denial, the worse the situation becomes. Accepting the TRUTH OF WHAT IS, IS THE BEGINNING OF LIFE and the meaning of life.

Sometimes one gets caught up in partial truths. The more open we are to seeing and searching and growing, the more truth we see in all situations.

This must begin with a simple acceptance and definition of who you are and what your identity is. Seeing the person you are, verifying the authenticity of the role you play in this world. Being comfortable in one's own body. This includes changes and the ability to grow. Change is not always growth but many times growth is an expression of change.

While the focus of learning one's identity is simple and the first step toward becoming the ultimate we are capable of expressing, it is far from easy and most people only touch on the fringes. We say we like or even love ourselves and it is true to some degree, but for most of us, it is more an expression of what we WANT to feel than what we DO feel.

Once I have defined who I am to some reasonable degree, the next step is to expose it and experience it with others.

NO DEMAND REVEALING

I have a need to share ME. That will bring me pleasure. My only request from you is to listen and understand, that it brings you pleasure that I want to share.

There is NO DEMAND FOR A PRESCRIBED RESPONSE and no desire to manipulate your feelings or behavior. Whatever happens will be O.K. because I am real and authentic and that is all I am responsible for. Whatever you do or feel will certainly have an effect on me - such as happiness or disappointment - but cannot be construed as failure or success on my part - that is your integrity and responsibility. My success or failure can only be measured in how true I was being to sharing the true self.

Under stress especially, most people attack motivation and character rather than reveal self. This is a psychological "charade." "I will tell you how bad you are and you guess that means I am angry or hurt."

Character assassination generally starts with the word - YOU. YOU..., are bad, vicious, deliberately hurt me, do not want to change - don't know how to love - ALWAYS CRITICIZE.

In a therapy group once a woman viciously went after her spouse for quite a few minutes about how badly he treated her. In spite of the viciousness, it was obvious she was very hurt and had a legitimate gripe against her husband.

I told her I felt her pain and was sympathetic to her complaints. The approach, though, would tend to make her husband defensive. Could she repeat that with the same intensity and anger but from the standpoint of HER FEELINGS. "Talk about his behavior and how it affects **your** feelings."

"I don't understand what you want me to do."

"Start your sentences with 'I feel'..."

She thought for a moment. "I feel you are vicious!"

She couldn't let go of the need to attack and blame. She could not take responsibility for her feelings.

I feel: hurt - angry - defensive - tied up in knots - confused - etc.

What makes it so difficult for us to just tell the truth and take responsibility for what hurts us or affects us? There are several common reasons.

1. I don't want the other person to know the power he has to hurt me.

2. I can't accept weakness in myself.

3. The other person will finish me off if I admit to being vulnerable and wounded.

4. It won't do any good (you won't change anyway so why bother?)

I WANT TO REVEAL MY FEELINGS BECAUSE I NEED TO SHARE WHO I AM, NOT BECAUSE YOU NEED TO CHANGE WHO YOU ARE.

When we insist others change so that we can be healthy, we give them total power over our lives.

I have no power to demand anyone else change. I can only change myself! I am only responsible for the actions of myself.

I must be totally responsible for my own happiness or the lack of it.

THEREFORE:

I must change the way I relate to you.

I must share myself and my feelings and reactions with you.

I must be open to you - even to hurt and disappointment from you.

That's my responsibility to myself, to you, to the relationship.

Often that will lower the defense mechanisms of the other - evoking you to be more real and truthful in return.

Being honest and telling the truth about oneself and feelings often entails admitting things we don't like - that make us embarrassed or uncomfortable - about ourselves and others.

When this happens, the tendency is to talk ourselves and others OUT of these negative and uncomfortable feelings.

"You shouldn't feel that way because..."

How can you change and grow till you admit WHAT IS? I DO feel that way. There is a very good reason I feel that way whether I understand that reason or not. Once I bring all that to awareness I have new options for response and perhaps this awareness itself will cause my feelings to change.

The results of "no demand revealing" are so simple as to be deceiving at times: once pressure for performance or change is removed and replaced by a sharing of information, better understanding of ourselves and each other is a natural consequence AND change generally takes place. BUT even if it doesn't, we feel loved, listened to, understood and cared about.

NO SOLUTION RESPONSE

If no change is demanded and no change is required of me then what am I supposed to do?

My spouse, child or friend comes to me with a problem, need or complaint. Why would this person come to me unless he expected me to DO something?

Calm them down.

Solve the problem.

Talk them out of their feelings.

Agree or disagree with their position.

By all means, give advice.

WAIT!

DON'T perform, solve problems, give advice, judge right or wrong, AND don't run away.

"You've left me nothing else to do. I'm stuck with the anxious, angry, needy and expectant person, whose situation and attitude have made ME anxious and scared. I have to do SOMETHING to relieve him so I can also calm down. What can I do?"

1. LISTEN to the message

   Even if it is painful, distorted and attacking YOU, shut up and listen. You can't help if you don't hear the message. Listen to the words and listen to the total message of the words. (If the person is incoherently screaming, the

total message might be how angry or frightened he is in this moment.)
Watch the body language and read between the lines of the actual words.

2. FEEL the emotion

"If I were expressing the words and feelings that this person is, how would I feel?" Put yourself in the other person's place. Do you feel frightened, angry, misunderstood, deceived, bitter, etc., when in that situation?

A man and wife once came to see me for the first time and the gentleman spent over 30 minutes sharing one catastrophe after another that had befallen him in the previous six months. Most of the events were totally out of his control such as several deaths in his immediate family, two businesses he worked for going bankrupt and car accidents where he was not even moving but got hit nonetheless.

When he stopped to catch his breath I said with some feeling. "Wow, you must have felt the whole world and God were out to get you and there was no escape!"

His eyes flashed panic and paranoia. "How did you know that? I never even told my wife I felt that way - How did you know?"

"Simple. I just put myself in your place and that's how I felt. I figured you must have felt much the same."

3. FEEDBACK how you feel

That's what I just illustrated with my client. First I let myself feel the emotion and then I simply shared that response. The key here is in feeling the pain of the other. Not taking the pain away from him or making it your own, but having the empathy to feel and understand.

This seems difficult for most of us to do. We RESIST feeling pain because it makes us feel guilty. "If YOU have pain, I feel guilty for hurting you or for not helping you."

In our society, so many men are afraid of painful emotion and feel it is unmanly to show this. Enculturation has convinced many women this is true and they also tend to see men as weak when they express these emotions.

WHAT DOES A HURTING PERSON NEED?

LOVE AND COMFORT.

Most people don't understand those terms. If you asked if they loved and comforted, they would say "YES" because they gave advice or talked you out of your feelings.

Someone feels my pain...

Loves me anyway...

Shares that moment - I'm not alone...

THAT'S ENOUGH! BELIEVE IT!

"I feel so hurt, angry, upset."

"I know you do."

"You DO? I thought no one cared or understood."

Healing phrases that comfort have to be sincere to be believed.

"I understand."

"That must be frightening."

"I feel your anger."

"Tell me more about that."

"Do go on - I want to understand."

"Talk about that."

Repeat or rephrase the person's statement to show you are listening and understand. Ask questions to clarify - not to challenge. "What did you DO that for?" always comes out "Why are you stupid?" That's not a question, that's an accusation. Ask "WHY" in a complete sentence, without using the word and you'll usually get an answer. "What were you feeling when you did that?"

Ask "WHY" and the person gets mad or plays dumb - "I don't know." "It all sounds good, Leviton," I hear you say, "but, you don't know my (fill in the blank - husband, wife, parent, child or friend). NO ONE TALKS THAT WAY." Perhaps not many, that's true, and therefore, the purpose of this book.

Comfort your loved one's hurt. Provide a place of safety and love. You'll have little need to give advice, solve problems or get blamed for lousy results. AND they will see us as psychic geniuses who read minds (no one understood before) and give us credit for solving all their problems.

THIS IS INTIMACY. When a person feels understood, cared about, important, no longer alone and loved... and wants to give the same to you.

YOU DON'T REALLY WANT WHAT YOU WANT, BUT YOU DON'T KNOW IT.

WHEN YOU KNOW WHAT YOU WANT, YOU CAN GET IT.

IF YOU GET WHAT YOU WANT WILL YOU HAVE IT?

IF YOU HAVE WHAT YOU WANT WILL YOU KNOW IT?

NOT ALWAYS

PRACTICAL APPLICATION

Most of us have a difficult time with the concept of NO DEMAND REVEALING - NO SOLUTION RESPONSE because we are caught up in what we THINK we want or need and not really in touch with our deepest feelings and desires.

How can I find out what I really want - what the real issues are - so that I can offer to share that with you. I can't share what I don't know.

STEP 1: DENY THE SATISFACTION OF THE WANT

(Often your spouse has done that for you.) To satisfy the WANT brings instant gratification, temporary relief and a masking of the inner pain - like a drug. Deprive yourself and let the pain speak to you.

STEP 2: ASK YOURSELF TWO QUESTIONS

A. If I meet this want how will it affect me and how will I feel? (the easy part)

B. If I don't meet this want how will it affect me and how will I feel (the hard part)

EXAMPLE: I will feel like a loser, unloved, or lonely. In most cases the real need or want is to FEEL LOVED. If my partner chooses not to change then I have evidence I am not loved, or worse yet, not worthy of being loved. Since my partner has the same general need, we both fight to WIN and wind up losing.

A couple came once with a very simple but irritating problem. The wife needed to buy "extra" food each month to feel secure. Answering "A" above, it saves time (fewer trips to the store), money (prices keep going up), and food is there for emergencies (unexpected guests or loss of job): at least we'll eat.

Husband's issue was to save money. "A" we can save over $100 per month on the budget, buying more than we need is "waste", if it's there we'll eat it and gain weight, or it will spoil and be thrown away. If I lose my job money is more important than food for flexible choices.

Both of them are reasonable people with good explanations of why they need what they need.

"B" if I don't get my need met how will I feel? Wife felt very insecure and vulnerable, unsafe and afraid. Something in her background made food an important aspect of feeling loved and secure.

The husband would feel like a loser, a small child being controlled by an unreasonable mother. So for him it is now a power struggle.

WHAT TO DO? SOLUTION?

REVEAL!

1. I reveal my deep fears and feelings to me.
2. I reveal my deep fears and feelings to you.
3. You reveal your deep fears and feelings to you.
4. You reveal your deep fears and feelings to me.

We both understand each other's motives, feelings and behavior and no change is necessary or demanded. Since we are now understood we both feel loved. The love was really supplied by me for me and by you for you, but also for each other.

If all I have to do to make you feel loved is buy an extra box of salt, I can do that for you as my expression of love. If all I need to do to make you feel loved is cut down on the budget, I want to do that for you as well. Now it's a gift rather than a demand or power struggle.

ANSWER THE FOLLOWING QUESTIONS:

1. What 3 changes is my spouse constantly asking for that I don't want to give or have difficulty giving?
2. What 3 changes do I want from my spouse that I feel would change the relationship in a positive manner?
3. What do I feel would realistically be the result of my changing the above 3 as requested by my spouse?
4. What does my spouse say would be the result of these changes?
5. What is my conscious, stated reason for not making these changes?
6. What do I feel would realistically happen if my spouse changed as requested?
7. What does my spouse feel would happen if she changed?
8. What is my spouse's stated reasons for not changing?

You will find the stated reasons for not complying with requested change quite creative at times, as we go to great lengths to show why these changes or requests are not a good idea.

"If I give you what you want, I feel like a loser, you are now right and I am wrong. I am a wimp, and wind up in the inferior position."

"If you give me what I want the situation is exactly reversed. I win and you lose."

"If I withhold what you want and don't get what I want, at least I haven't lost - it's a stand off."

So the whole issue is no longer the truth or reasonableness of each other's request, but has deteriorated to a POWER STRUGGLE.

To break this impasse we must remove the power struggle.

NO CHANGE REQUESTED - NO CHANGE GIVEN

What we are now after is INFORMATION -

> What did you want the change for?
>
> What would it make you feel?
>
> How do you feel without it?

Now that we each have that information with no pressure to respond in a particular way, we are free to explore the same questions from the receiver's point of view - "What am I refusing?"

Do I want my spouse to feel loved? Now that I am not required to give these changes am I willing to give them as a LOVE GIFT? You will be surprised how much easier it is to give a LOVE GIFT than to respond to a threat or demand.

If for some reason you still can't give the changes, you can be free to tell the person why and that you DO love them and want to find a way to show your love and you are sorry that they have identified your love with that request for change.

Now go to worksheet B and take the test. Answer these questions fully on at least one requested change and have your spouse do the same. After you have honestly answered all the questions, write a summary on the back describing what you learned about yourself and your spouse and how this exchange of information impacted your relationship.

Worksheet C is a slightly different approach to changing relationships. Wait a week or so and then try this approach and write down the results on the worksheets provided.

LOVE:

THAT OVERWHELMING EMOTION

THAT SHOOTS THROUGH YOUR BODY
AND SHUTS DOWN YOUR BRAIN

Chapter 14

Love and Its Impact on Self

" Life is a banquet and most poor sonsabitches are starving to death" was never more true than in the area of love.

The one area of life we all agree is important, is loving and finding a love partner to share life with, but just as most people are not especially successful in living as individuals, most are also not particularly successful in a couple relationship.

Not surprisingly, researchers are finding that individuals fail in marriage in the same general areas they fail as persons. The problem within me is the problem between us, and vice versa.

"Love experts" such as authors Herb Goldberg and Sam Keen, tell us that "romantic and passionate love are opposites". "Romance is a drug high, a fantasy trip. The higher the high, the deeper the crash."

On the other side, Nathaniel Branden declares that "Romantic love is a passionate, spiritual, emotional, sexual attachment between a man and a woman that reflects a high regard for the value of each other's person."

I'm not prepared to throw away romance, excitement and exaggerated pulse rate. It is a "high" and why apologize for that. Romance may not be enough to DEFINE love or sustain it, but it is a great place to start...and an even better place to finish.

Earlier in the book, we discussed the concept of subpersonalities and how people often relate from distorted or partial aspects of self rather than from the true self. This is a good metaphor for love. Rather than relating from the essence or core of TRUE

WEBSTER DEFINES ROMANCE
AS BOTH
"A LOVE AFFAIR" AND
"THE TENDENCY TO DERIVE GREAT
PLEASURE FROM ROMANTIC ADVENTURES"

HE ALSO CALLS IT . . .
"AN EXAGGERATION OR FALSEHOOD

I GUESS HE HAS BEEN IN LOVE

LOVE, most people relate from a "subpersonality" or partial aspect of love such as romance or sexuality - confusing it for the real thing.

One of the clearest explanations of this comes from Robert J. Sternberg, IBM professor of Psychology and Education at Yale University. He identifies three core aspects of love that break down into eight different types of love expression.

Sternberg's triangle consists of the three faces of love: **intimacy**, **passion** and **commitment**. In brief outline form, the eight types of love expression are as follows:

1. NON-LOVE - the absence of all three components. This describes the large majority of relationships which can be summarized as casual interactions.
2. LIKING - just intimacy. Sharing beyond the casual, talking about your life, true friendship, closeness and warmth but without the intenseness of passion or commitment.
3. INFATUATED LOVE - only passion. This is the "love at first sight" that can arise instantaneously and dissipate as quickly. It involves a high degree of physical arousal but no real intimacy or commitment. It can be the product of love or from horniness or indigestion.
4. EMPTY LOVE - commitment without intimacy or passion. This is the kind of love sometimes seen in a thirty year marriage that has long since become stagnant. All that remains is the commitment to stay with the other person no matter what. This may be the saddest of all as people settle for the **illusion** of love and security rather than face the fears and insecurities of admitting they are alone and starting over.

5. ROMANTIC LOVE - a combination of intimacy and passion. More than in-fatuation, it's liking with the added excitement of physical attraction and arousal but without commitment. A summer affair, perhaps.

6. FATUOUS LOVE - passion plus commitment. Hollywood love: Boy meets girl, a week later, they are engaged, a month later, they are married. They are committed on the basis of their passion but because intimacy takes time to develop, they don't have the emotional core necessary to sustain the commitment. It usually burns out as quickly as it flamed up.

7. COMPANIONATE LOVE - intimacy with commitment but no passion. It is a long-term friendship, where the sexual feelings have died or never existed, but they continue a "family or brother-sister" love.

8. CONSUMMATE LOVE - complete love, the real thing or total package of intimacy, passion and commitment. Achieving this is like trying to lose weight, difficult, but not impossible. The really hard part is keeping the weight off after you have lost it or keeping the consummate love alive after you have achieved it. Consummate love is possible only in very special relationships.

As you can see from Sternberg's descriptions, not everyone "loves" the same or brings the same needs and elements to a relationship. Another contributing factor is that relationships of love generally go through six STAGES and can and do break down and terminate at various points.

Most of us start with romance, which is exciting, passionate and almost always irrational. We are driven by desire, hormones and the exploration of someone new. As this satisfies and fulfills our immediate fantasies and concerns we make an early commitment to be exclusive in our dating and agree this relationship has potential for the future worth testing out at greater length.

At some juncture in this early commitment, we pass the point of "putting our best foot forward" and need to "always look good in the eyes of our partner" to come face to face with some negative realities. All is NOT perfect in this person and relationship. There is testing and anger, doubt and anxiety. There is establishment of territory, the negotiating of space and togetherness, power struggle and conflict.

Possibly the great majority of relationships falter or end here. The bubble is burst, reality sets in, "You are not 'what I thought' you were."

The emotionally secure and reasonably healthy person expects this reality and is prepared rather than shocked or hurt by it. This is a challenge to be met, not a tragedy to be avoided. The next stage should be resolution and acceptance. Listen, care,

SCIENTISTS HAVE
DISCOVERED THAT
THE DISEASE CALLED
LOVE
IS THE RESULT
OF AN OVERACTIVE
GONAD

negotiate, drop defenses, admit weaknesses, accept differences and state your needs and limits.

If you survive that and are still together, there is a great chance for the final steps.

The next one is commitment or ethical love. This is the decision to CARE about this person and the relationship regardless of whether I feel like it AT THIS MOMENT in time. Rational choice is based on character (who the person IS), rather than situational behavior (what the person just DID). The total relationship carries more weight than the individual or situational problem. This includes the elements of tolerance, forgiveness and understanding. Understanding and forgiving are very different from being a "nice guy" who pretends to ignore hurts and represses resentment and hostility.

The final step is mature, consummate love as described by Sternberg - functioning as a couple, providing a safe environment for each other, giving out to the world as a team and inspiring each other to be creative - a refuge from the world outside.

Why do some make it and others not? Some lack the proper elements of love while others can't struggle through the stages of love.

As you can surmise most relationships make it or break it in the all important stages of conflict, power struggle and resolution.

This is the time when each authentic self must come to the surface and be expressed. "I want you to see and know who I am in my entirety and I want the same of you. Let's see if our authentic selves mix and match in such a way that creates a desire to spend our lives together."

This leads us to the next chapter. It is not enough to understand the semantics of love and the theory that supports love.

How do we work our way through the stages? In what manner can we locate and utilize the passion within us? On what basis can we effect commitment? The next chapter deals with the nuts and bolts of intimacy and the struggles of achieving it.

"Love is the substance that life is made of,
the evidence that life's worthwhile,
For by it, two people unite as one,
Through love we understand the integration of
diverse personalities, so that the final
end is greater than the separate two.
By love, one person offers to another
the sacrifice of a giving spirit,
the complement of respect and admiration,
the fulfillment of his innermost self.
By love we thrill daily to the exploration of
the other's mind
Therefore, through this inner-stimulation and
emotional exchange
We have the knowledge that we have pleased our mate.
Without love it is impossible to please him.
He that loveth must first believe in himself,
and then give of himself to his partner."

I fell in love with you tonight...
Oh, not for the very first time.
I like to fall in love with you...
over dinner...or with wine.

I like your little girl smile,
that sophisticated grin.
The laughter so spontaneous,
from your head down to your shins.

The business woman at her desk,
efficient and sincere,
The look of joy when hunger hits...
delight from ear to ear.

The silly kid indulging
in chocolate scoops galore,
Soft icecream and gooey cake
'till the body sighs ' "Nomore".

The angry and the vulgar
always at your beck and call,
But you also curse in humor
you can "fuck off" with them all.

There are tears that miss your parents,
frustrations over life.
An anguished cry of sorrow
from the constant blows of strife.

Still you feel the heights of passion
as no other surely can.
Riding rapids and crescendos
as they sensuously expand.

You are caring, you are thoughtful,
and so generous with love.
You have a gift for healing
and are gentle as a dove.

There's a strength that brings survival,
an integrity and will.
*So **much** that I admire,*
both simplicity and frills.

You are woman, you are child...
ever anxious, or so still.
You are beauty, you are passion
*I love you **now**...and always will.*

I took a look at you tonight
from my being to my soul,
Bringing trembling satisfaction
you have made me feel so whole.

And I fell in love with you tonight,
as I did the very first time.
That magic touch on a silent chord,
a symphony sublime.

If this is what the poets feel
when they speak their words of love,
Then life has found its richest form
AND NOW I KNOW OF LOVE!

Chapter 15

Love and Intimacy as Expressions of Self

How To Make Any Relationship Work - Even Yours.

Everybody talks about intimacy...but sex is as close as most people get.

Everybody wants intimacy...but no one seems to know what it is.

People avoid intimacy...for fear of losing something they don't really have...themselves.

True intimacy is sharing my deepest, most real self with another human being...and having the other to do the same with me.

Intimacy is loving, but I must first love myself.

Intimacy is trusting, but I must first trust myself.

Intimacy is revealing, but I must first reveal to myself.

There are NINE vital aspects which help create intimacy in a relationship and will be discussed briefly. They are:

1. Feelings - Yours and Mine
2. Self-revelation
3. Honesty - a Caress or Club?
4. Trust
5. Openness to Life
6. Listening

LOVE:

*THE EXCUSE THAT
MOST PEOPLE USE FOR*

"FALLING IN BED"

7. Acceptance

8. Giving

9. Receiving

1. FEELINGS - YOURS AND MINE

Every feeling you have is important and has meaning for you. Dorothy is constantly revealing deep insightful feelings in the process of her therapy and then lightly dismissing the subject with the casual, "Isn't that silly?" Because the feeling is in apparent contradiction to her conscious motivations, life-style, and general way of thinking, she dismisses this contrary feeling as being silly.

If feelings did not have a cause, they would not be there in the first place. So, even the most irrational feelings must have a legitimate source that is meaningful and important. Feelings will reveal a lot about the person if we can dig down deep enough to find the source and understand it.

Every feeling you have is either trying to reveal something to you or to hide something from you.

The only reason we don't want to reveal our true feelings (to ourselves or someone else) is fear...the fear of destroying, or being destroyed, of hurting, or being hurt.

Betty is thirty years of age, single, aggressive, and independent. Highly intelligent, she is something of a rebel and sees herself as a very strong and dominating woman. Strangely enough, the only area in which she feels competent as a person is sexually in bed with a man, and she is rarely able to relate to them well on any other basis. She has no close women friends and finds it very difficult to be open and friendly with women.

Betty's mother is fifty, attractive, and divorced. She is a very successful business woman with her own career, and very well known in charity and social circles.

Within thirty minutes after the start of an all-day marathon in group therapy, Betty was feeling extreme anger and hatred toward her mother, describing her as weak, inadequate, stupid and totally incapable of being a mother. Even Betty seemed rather surprised and overwhelmed by the intensity of her angry outburst. She seemed sincerely surprised to find that she had been harboring such intense hatred regarding her mother. When asked if she had ever talked with her mother about these feelings, she replied with disgust and contempt, "If I told Mother how I really felt about her, she'd have a heart attack and die."

As the issue was discussed further, it became more obvious her deeper fear was that if she confronted Mother with this hatred and hostility and told her how Mother had failed to meet Betty's needs, Mother might simply say, "That's tough, and you can go straight to Hell."

Betty really expected that Mother would draw into a shell, become defensive and unhearing, and, therefore, reject her without being touched deeply by Betty's feelings at all. Then Betty would be left with the problem of not having a mother. She was very frightened that her mother's rejection would destroy her.

For most of us that's where it is - fear is the barrier which keeps us from being intimate - fear of destroying and more probably and most often, fear of being destroyed.

This is due to an inner anxiety that says to us, "You can't handle that particular situation. You do not have the inner strengths to survive that potential hurt, so don't venture out and take the risk. The pain will be unbearable." Or, in contrast, the message may be: "Your spouse (friend, parent, etc.) will not be capable of handling your feelings and will suffer a nervous breakdown or at least insufferable pain and you will be stuck with the guilt of that as a burden the rest of your life."

All of us have different levels of tolerance to emotional and physical pain, but it is the fear of pain that controls our lives...not the pain itself. If we believe we can handle the pain and do not fear it, we succeed quite well. In fearing the loss of love or relationship with the other person, we are making them more important than we are. If I lose the love of my friend over a disagreement, that will be a loss; I will experience that loss and not minimize it but with the awareness that I can and will survive without that person. I hope we can work it out, but if we can't I don't want a phony relationship anyway.

It is true that the other person can retaliate by punishing you with guilt, by playing "destroyed" or making it look as if you have destroyed him by getting sick or having a heart attack or going into a deep depression or even committing suicide....that is their right and their choice, and you have no power or control over that person's response.

You do not have to accept this guilt or believe yourself a bad person just because someone else lays that trip on you. Your feelings are either trying to reveal something to you or to hide something from you. We often watch what people do in order to find clues of what they are feeling, but sometimes it is better to watch what they don't do for even deeper information.

If you are an extremist, the opposite extreme is usually what you most fear. People who cry easily, as an example, may be very angry on the inside and most afraid of this anger. People who are easily angry, carrying a constant chip on their shoulders and exploding in very irrational and inappropriate ways, are most often afraid of being hurt.

The solution to the dilemma of extreme feelings is to allow yourself the luxury of experiencing whatever emotion you fear the most, whether hurt or anger, and thereby convince yourself that it will not be destructive to you and will not be painful beyond your ability to endure. Once convinced enough to let the anger or hurt come to the

WHEN A WOMAN SAYS

SHE WANTS A
"FEELING MAN" . . .

MOST MEN PREFER TO
BELIEVE SHE'S HORNY

surface, a person is able to experience the deep satisfaction of his real feelings and the surprising and new reaction received from others.

It may seem rather strange in a chapter on intimacy to spend so much time on knowing one's own feelings and being honest and direct with one's own feelings rather than talking about the feelings of others'. However, one complements the other.

That's the key: when we are deeply in touch with our own feelings and what's going on inside our own emotions, we are very, very much in tune and in touch with the other. Whenever we can be open to all our feelings, whether negative or positive, we can then be open and receptive to others. When we can allow ourselves to feel the full range of our own emotions: anger, hurt, confusion, happiness, pride, disgust, etc. - we can be open and available to these feelings in our friends.

2. SELF-REVELATION

You have a responsibility to be real...this responsibility is primarily to yourself and secondarily, to others. You have no responsibility, control or ability to predict what type of response you will get from others when you are truly real with your feelings.

All phoniness, defensiveness, game-playing or whatever else keeps us from being real with our feelings is protection against our innermost fear. All fear, as stated before, really goes back to the fear of being destroyed or destroying another. Probably the most basic fear is that of being destroyed and that is precisely the reason why I must begin with myself in any type of therapeutic growth and intimacy with others.

The first thing I have to do is know myself. There is no way I can reveal myself or be intimate with others until first I reveal myself and am intimate with me. Some of us are past experts at kidding ourselves about almost everything. We are very good at deceiving ourselves on a conscious level from knowing what's really going on deep inside. This process can be reversed, but it is hard work, and you really have to want to do it.

It sounds overly simple, but you can start by asking yourself a basic question over and over and over again until your subconscious hears and believes it: "How do I really feel right now? What is really going on inside me? What do I really want to do? Why am I reacting the way I am reacting?" If you really want to now and will take time to stop, ask, and then listen, you'll get the answer.

It may take weeks or even months, but eventually you'll get to the place where this will happen more or less automatically and on a subconscious level so that you always have a pretty good idea of what you are feeling and why. The important point here is not that you are totally aware at all times consciously of what's happening on a feeling level, but that you are open to this information at all times. If you arc constantly open, the information will come to the surface whenever it is necessary for you to know it. If you are constantly closed, the information will never surface except under extreme pressure or because you consciously want it to.

Surprisingly, this may be the most difficult step of all - the step of self-revelation. Most of us do not want to know our true feelings or to be familiar with what's really going on inside us because we are afraid we will not be able to live with this information. If we do anything with the information, we are afraid of being hurt. If we don't do anything with the information, we are afraid of being frustrated...therefore, we'd rather leave it buried.

The problem, of course, is that even though the information is buried, it goes on affecting our lifes and relationships, but because it is operating on an unconscious level, we have little or no control over the behavior connected with it. When we bring the information to the level of awareness, then, and only then, do we have the choice of what to do with it and conscious control of the behavior connected with it. Once I know what I'm feeling, I have the choice of how to handle this information and whether or not to pass it on to others and, if so, in what manner.

3. HONESTY - A CARESS OR A CLUB?

Honesty can be used as a club to hurt or as a caress to heal. Motivation plays a very important part here. If you are deliberately revealing your deep, honest, and real feelings to the other person for the express purpose of punishing, hurting, destroying or with any other kind of malicious intent, then perhaps your guilt is legitimate. Even so, while all of us have the power to hurt other human beings, particularly those who are important to us and to whom we are important, we still don't have the power to destroy even if we want to. The other person can either protect himself, retaliate in turn, or simply walk away from your life. While it may be hurtful to lose you, they won't be destroyed by it. So, even if we wanted to destroy another human being, each person has the power to protect himself against you and cannot be destroyed unless he chooses to let you do so.

On the other hand, honesty for the purpose of revealing who I am, where I am and why, for healing or improving relationships is not destructive and does not deserve the resulting guilt. Any guilt connected with this type of motivation and approach is neurotic guilt, thrown on you by the other person who does not want to hear your feelings.

Honesty is not telling everything you know. It is telling what is important to you, to the other person, to the relationship. Many therapists and theorists insist on total honesty...complete vomiting of all feelings, thoughts, past deeds and activities, etc. Possibly this is because most of us are very good at deceiving ourselves. If you vomit all, you don't have to be responsible or worry about choosing...it's all on the table for the other person to see and experience. We believe this can either be helpful or very hurtful.

A person has an affair and comes home to confess to their spouse and clears their conscience. In confessing, they feel relieved and forgiven...cleared and clean. Now, what is the spouse going to do with this information? What are they going to do with their own guilt and bad feelings? They are not supposed to use it against the confessor because they have confessed, and yet, the spouse holds inner feelings of self-doubt, rejection and hurt that surely accompany that type of confession. Clearing your conscience at the expense of someone else is unfair.

If there is an affair and in the process something important is learned about the marriage (pro or con), it makes sense that the learning partner share that new understanding with the spouse in order to improve the relationship. For example, people in such a situation learn that there is more love in the marriage than they were aware of; that the relationship has lost its courtship or fun or spontaneity; that anger or resentment or fear has driven them apart, etc. It is this kind of feeling information that should be shared...either for the purpose of improving the relationship or at least revealing what is wrong or bad about it. The fact that there was an affair and the information came as a result of that affair is not necessarily to be revealed.

We are not suggesting, condoning or criticizing affairs. It is evident that a lot of people don't have the courage to confront issues and needs in their marriages on any kind of consistent level and so allow resentments and subsequent distance to build up. Then they often create a crisis, such as an affair or a bitter violent fight to bring things to the surface. This is usually done at a subconscious level of motivation. Rather than condemn or judge people for their counter-productive behavior, we prefer to help them learn from it by pointing out why they needed it, what was learned or accomplished and what their options are now. Many people require a crisis before they are able to even ask for the help of therapy. Unfortunately they accumulate many handicaps to success through this delay. A day-to-day honesty that tries to improve the marriage before it gets out of control is the best kind.

Being able to discriminate between what is legitimately private information and what is important to be shared is not easy. Often when we "protect" the other person from the truth, we are insulting their capacity for being real or strong.

In a family with five daughters, the father was constantly treated as the outsider. The favorite expressions went something like this: "Don't tell Daddy; he wouldn't understand...Don't tell Daddy; he'll get angry...Don't tell Daddy; he'll be hurt...Don't tell Daddy; but don't let him know he's not being told." In their desire to protect him, they were insulting him, rejecting him, and leaving him out, assuming he was too weak to handle it. What could be more castrating than not being included in one's own family circle? Instead of showing unconditional positive regard for their father's strength and potency as a man, their protecting him "for his own good" was simply a statement of his inadequacy.

One daughter, in the process of her therapy, decided to be honest with her father and, as might be expected, he was very defensive, and it was difficult for him to respond. The daughter's predictions were all correct - he got angry, he didn't understand, he was hurt, and he did not know how to respond.

With strong feeling, the son-in-law proclaimed to this father that his wife was the only daughter who was treating him like a father...that they were tired of treating him like a baby, protecting him, and making him as an outsider in the family. For the first time in his life, he was going to be included by someone. They believed in his masculinity, in his ability to be a father, and his ability to respond to feelings...and intended to relate to his strength and not his weaknesses. They refused to relate to him as a weak and inadequate man and expected him to respond with strength and feelings.

4. TRUST

Another problem with intimacy is that of trust. Many of us do not want to be intimate in sharing our deeper feelings of anxiety, fear, inadequacy, or desire because we cannot trust the other person with the use of this information. We are afraid they will take this information and gossip about it or use it against us to hurt us in some way at their pleasure or discretion.

My protection at this point is my ability to trust myself. It is much easier to trust others, even strangers, if I have a deep sense of trust in my own judgment and in my feelings regarding myself. If I have true self-love as discussed earlier, I will not let myself be destroyed. If I have trust and confidence in my own strengths, in my ability to withstand pain and to handle crisis situations, and know what my own limitations are, then I can take risks I could not otherwise afford.

If I am acquainted with the healing benefits of grief, suffering and pain and am not afraid of feeling these, I can allow myself to be intimate and thereby vulnerable to the possibility of hurt. I trust my judgement that once I discover the other person is being vicious or malicious or deliberately punitive and hurtful and destructive to the relationship, I have the ability to stop them or to withdraw from the situation, thereby not allowing myself to be unduly hurt or eventually destroyed. Once confident that I can either handle or avoid destructive situations, I am more comfortable in being intimate and revealing myself or sharing myself with others.

If I love myself, trust myself, and am revealing of my true feelings to myself, I am ready to be intimate with others.

5. OPENNESS TO LIFE

To be totally open to all the realities of life...internally and externally...emotionally and intellectually...is to be a truly healthy person. To experience these various emotions and realities with little need to defend, deny, or distort, is to be fully human.

A healthy person is open to the totality of human experience - both good and bad. All human experience is available to him, and he has little or no need to defend against the knowledge of its existence.

He knows the healing benefits of true pain and grief and has little need to ever defend against these, because he knows them to be beneficial to his growth and not destructive of his person.

He is very much in touch with his full strength potential - both physically and emotionally - and therefore can take whatever risks are necessary to his continued well-being.

The process of stripping away these layers of defence can be any method that helps a person to experience emotional pain, fear or discomfort in a supportive environment. He experiences what is there and comes out of this trauma without being destroyed as he had feared would happen. This leaves him in a state of relaxation, calmness and experienced personal strength.

As he successfully works through these layers, the person becomes less fearful, more confident of his own strength and more in touch with his deep inner self-hood. Obviously growth never ends, but all of us can certainly reach a level of openness at which we can continue the growth process without a helping agent.

Once you've accomplished what was just described, regarding contact with one's deep feelings and emotions, being aware of them and expressing them to others, the next step is to be able to give the same to others.

6. LISTENING

We need to be able to listen at a deep level to the other person's needs. This entails forgetting for the moment your need to defend yourself against the other because you are no longer afraid of him and know that he cannot wipe you out.

The other's needs must be important to you and it is important that he know this. Our defense usually is to weigh the other's need or requests through our own value system and judge their legitimacy. If we feel it is illegitimate or we are incapable of fulfilling this need regardless of its legitimacy, then we tend to deny the legitimacy of the need. In the process of rejecting the need, we are really rejecting the other person.

A common example of this might be a husband who has to work nights and weekends in order to make ends meet and whose wife is constantly complaining and nagging him regarding this. His wife's arguments sound very legitimate: he doesn't spend enough time with her or the children, they never go anywhere, she spends lonely hours doing nothing and feeling rejected, he comes home too tired to meet her sexual needs, etc.

Her husband's reasons also seem legitimate: he is working overtime for more money, he is trying to take financial care of his family, jobs like this are not plentiful, he is not qualified to do other work, this is the price he has to pay for advancement, etc...

We seem to have an insoluble situation - the man can't quit his job, and the wife feels lonely and rejected. When she constantly nags her husband about this situation, he becomes defensive and guilty. He knows she is lonely and her nagging has validity. He feels guilty everytime he goes to work because of what he is doing to his wife, and he feels guilty if he doesn't or if he leaves the job because of what he would be doing to himself.

He resents her for putting him in this conflict, and his answer is that she has no right to bother him about this when she knows he cannot change the situation and is doing it partly for her. He can't do anything to change the situation and so she has no "right" to be hurt, or to feel badly, or to nag him about it. In rejecting the legitimacy of her need, he is telling her that she has no right to her feelings.

What his wife may really be asking with all of her nagging and bitching about the job is whether or not her husband really loves her, is aware that she is alone and hurting, whether he cares that this is a very difficult situation for her, whether he recognizes that she is sacrificing for the family as well as he. Does her husband appreciate her sacrifices and the fact she has to take care of the kids alone and has to do without her husband a great deal of the time?

Perhaps if the husband were able to let his wife feel and express her hurt, loneliness and disappointment and accepted the legitimacy of her feelings, he could respond to her needs. If he could tell her sincerely that he cared for her and wished he could change the situation and didn't like it any better than she, she might be able to relax and stop nagging. The deepest need of the wife is to be heard and understood, and for her feelings to be accepted as natural, normal, and legitimate. If the husband can do this, then usually he does not even have to solve the problem. (That means both their feelings are not wrong or bad but have a legitimate reason for their existence. Their real issue is acceptance of these feelings.)

7. ACCEPTANCE

First, we accept the legitimacy of the other's feelings. Second, we express our caring about these feelings (they are important to us); third, we say we're sorry that we cannot change it (if we can't); and last, we both are able to accept the reality of the situation and to live with it much more easily.

Unfortunately, our tendency is to feel that admitting a person's feelings are legitimate is saying that we have to supply a solution to the problem. Many times we cannot change a hurtful situation, but we can still accept the feelings connected with it.

Usually for most of us, this is all we really need or want from the other...whether it be a parent or a spouse or a friend. If you can sincerely and positively respond to a person's feelings first, this will leave you all the time necessary to try to work out a solution to any and all problems.

Looking again at the husband who's working nights and weekends, if he can meet his wife's needs by sympathizing and caring about her loneliness and hurt and she is, therefore, able to feel loved and comforted and to relax and quit nagging in return, a strange thing often happens. Before you know it, he finds he can spend more time at home because he has been using this legitimate excuse to get away from the strain and stress of his relationship with his wife and children. At this point, he needs to express his needs and to honestly tell his wife why he hasn't spent more time at home, and what his problems are with her. It is now his wife's turn to be non-defensive in listening to him and in an honest exchange of real feelings and caring for each other.

When it comes right down to it, in spite of what we may insist on from other people, most of us don't really need anyone to judge us, correct us, interpret us, explain us, deny us, argue with us, encourage us, or even reassure us. We all need someone to care about our feelings and try to understand how we feel. The happy truth is that we can cure ourselves and make our own decisions when we are given this type of atmosphere of acceptance, caring and love.

8. LOVING IS GIVING

Our contemporary spiritual guide CHARLIE BROWN puts it in perspective when he says, "It may be more spiritual to give than to receive, but receiving is good enough for me." For many of us giving means "giving up". "How much of myself do I have to sacrifice or give up to be loved by you? And what are you going to give me to make it worth my while?"

For the person who already feels deprived, it is difficult, if not impossible, to see love as primarily giving. The deprived person, like the infant child, sees life basically as the process of BEING loved and RECEIVING from others.

For the person whose basic needs have been met and is not a deprived child, giving becomes the highest expression of his potency. In the act of giving, the productive person experiences his strength, his wealth, and his power. To be fully human and to love maturely is to give of what's alive in you. To give the best that you can; your joy, interest, understanding, knowledge, humor, sadness, or whatever you are experiencing at any given moment. Giving is in itself exquisite joy - giving is its own reward.

Therefore, the first principle of giving in love is that you RECEIVE PLEASURE FROM THE GIVING. The primary driving force is YOUR NEED TO GIVE from the abundance of self - not your need to be appreciated or seen in a good light.

The second principle of giving in love is that you care enough to want to give what the spouse wants to receive.

A wife states that flowers given on occasion make her feel loved and special. Her husband responds, however, that flowers are a waste of money - they cost too much and shrivel and die. His expression of love is to give candy - something that will last awhile, taste good and bring nourishment. Her response is that candy makes her fat and she prefers flowers. Is it more important to win the argument or to make your wife feel loved and special? If flowers do the job, bring her flowers. On the other hand, the wife can acknowledge that she understands candy is an expression of love for the husband, but still prefers flowers.

If I give a dime's worth of love in order to receive a quarter's worth in return, that would be exploitation. If I give a quarter's worth of love to get a quarter's worth in return, that's bargaining. If I give a quarter's worth of love and ask for nothing in return, that's love.

9. LOVING IS RECEIVING

There is another side to the coin. Love is receiving. Giving implies making the other person a giver as well. They both share in the joy of what they have brought to life. Love is a creative quality that produces love; impotence is the inability to produce love.

If my love is a mature, productive love that comes out of a person who cares for himself and has no need to exploit others, it will be returned. This is not to say that one hundred per cent of all people will love me in kind, for that would be impossible and unnecessary. Love comes in many intensities and versions.

The first step in receiving is appreciation and acceptance. To accept and appreciate a gift is of itself a love gift in return. When you are embarrassed or for any reason refuse a gift of love, you have cheated the giver out of some of his joy. "I don't want to be in debt to others. I feel controlled or obligated when given to. It embarrasses me" are some of the reasons given for refusing a gift. "I'd rather give than receive." Does that mean you are obligating or controlling the other when you give?

If you believe receiving puts you in debt perhaps you need to explore your own reasons for giving.

The second step is reciprocation. We are not in debt or obligation to return a love gift in kind, BUT a gift received produces a feeling of being loved that should cause a desire to show your love as well.

Most of us are better at one than the other. A truly healthy person has a pretty good balance of ease in giving and graciousness in receiving.

You can be happy, successful enriched, fulfilled, and find meaningful life, purpose and direction...and share all this with the important others in your life.

EQUAL MARRIAGE

WHERE WOMEN TAKE ON
ALL THE BAD HABITS OF MEN . . .

AND MEN LEARN TO DO HOUSEWORK.

Chapter 16

Marriage and the Self

The music plays warmly in the background as the men file slowly to the front of the church. It is easy to spot the bridegroom to be. As the minister in flowing robes takes his place in the center, the man of the moment takes two steps forward as the others line up to his left and behind.

His chest swells with pride and anticipation. The back straight and legs planted firmly, this is a true gladiator in heat. The silly smile of conquest covers his face as he glances over the audience. No man has been so happy or proud. This is the moment of triumph, the taking of his bride, the most stunning, beautiful creature in God's world is soon to be his.

The music swells and the congregation stands in excitement. Here comes the bride. The bridesmaids have preceded her, flowers have been strewn, the moment is now.

The tradition of father escorting daughter down the aisle is immediately apparent - she'd never make it without him. Her wan smile suggests the need to faint - or throw up. The father is frightened they won't make it and she'll NEVER leave home. Together they lean heavily on each other and slowly forge to the front.

The groom is in ecstasy. No one has been so radiant and fine as this woman he is about to claim. They join hands and a warm ritual of love begins as both space out and hardly hear or experience the words spoken. The ceremony concludes with prayer and an introduction for the very first time as MR. & MRS. RONALD T. JONES.

There is a lingering kiss, an audience murmur of relief and a brand new couple has been born. An amazing transformation has taken place. The hesitant, frightened little girl of a few moments ago, about to toss this morning's breakfast, now radiates a triumphant smile of success. Strength and power abound in every stride. Eyes are alert and alive. "I did it, I got him, I'm married!" Flashbulbs pop as cameras click and no picture will ever again show her beautiful aliveness like this one. Next to her stumbles a deflated stranger. On the groom's face is a confused look of anxiety and distress - "What the hell have I done?"

This is called "The Miracle Transformation of Marriage."

Don't believe me - look it up. Choose ten wedding books of your friends and family at random and look for those magic "before and after" pictures of the bride and her father just starting down the aisle - and then the triumphant return with her reluctant prize.

PEOPLE AND RELATIONSHIPS CHANGE
WHEN THEY GET MARRIED.

Marriage is a powerful institution. It tends to bring out the closet craziness in us, to reveal weakness and faults we had even hidden from ourselves.

Differences between us become exaggerated and intense. The every essence of attraction may surprisingly become the irritant of discontent. "Why don't you think,

MARRIAGE:

AN INSTITUTION WHERE YOU SYSTEMATICALLY PUNISH YOUR SPOUSE AND KIDS FOR ALL THE REAL AND IMAGINED PAIN INFLICTED ON YOU BY PARENTS AND SOCIETY OVER THE YEARS.

feel and act like I do?" we wonder, or as the esteemed Professor Henry Higgins bitterly complained, "Why isn't a woman more like a man?"

Possibly no other decision so changes, impacts and influences our destinies like the one called marriage. Consider the framework of our culture and the programming over centuries of time.

(Anytime you talk about "Generalities of Truth" you are leaving out exceptions and individual differences, but stereotypes exist and serve a purpose because THEY TEND TO BE TRUE more often than not. The culture is in transition but no clear-cut new stereotype has yet evolved.)

Men tend to feel more FREE before marriage and women usually have to work harder to keep it going. There are some built-in paradoxes here.

Women are still primarily programmed for marriage as the ultimate career, even if they plan to pursue a secondary career as a breadwinner. This was emphasized recently by the 1986 "Marriage Patterns in the United States" demographic study. This study reported that college educated women who are still single at the age of 35 have only a 5 percent chance of ever getting married. PANIC RULES THE LAND.

These were women who put self satisfaction, education and careers first - not the old maid spinsters of yesteryear - but attractive, sharp, sexual, cream of the crop ladies who were not panicked to marry young, not desperate or dependent. They had figured to marry in good time! When they were ready, when other priorities had been explored, when the appropriate man who appreciated them and their life style came along.

Now they are told it won't happen - TOO LATE - there just aren't enough men to go around, and the gloom and doom hits hard. Suddenly a source or situation out of their control takes away the choice and panic prevails. The thought of no choice is an empty one.

In the next six months half of those women "fell madly in love" and got married, blowing the whole study out of the water. The embarrassed authors of the study said they made a mistake and revised their statistics. They were basing their study on old dating patterns when the average marriage age for women was 18 and men was 21. Now it is closer to 25 and 27. But the panic of never getting married and spending life alone was the biggest factor.

While the career single women of today is not as programmed for financial dependency as her predecessors, we still hear worry about making it alone on one salary, paying the bills, surviving in an expensive world. If a child is involved, this is an even heavier burden of financial and emotional responsibility and there is a longing to share it.

Men are programmed to be career oriented as the primary function of life and that eventually there will be a wife and family to support and "if I'm lucky my wife will work too and help out."

Men are programmed to chase women and delay or postpone marriage while women are programmed to run away and get caught. We may or may not fulfill our programming but it's there. For you women who might be offended by this, read "THE CINDERELLA COMPLEX". This is a modern book by a modern career woman who says very well what I'm struggling with here. Women tend to be strong, independent, free, and capable when living alone (either before marriage or between marriages) but once married there is a stronger, underlying pull to become weak, dependent, helpless and controlling.

Men also feel free, strong, masculine, alive and independent in the single state. Even when it wasn't true, men took the attitude with women that "there are dozens of others in line behind you, just waiting their turn at my desirable substance, so get with it lady. Make me happy and keep me happy or I'm gone to the next in line".

This has always worked as a tactic to encourage women to work harder than men to keep the relationship going, with the added attractiveness of the challenge to succeed. Women seem very attracted to men who aren't overly needy of them and suspicious of men who are.

The sad truth is that women have always been more interested in romance, intimacy and togetherness, while men are satisfied with sex and the absence of hassle. Hence more pressure on the woman to make it all work.

Compounding this is the new revelation that the man IS in a buyer's market and that there ARE as many as two women for every eligible man in some communities and therefore he is more cocky and confident in his approach to relationships. In summary, before marriage the man is more psychologically free than the woman, more strong, in charge, safe and free to leave if it's not working. In that environment he SHOULD be at his best.

Knowing this - and being fully aware of the well deserved reputation of fragile male ego - the woman shapes and turns the relationship with the skill and expertise of a master craftsman.

Men like the feeling of freedom and possibilities, while that leaves women feeling in limbo and pushed toward closure. And then they marry. There are various steps toward marriage on the bouncy road of romance. Each prepares for the next one but is NOT the same and unique to itself.

Casual dating leads to serious dating, "going steady" or commitment, sexual involvement, engagement, living together, finally marriage. In today's society, there is no particular order to the above.

At each step, we learn more about the other, more about ourselves, fine-tune the relationship. The modern step of living together (at the beginning it was referred to as trial marriage) adds a dramatic new intervention, but for MOST it is still not the same as marriage. Living together is logically and potentially one of the great innovations of the new age. Moral considerations aside, look at the advantages.

You DO get to practice being married without the life or death consequences of divorce hanging over the door. Living with someone on a day-to-day basis provides opportunity for full disclosure of faults, quirks, and idiosyncrasies, such as neatness, housekeeping and habits. Expectancies on a 24-hour basis are often different than a dating arrangement.

This is a day of serial marriage - one at a time till I get it right. But no one likes divorce and divorce means keeping score. Serial living together - till you get it right - is not a score-keeping operation - no one asks how many times you've shacked up when you apply for a wedding license, but they do ask how many times you've been married.

One or more live-in situations gives opportunity to discover what you want and don't want in a relationship, what to LOOK for, what questions to ask, something that requires a couple of divorces for some folks to discover.

Delaying first time marriage gives people a chance to grow up and mature before they take the plunge rather than after the fact. That has to be an asset circumstance for most people. Delaying marriage by living-in often (but not always) delays having children, again upping the maturity factor, and mature adults are better parents than their immature counterparts.

So the logical conclusion is that living together is a great preparation for marriage, works the bugs out before the event, rather than after, removes the mystery of what you are choosing. But statistics tell us (who wants to be a statistic?) that it doesn't help or hinder. People who live together first have no better (or worse) track record than those who don't.

This is very disappointing to me. It simply means that people are failing to learn from and take advantage of a wonderful opportunity for growth and education. The man apparently is still basking in his "one foot out the door" sense of freedom and control and the woman is working even harder to please and close the sale.

They then get married and the world shifts into reverse. Now the woman is free and the man under obligation. She has accomplished her objective, proven she is desirable. The marriage certificate in today's society is rather a "degree of proficiency". She passed the test. Where she felt obligated to protect the fragile male ego before, to keep him from running away, there is no such need now - he's MARRIED, committed, for better AND worse. Now she can let her hair down, tell how she really feels, overhaul his emotional motor to where he runs more smoothly, gain weight, whatever. The game is over - relax.

On the other hand, the man IS obligated and trapped to some degree. There is no law on the books requiring a woman to support either her husband or her children. A man can go to jail for failure to provide. (The new ERA laws in California and some other states say you can no longer discriminate according to sex but try applying it to support).

Now unconsciously the role reversal seems to shape up that it is the man's responsibility to work harder, prove himself a worthy husband, and live up to the expectations of success according to the measurements of husbands. He has passed the apprentice level of "potential". Before he didn't have to put up with her lip - now he does - she's his wife. That great marriage authority, Eddie Fisher, whose marital parlay segued from Debbie Reynolds to Elizabeth Taylor to Connie Stevens, before moving on to lesser lights, bitterly complained a few years ago that "marriage destroyed relationships." (If you have to be destroyed, what a way to go!) "Women change when you marry them. Before marriage, they adore you, chase you around the world, wait on your every whim, can't get enough of your singing, can't do enough for you. The second you finish your vows, they turn to demanding, castrating bitches who now expect you to do all that for them."

There is some truth in what he says. Compounding this is the added truth that man tends to lose a degree of confidence and strength, now is more intimidated than intimidating, and is confused by the instant TESTING that wasn't there before. The woman often jumps on this confusion and "nice guy" response as weakness, rather than the desire to please, and finds herself exploiting it.

She was never "free" to test the boundaries of the relationship before - she was too busy protecting it. Now she feels a need to test, stretch, experiment and discover. It is difficult to feel comfortable within the framework of a relationship without knowing the outer limits of that framework. How far can my spouse be pushed, under what circumstances, and how often? For some women this need to test and push limits till abruptly stopped is an obsession.

Paradoxically, the angry wife beater with a short fuse may put a stop to "this testing nonsense" in a hurry and go on to a more comfortable marriage than the "nice guy" who wants to take his wife seriously and give her what she demands or needs. If she sees this as fear and weakness - "look out below".

IS THERE NO ANSWER?

IS MARRIAGE MERELY GROUNDS FOR DIVORCE?

SHOULD WE ALL SIMPLY GO ON LIVING TOGETHER?

I'm a pragmatist - whatever works! I also have an obsessive need to understand and simplify. If something works WHY does it work? What are the properties of success? How can I apply it to other areas of my life?

There are two general reasons for relationships succeeding before marriage where they don't after. One possibility is phoniness. Both partners being on best behavior, courtship, doing what you know will please, ignoring the petty irritations, hiding the areas of self you are ashamed of. If that's your approach and you want your marriage to work, then continue to do what worked before - DON'T CHANGE.

I had a psychology professor in college who advised us to "do nothing before marriage (such as the courtesies of opening doors, seating the lady or what we've mentioned above) that you don't intend to continue after marriage. Otherwise you are perpetrating fraud - you are courting someone under fraudulent conditions." That is the EXACT reason for the failure of most marriages - the romance was partially fraud. "What you see is NOT what you get."

A second possibility is expectations. There is no stereotype with a stranglehold on values and belief systems quite like that of marriage. A husband IS and DOES. A wife IS and DOES. The Gospel according to THEY - "They say" - and no one knows who "they" are to be held responsible. Interesting enough these stereotypes don't always carry over into living together or even dating. People live together five years in perfect harmony and agreement. They share household chores, go 50/50 on the budget, treat each other to meals and gifts, negotiate decorating and overall decisions, blending a nice mixture of togetherness and individual privacy and friends.

The day after they get married the woman may be in for a shock - now she is expected to do the housework, and she's no longer free to go dancing or even to lunch with her girl friends even though she's been doing it with no repercussions for five years. WHY NOW? "Because you're my wife. I didn't like it before but I had no right to say no. Now you're my wife and wives don't do those things."

Or the wife whose new husband is the weekend, macho athlete, once married doesn't want him to risk injury or take time away from her.

One very jarring example was a 40ish professional who moved into an apartment with his divorced lady friend and her two teenaged children. He was warm, caring, supportive, low key and noncritical. The relationship went on for three years under "tight" conditions in a small apartment with no stress. So they married, moved out of the apartment and bought a large home. A pre-nuptial agreement protected the assets of both. He supplied the down payment and bought the house furnished. When before he paid "rent" to her and it was "her apartment", now it is HIS home and furniture.

"DON'T EAT IN THE LIVING ROOM, TURN OFF THE LIGHTS, WASH ONLY WHEN THE MACHINE IS FULL BECAUSE I'M PAYING THE BILLS." Suddenly he becomes critical of her discipline and the kids are brats.

The difference here was money and responsibility. When it's your apartment and responsibility, do your thing. If it's my money and reputation (my wife and my step-children) I run the show.

Speaking of expectations, an interesting survey of the 80's sought to determine through numerous interviews which group of people were the happiest - married men, married women, single men or single women.

The order turned out to be: 1. married men; 2. single women; 3. single men; 4. married women.

Do you need a better explanation for the divorce rate? The happiest people are married to the unhappiest. Is this possible?

Sure. Their expectations are different so thus their level of satisfaction. If both of us are looking for a job and I expect $1000 a week and you expect $500, we have very different expectancies. We both get hired the same day for $750 a week. You are overjoyed with a feeling of success and well being. They are paying a third more than you expected. I am devastated and angry and feel a 25% cut in my self worth. It's all relative.

Men tend to look to marriage for rest and relaxation - a home or castle, a safe refuge if you will, where refreshment from the battles of life come with food, comfort, sex and companionship. The absence of hassle is heaven. Men get their self worth and value from career, productivity and financial reward.

Women tend to get their identification, self worth and personal satisfactions from the intimacy and sharing of love and marriage. Even a career woman who gets the same "goodies" as men from work still points to love and marriage as her reason for living and personal identity.

Neither position is right or wrong. They are simply DIFFERENT. If both parties understand these differences they will not feel personal rejection from the other.

When the absence of hassle, reasonable sex and pleasant conversations are enough to please you, it's easy to see why married men are happiest. When continued courtship, rapt attention and personal satisfaction are required, more is at stake and disappointment comes more readily.

A third possibility is AUTHENTICITY. Let it all hang out. BOTH PARTIES NEED TO BE FREE BEFORE MARRIAGE AND STAY FREE AFTER MARRIAGE.

If you do this there should be no dramatic change during or after the ceremony.

Don't let some stupid stereotype dictate your marital values. Decide the standards and values YOU want to live by and live by them. It doesn't matter what other husbands or wives do, it only matters what works and is comfortable for the two of you. Create, design, negotiate and fashion a loving, accepting, flowing life style that meets the needs of both. Write your own job description. Put it on paper. This may be more important than a pre-nuptial agreement about financial assets.

BEING FREE means free to be, act out and express one's total and true self - all of oneself. If there are "undesirable" habits and feelings you plan to share AFTER marriage, share them FIRST. Take the risk. If there are petty irritations you can't wait to correct in your mate, DO IT FIRST - BEFORE MARRIAGE - if you both survive, perhaps the marriage will too.

WHAT IF I LOSE MY LOVER DOING THIS?

What have you lost? You'd either lose him anyway with the subsequent pain and discomfort of a divorce or you are doomed to the marital resentment of courtship fraud and the anger that your spouse refused to change for you.

Be true to yourself BEFORE marriage and DURING marriage. Nothing bad can come from that.

AUTHENTICITY, GENUINENESS, REALNESS, BEING OPEN, HONEST AND INTI-MATE.

All the things we have discussed about the self and its possibilities apply at their most important here. No other decision is this important. Nothing else in your lifetime will have the total effect that comes with your choice of a marital partner.

DON'T DO IT "SOMEHOW". "SOMEHOW, SOME WAY, BY SOME MIRACLE OF FATE IT WILL WORK OUT"

DO IT TRIUMPHANTLY!

DO IT AUTHENTICALLY!

DO IT RIGHT "WITH INTELLIGENCE AFORETHOUGHT"

Chapter 17

The Loving Couple

Life can readily be defined as a series of relationships. It is important to all of us that these relationships can be productive and meaningful - that we love and be loved - like and be liked - respect and be respected. So often we are taught that this entails being "nice", being sensitive to the desires of others so we can "please" them; and we try to become skilled manipulators so others will think well of us. To this end we become more concerned with how we "ought to feel" and what we "should do". We weigh the "rightness" and "wrongness" of our own personal feelings and needs in the light of the expectations of others.

The basis for all productive and meaningful relationships is honesty and love. But before once can be honest in his relationship with others, he must be honest with himself. Before he can love others, he must first properly love himself so that he is a person with love to give. Before he can respect others, he must respect himself.

Possibly the most difficult chore for many of us is simply knowing what we really feel and why. We get so caught up with the rightness or wrongness of our feelings - personal guilt - and how we should feel, that we don't really know what we do feel.

The emphasis of this book has been less concerned with the goodness or badness of our feelings than with simply exploring and examining how we do feel. As we discover what we really feel and learn to live on a conscious level of feelings and needs, we discover why we feel as we do about ourselves, our parents, friends and acquaintances. Knowing why helps us to understand and accept our feelings as legitimate and rational. This in turn gives us complete freedom of choice in acting on our feelings. We are free to be angry or not - to be sad or happy - to withdraw or communicate - to overlook or confront. Until we know and understand our feelings and needs, we cannot be free in choosing our relationships but are shaped by circumstances and entrapped by unconscious motivations over which we have little or no control.

Self-awareness then tends to self-acceptance and unconditional self-love. (I love myself and believe I have self-worth and value because I exist and need no other reason.) Once we can be comfortable with ourselves, we have a real freedom and little or no guilt because we no longer have to be dishonest with ourselves and others.

This in turn makes it easier to see and understand the real needs and feelings of others - to know what they "really mean" underneath the fear or hostility. Living on a level of self-awareness we can relate to people on the basis of their needs and feelings, honestly giving them our interest, care and concern.

Self-awareness then becomes the key to living by one's own integrity, doing what is constructive and best. This, in turn, should also be best and most constructive for the important "others" in one's relationships.

By knowing and understanding our own feelings and needs we honestly relate to the feelings and needs of others. The productive and meaningful relationships we achieve give meaning to life itself.

Healthy relationships don't just happen. They are products of relatively healthy and reasonably well-adjusted people who are willing to take the calculated risks involved in the complicated process of loving and being loved.

The best reason for having a self that is mature, capable and independent, can stand alone and does not need others for survival, is that one then is truly free to LOVE SOMEONE ELSE. It is impossible to love someone we need for survival. Where there is no choice there is no love.

Once one is free to BE, one is free to LOVE.

What kind of couple would we expect from this maturity? What type of interaction, mutual support, inter-dependence would emerge?

I believe the effect is enormous. We need each other - not to survive - to ABOUND.

not for dependence - for ABUNDANCE.

not for basics - for the ULTIMATE.

In the next few pages I'd like to describe what the benefits of this kind of love really are. Twelve attributes or examples of what the self-actualizing, self-sufficient and satisfied loving couple would be like. Keep in mind these are not necessarily super-people, idealistic to the point of mysticism. This kind of relationship is readily available to each of us. For most it will certainly require effort - a stretching, growing, risk-taking advance that passes through corridors of fear and uncertainty, disappointment and failure - but an effort that refuses to be discouraged until the goal is accomplished.

This is a goal of comfortable expectancy, secure in what we have, looking forward to the mutual challenge of the future, basking in the pleasures of the past, a relationship based on the following qualities:

1. A lack of defensiveness that allows each to perceive circumstances as they really are; not "as I need them to be".

Our individual perceptions must either complement each other or be seen by each in the same general context. People who approach life from very different frames of reference can both be "right" but totally miss the point of each other's reality. Even more common is when husband and wife each share what happened in their argument last night and the stories come out so differently from each other that is sounds like two different families.

Jane: We got in a bitter dispute over who was going to do the dishes.

Bob: (interrupting with obvious irritation) It was before the dinner and it was over your mother. The dishes never came up.

When we can't agree about simple facts, how can communication begin or issues be readily identified? This is not an uncommon experience and can only mean that one or both are so frightened of being blamed, wrong or bad, that they cannot look at any situation in search of truth. Instead they find ways of distorting the issues in order to protect self and make the other the culprit.

When one is not threatened by someone's judgement, it is possible to perceive others as they really are, and interpret their behavior as it was really intended.

Love consists of two people with good judgement who see things as they really are and don't play games. They have enough ego strength to protect their individual self worth, so that defensiveness between them is minimized.

Without this need to protect oneself from blame and accusation, both are free to perceive life situations with a minimum of distortion and a maximum of desire for understanding and truth. Problems between them are therefore more easily understood and resolved.

This kind of couple can tolerate uncertainty and ambiguity more easily than others do because of their own inner peace. They do not lead the rigid, structured life style that some people do as an armored protection against the uncertainty of not knowing. Not being constantly overwhelmed by anxiety regarding themselves or their relationship, they are not forced to press issues to premature conclusions or to make impulsive and inflammatory accusations.

Tolerating uncertainty and not always needing immediate gratifications gives them room for flexible searching and the patience to allow events to naturally unfold.

2. Strong, positive feelings of self-love and acceptance, combined with a non-possessive love for others.

Emotionally crippled people create emotionally crippled relationships. It takes two individuals who bring a sense of self-worth, love and pride to the relationship to make it special and enhancing.

Honesty with oneself about what is done and why it is done creates feelings of self-worth, leaving little need for guilt, shame or anxiety. One can freely give and receive this type of sharing and believe in the essential inner goodness of the individuals and the couple relationship itself.

This couple can separate individual and isolated behavior situations from the basic character of what each person is. "I may not always agree with or approve of what you do but I love, appreciate and believe in what you are."

Some people have difficulty with this concept of separating behavior from character, insisting that the behavior is a direct reflection of the character. If one judges the behavior bad, the character must be bad as well. Two factors are involved here. Who is to judge the "goodness" or "badness" of the behavior? This often falls into controversial areas of value judgement and what person has the right to impose his or her value judgement over that of the spouse?

Areas of religious faith, war versus pacifism, sexual conduct, economic policies and habits such as drinking and smoking are just a few of the examples where value judgements may be violently opposed.

Since none of us is perfect nor should need to be or act in a perfect fashion, there must be room for imperfect or negative behavior without that person's character being permanently defamed by it. We can tell a lie without being a confirmed liar or commit a vindictive or hurtful act without being forevermore a vindictive and hurtful person. When one can believe in what the other party is and their essential goodness as a human being, their positive motivation to be appropriate, it is fairly easy to forgive, to be tolerant of and even understand behavior which disagrees with or seems in conflict with their character.

The structure of the relationship - open or closed, permissive or demanding, set roles or household sharing - does not determine its success or failure; but the key to success is the ability of the two persons to choose, define and flexibly flow with a life-style that consistently reflects their values, encourages their growth and meets their needs.

This combination of self love and non-possessive love creates such as environment.

3. An openness to the totality of human experience, both inner and outer, positive and negative.

A loving couple welcomes each day and experience with an expectation of OKness rather than a sense of dread or concern. They are not necessarily "high" or in a hyper state of ecstasy, that would be unreal on a continuous basis, but with solid feelings of comfort and goodwill. "I can handle it, learn from it, flow with it, do whatever is appropriate. My backlog of responses is sufficient to the day and I'm glad to be alive, in a world I experience as generally friendly and reasonable. I will not be overwhelmed by the extremes of life, either positive or negative. Because I am reasonably in touch with my feelings, I can truly be spontaneous in life and feel certain my reactions will be appropriate and not just impulsive."

Having a spouse to share in this confidence and strength certainly provides an additional safe environment or increment of strength to add to this reassurance of sufficiency.

We might add that spontaneity differs from impulsiveness in that it is always appropriate to the reality of the moment. Impulsive behavior may or may not hit the target. If it does, it's pure coincidence. Spontaneity comes from being in touch with one's integrity - operating from the inner core of one's being. When this is true, perceptions are correct, feelings are appropriate, and behavior fits the occasion.

The spontaneous couple is one that provides a consistent spark of electricity that flows between them. Each one has the potential to "turn on the other one" and is consistently "turned on" by the wit, warmth, and individuality of the other. "Your love of life inspires me and makes me glad to be alive. You bring a sparkle to my eye and a spring to my feet." There is a constant energy flow that continually recharges each other as though they have found the secret to total and unending source of supply, a real perpetual motion.

At the same time, each has his own source of supply and is not totally dependent on the other. That's where the spontaneity comes in - an extra spark that motivates, but not great depression or anger if it is missing.

For these people, familiarity does not breed contempt but they can see value in and be inspired by the basic, everyday experiences of life.

Perhaps this explains why some marriages seem to breed boredom and discontent, while others are always new, exciting, and stimulating. People who primarily look to others to supply most of their excitement and reason for living are bored with themselves and are more often than not, boring people. So they must constantly search for change, diversion, or escape.

Those who primarily look to their own inner being for stimulation and excitement, who like to grow and learn from life, are exciting to be around. When two such people are married, they stimulate each other to new heights and do not tire of each other's company. Since they also have privacy and right of movement within the community, there is no claustrophobia or need to run away. They are busy, active people who keep a proper place for escape and nurturing the child within them, but not to excess.

4. Problem-centered — rather than ego-centered.

"The meat is tough" brings a reaction from the cook that causes one to wonder if it was cut from his or her own leg. "Your breath is bad" is not a comment on your character, but on what smells.

The ego-centered person cannot separate his ego from whatever the problem may be. He keeps feeling, "Why don't you like me?" and responds with, "I am too a nice guy."

A teacher writes a test for her class and feels it is an excellent sampling of the material covered. Her class claims that the test is tricky, irrelevant and unfair. If the teacher is ego-centered, her reaction will be: "Why don't you like me?" How can you hurt me like that? How can you call me a bad person and teacher (without socially redeeming features) when I work so hard for you and try so hard to be liked?" Those are her inner feelings, which will probably never be revealed to the class. What the class will probably hear is an angry, defensive, impassioned dissertation designed to prove that they have no right to feel that way, the test is a good one and they have poor judgement. Why the violent reaction to criticism of a simple test? Because the teacher cannot separate her ego from the test. She is on trial, her integrity, intelligence, character and self-worth and this is what she is defending.

A problem-centered person might feel disappointed or surprised at the class reaction but would not tend to take it personally. "If I am a good person and a good teacher, I can afford to blow a test now and then without loss of personal worth." She would respond to the class by asking for clarification of their feelings and share her own personal views regarding a solution to "their mutual problem and concern". That would bring about a reasonable compromise for all involved. All of this has nothing to do with whether the class "likes" the teacher or the teacher "likes" the class members. They simply share a mutual problem to be solved.

Put that principle into a couple relationship and the emotions become even more intense as the stakes become higher and the egos more on the line. Mention that the food doesn't taste good or that the sex was not overly exciting last night or that there won't be enough money to pay the bills this month and your spouse may immediately jump to the conclusion that your comment is an indirect but vicious attempt at character assassination. They respond by fighting for their lives. Sometimes it **is** indirect character assassination and sometimes an innocent comment or mild complaint without critical intent. The ego-centered person will be offended regardless, the problem-centered person will not.

A problem-centered couple is one that can look at a situation regardless of how personal it may be, and say, "We have a problem to solve between us, let's go to work on it." No judgement, just looking at what is and how it affects us and why, and how we might modify the situation to affect us differently.

If you judge my behavior or approach as inappropriate to your needs or feelings, that does not necessarily determine that I have, therefore, been judged bad as well. The judgement-ego response is so common it seems "natural", a part of inborn nature, but to be defensive is undoubtedly **nurtural**, part of our cultural upbringing.

When a person really likes himself, he expects others to feel the same, so he is more objective about his work or behavior and others' acceptance or rejection of it. This is especially true in a relationship where there is abundant evidence of love and feelings of well-being for the other.

Remember, we are talking about attitudes and motivations. One can appear to have a mission in life and be a service to others and really do it for purely selfish reasons - to "buy love" or look like a generous person when he just wants to feed his ego or pocket book.

The problem-centered couple has their relationship in overdrive and it requires only minimal attention. At the beginning they may have concentrated all their energy to solving problems between them, learning a new language, discovering new methods of pleasing each other and making the relationship a functioning one. Once learned, maintenance may require little effort.

Because this couple is not wasting energy being defensive or protecting themselves from the constant fear of attack they are often generously involved in solving problems "outside themselves" - community projects, charity events, public affairs.

A loving couple finds it necessary to share elements of this love in the same manner a loving person finds it necessary to have someone with whom to share his or her love.

5. A need for physical and psychological space, as individuals, as a couple and as a family.

These people not only do not mind solitude, but actually seek it. This detachment is expressed in their ability to be objective in their viewpoints about others. It is not that they do not like people, for they do. They also like themselves and do not mind being alone with themselves. What we are saying is that they really don't need people as a crutch but can enjoy them for what they are when together. Those who cannot stand to be by themselves and are constantly seeking out others to fill a void or a vacuum in their lives, can't really like or love people, because they need them too badly. If you need someone for a crutch, you don't really respect that person for being your crutch, and you feel hostile towards him because he reminds you of your own dependency.

This couple's needs can be expressed in a variety of options. Each of the individuals has a need for and takes the opportunity to be alone with himself - to retreat for his own recharging process - without having to fight his spouse for it, or feel guilty for needing and taking this time; and can freely give it to the spouse. People who freely give and receive privacy, do not have a need to withdraw from the other as an escape from responsibility or confrontation.

Privacy should not be confused with withdrawal. The couple will often have a need for privacy as a couple - apart from family, children, friends, or outside commitments. This is a time to be alone with and totally experience each other. Another time may require an aloneness that includes the children - a family intimacy.

Privacy may call for time away from your spouse to explore other worlds or people as opposed to being alone by yourself. This is an area that frightens a lot of people. "If my spouse is allowed time alone with others, it is inevitable this will lead to sexual involvement."

It stands to reason, many of us don't want most of our time away from the other or why would we want to be married? It is also clear that no one person can meet all the needs of another and that is too much to ask. Freedom to explore our world, to meet and enjoy others without the restriction of possessive jealousy is an important quality of growth. If self-actualizing people need and have this detachment, the actualized couple must have this freedom as well.

In most cases when a person expects sexual involvement to result from every friendship between the sexes he is really speaking of his own needs and feelings. "That's what I want or would be tempted to do in that situation, so everyone else does, too."

Jealousy is not based on love, but fear. The irony is that the most possessive people generally enjoy a double standard that allows and excuses their own infidelity while condemning and controlling the spouse.

"Perhaps I'm not person enough, good looking enough, successful or loving enough to keep my spouse. And someone out there may meet my spouse's needs better than I can. So, I better keep a tight reign on my spouse so he or she will not have the opportunity of finding that person. It is better to keep a person by a destructive method than to lose them by a good method of relating and wind up being alone and rejected."

Is that really true? Is your survival as a person that tied to someone else? Keeping a spouse under lock and key brings feelings of claustrophobia and actually pushes them to try to escape.

Possessiveness of mate always leaves a lingering doubt of whether they remain with you out of love and loyalty or because you successfully maintained control.

Allowing space or freedom in a relationship does not mean you don't care what the other person does. Freedom is not an invitation to infidelity. But why does fidelity have to be demanded or controlled? Fidelity can only be a gift of love - whether it is emotional or physical. It cannot be demanded or controlled.

The issue here has nothing to do with sex outside marriage. That subject will not be covered in this book. What we are talking about is freedom for each spouse to explore his world without restriction by the other. "If your behavior frightens, confuses or upsets me, I want the right to share that with you and resolve it with mutual concern for each other's feelings. As a result, you may choose to modify your behavior or I might better understand, but I do not wish to control your freedom to be you."

The best protection against breaking a trust is the trust itself. I would like to share with you what that trust means to me.

A COUPLE'S CREED OF TRUST.

"I TRUST YOU. I TRUST WHAT YOU ARE. I TRUST YOUR GOOD JUDGEMENT. I TRUST YOUR LOVE FOR ME. I TRUST YOU WOULD NOT DELIBERATELY HURT ME. I TRUST IF A MISTAKE IS MADE, WE CAN WORK IT OUT BETWEEN US.

"I TRUST ME. I TRUST THAT I CAN LIVE THROUGH ANY GRIEF OR DISAPPOINT-MENT THAT OCCURS. I TRUST IN MY OWN ABILITY TO SURVIVE.

"I TRUST US. I BELIEVE IN WHAT WE HAVE AND GIVE TO EACH OTHER AS INDIVIDUALS AND AS A COUPLE. I TRUST THAT WE ARE REAL WITH EACH OTHER AND EACH IS BRINGING TO THE RELATIONSHIP HIS MOST AUTHENTIC SELF.

"SINCE I CAN TRUST, IT IS THE VERY BEST OF MYSELF, THE MOST GENUINE ASPECTS OF MYSELF THAT I SHARE. IF THAT IS NOT ENOUGH FOR YOU, I MUST ACCEPT THAT, EVEN THOUGH THE DISAPPOINTMENT WILL BE GREAT. I CAN ONLY GIVE WHAT I AM. YOU CAN ONLY GIVE WHAT YOU ARE. I BELIEVE THAT WILL BE ENOUGH".

6. I AMNESS - a sense of personal authority and independence that transcends the relationship and the mutual environment.

We're not talking about defensive rebellion or selfish committal, "but what's really best for me, for my integrity, is really best for the important others in my environment." These are self-starting, self-sufficient, and creative people.

Many times when the issue of ultimate authority is raised, we hear the question, "What if both feel 'this is the best for me' and have opposite viewpoints? Doesn't there have to be an ultimate decision? Who will make it?"

Our society has always given that legal right to the men. A couple live in California and he's offered a job opportunity in New York that he cannot pass up, so he takes the job. The wife says she won't leave California and refuses to go with him. In the past, he could sue for divorce on the grounds of abandonment and she might not get much in the settlement because it was "her fault". A wife was required to follow her husband. With the new California divorce laws, either one can file for "irreconcilable differences" and since there is "no fault", property settlement is not affected.

Does a husband really have the right to impose his will on the wife? Does the wife really have the right to impose her will on the husband? The situation described above is being more and more reversed. Wives are getting opportunities for jobs that call for moving to a new community, pulling up roots, and forcing the husband to find a new position. Why not?

If it is important to the one who wants to move, it is difficult to imagine a loving spouse standing in the way of the move, even though there would be inconveniences. But, and this is a big but, if both decided this was an integrity decision (one to go and one to stay) and could not compromise it, then each would be obligated to his own integrity. A spouse cannot ask another spouse to go against his/her own integrity, even if the law gives them that right.

I feel this is a rare occurrence. Most situations can be compromised and whoever feels strongest about his particular opportunity or desire will generally win, which is fine if they are equally matched - not so fine if one is overwhelmingly dominant.

Loving individuals are looking for ways and means to meet both their needs and are equally interested in both needs being met, so they work hard to understand each other and not let this impasse happen to hem. People who want "masculine rule" seem to feel this is one of their strongest issues - someone has to break the tie vote. When either the man or woman takes that role of "ultimate authority", the integrity of the other is violated (providing both are standing on integrity at this point). If their integrity needs are that incompatible, perhaps the marriage should not survive. People come before marriage. This is more theory than concern because the issue of integrity conflict is rare, especially between those who truly love and understand each other. For those who don't, the difference might be a test of power or contest for authority, somewhat of a "king of the mountain" game, and that's manipulation, not integrity.

For something to be truly "best for me" we must consider the feelings and needs of the important others in our life to come to that conclusion. They won't always agree and it is our responsibility to be true to ourselves and not to lie to ourselves if we want to claim that decision. If we're kidding ourselves, all involved lose.

As for the couple's relationship to their world, they get along with their culture but are somewhat detached from it. They do not allow themselves to be "squeezed into a mold". They are not particularly rebellious nor do they agree completely with the culture.

Each can tolerate differences of feelings, needs, and ways of expression or life style in both their spouse and the world outside and enjoy finding ways to encompass the differences without a great deal of stress or discomfort. Where we agree and share, this is no problem. Where there are differences, we find a way. What we achieve as individuals heightens tremendously in the couple unity.

7. A generous and affectionate concern for humanity.

Even though they are aware of, and troubled by, the shortcomings of humanity, including their own, the loving couple is happy to be part of the human race and happy to be involved in this race.

It is precisely because of this point that couples can be open, tolerant, non-judgmental, and forgiving of each other; rather than gossipy, suspicious, and accusing. They can be aware of negative reality, without being carried away by it.

Some people try to handle this with a "power of positive thinking" approach. "Let's try to pretend that the negative does not exist or didn't happen." That is an escape from reality that doesn't work. You don't have to deny or distort reality to avoid negative consequences. Seeing things as they really are makes it easier to relate to them with an appropriate response.

8. A deep capacity for and need for intimacy at many levels.

Intimacy can be defined as the act of revealing and sharing private aspects of oneself which are not generally on display to most people. Intimacy also provides an atmosphere of warmth, safety, and caring wherein another person experiences the desire to do the same with you. Many people are good at one without the unifying balance of the other, causing a distortion of the relationship. How sad it is to be able to provide a safe environment where others are free to be themselves with you, but where you are not free to share yourself with them.

Intimacy is not only revealing facts or secrets but having an attitude of closeness that is often difficult to define. It comes in varying shades of depth and openness, depending on the current circumstances and the persons involved. There is everything from the casual intimacy of getting to know a new friend to the deepest sharing of lovers.

Some people go through life and have rarely or never experienced this on any level. Others seem frightened by it and deny the necessity for closeness. They seem to fear the vulnerability involved that leaves one open to pain, disappointment, loss, humiliation or exposure. It is safe to say the more one likes himself, the easier and more desirous it is to share that self. The less one likes himself, the more he feels the need to hide this negative information from the world.

The relations of a loving couple are deep and profound but with a few, rather than many other people. The couple probably has many acquaintances and social contacts but their deep and profound relationships are restricted to a few. They are able to take other individuals and couples into their intimacy and sharing, thereby extending their "family circle" and increasing the love power involved. This brings nourishment, support, and involvement into the couple relationship from outside and strengthens the bond between them.

The number one relationship would, of course, be with each other. These people are experienced at achieving a depth of intimacy and bring this to the marriage. This takes an ability to be open to sharing of oneself at an important level.

Any hostility they have is situational and not chronic. They will respond with anger when anger is appropriate to a particular situation and time and are not the kind of people who carry "chips on their shoulders" looking for an excuse to blow their tops or inappropriately over react.

Because their anger is situational and not chronic, they don't tend to "gunnysack" grievances and carry silent resentments that drain off love and closeness. Each can understand and handle the other's anger because it is directed at the situation and is appropriate to the moment. There is less need to feel attacked or to take things personally.

This is where an interpersonal relationship within ourselves is so valuable, as we mentioned in previous chapters; the need to understand the various subpersonalities within our nature. The integration and harmony within must evidence itself in the outer experience. Our inner growth and the quality of friends we find ourselves relating to are reflective of each other.

9. Dominant people, without a need to dominate or compete with others.

A dominant person is one who takes complete responsibility for his own life; a "take charge" individual who sees what needs to be done and does it: independent, strong, capable, and assured. This has no connection with a need to dominate or control others, which is generally associated with insecurity, jealousy, fear and lack of self-esteem. Both persons may appear strong and be successful but their inner selves are worlds apart.

When two healthy, dominant people join forces, they make quite a team.

They can respect people, learn from them, and relate to them regardless of race, creed, culture, position, etc.

This kind of person (or couple) does not feel a need to prove himself superior, compete to make a point, or put someone down in order to feel his own sense of authority. In a couple relationship, this is extremely important. Each is not only comfortable with his own sense of authority, competence, and accomplishment, but is also highly aware of and proud of those of the spouse.

There is no struggle to be boss, no hassling for position, no fear of being put down or discounted. Rather than jealousy for one spouse's success, there is a deep feeling of pride that includes both as part of the success.

In a couple therapy situation, the wife was proudly stating she had changed and matured over the past three years. Her husband sarcastically pointed out that he felt some part in that and would like a little credit but didn't expect to get any. She very quickly blurted out that he got none of the credit, "it was all my doing."

When asked why, she replied, "If I give him any credit, that would leave me worthless."

What a tragedy! She could not conceive of giving him any credit without "going in the hole" herself. Not only would it take away from her credit, but worse yet, leave her with no credit at all...worthless. Ironic in one who was proud of how much she had changed and matured.

On another occasion, where the husband worked and the wife reared five children during a 20-year marriage, the husband admitted the major reason he did not get a divorce was that he did not want to share his community property with his wife. It was his job, his success, his money, investments, etc. She did nothing to earn it and had nothing to do with his success, and he resented sharing one dime of it with her, regardless of the law. How sad.

Where both partners have sufficient ego strength and feelings of self worth, they can share in the whole spectrum of each other's growth and success, both being fortified and neither being deprived. A person who cannot learn from anyone, give another credit for accomplishment, or who even feels threatened or put down by the success of others, is truly a deprived person.

As a deprived person, he feels so empty inside that most of his energy goes to trying to fill that bottomless pit of emptiness.

10. A highly tuned sense of priorities.

For many people, "the end justifies the means" but not for the loving couple. It is more important to them "how they live" (their character values) than whether or not they attain their goals, even though their goals are very important to them. They also seem to enjoy the means to an end more than the average person.

This is one of the areas that keeps the marriage stimulating, exciting, and growing. It fights boredom and stimulates response. Not only are they learning from yesterday and building for tomorrow, but they are especially enjoying the wonders of today.

"Here and now" living incorporates all these values. Some folks live in the past and never see the fresh opportunities of today. They either glory in the past accomplishments because they now feel past their ability to produce, or use the "bad luck" of the past to excuse the failures of the present.

Others tend to build for tomorrow - saving, hoarding, looking forward to that someday when they will "arrive" at security or fun or whatever. But tomorrow never comes. It is always today, and a future that doesn't include today isn't much of a future.

The self-actualizing couple enjoys the planning and preparation for tomorrow, enjoys the event planned for when they are experiencing it, and comes home with a suitcase of happy memories when they return.

Many people set goals of success such as "President of my own corporation", "a million dollars net worth", "lead singer in a band", "married and parent of a child". They say, "Then I'll be happy," only to discover that the outside accomplishment didn't bring the happiness they expected, and they had to set a new and higher goal.

Actualizing people set goals to provide stimulation and structure to their lives and are pleased and proud to accomplish these goals. They feel satisfaction in their achievements and living up to value standards. However, their happiness comes from within. They enjoy living and even if they miss their goals or change them in mid-stream, the fun was in trying, in doing one's best, in purposeful and meaningful living, rather than keeping score. They tend to live in the here and now.

11. A warmly compassionate sense of humor.

Their humor tends to be philosophical and non-hostile, much in the manner of a Bill Cosby. It's laughing at the human condition without putting anyone down. The opposite of this, of course, is humor at someone's expense and humiliation.

Comedians who specialize in hostile put downs have their role in making us laugh, sometimes out of embarrassment or shock, but have probably found an indirect method of releasing their own chronic anger or resentment, without having to face it directly, and are being well paid in the process.

There is no better saving grace in marriage than humor. Those who can poke warm, loving fun at themselves and their partners can save many a bad situation from being explosive.

Sarcastic humor that humiliates one's spouse in front of others will eventually destroy love and the marriage.

Couples without a warm sense of humor take themselves, life, and situations too seriously and tend to get hurt feelings more easily. The ability to see humor in unusual or unexpected situations, such as spilling coffee in a restaurant or cigarette ashes burning through a new suit of clothes, can ease tension, relax others and soften disappointment. The alternative to this is often anger and finding someone to blame. When you don't have to be perfect and you can feel warm, humorous feelings of affection for your own faults and failings, you can more readily accept responsibility (rather than blame) and not over-exaggerate the consequences.

12. Positive, creative energy flow.

All of us seem to have a certain amount of creativity that varies in degree. Creative people do not waste their energy potential defending or explaining or being anxious, and so this energy is free to be used for creative activity. For most of us, then, the healthier we are, the more creative we can be; and the more tense and bogged down with problems, the more our creative energy is drained.

It is easy to see how this principle can be applied to couples. Creative people have creative marriages. They are not boring people but are busily pursuing life and sharing that excitement and energy flow with each other. When things go wrong, they are busy seeking solutions rather than defending against accusations or doing jury duty to determine the degree of guilt and terms of sentence.

They have a lot of positive energy to invest in life and each other, and each tends to supply or supplement the other rather than being depressing or draining. It is very difficult to live with persons who experience constant energy leaks of depression, guilt, shame, anxiety, and defensiveness. On the other hand, a positive creative energy flow can be exhilarating and expansive to both partners.

This is what the self-actualizing, self-sufficient, and satisfied loving couple would be like. Again, we emphasize these are not super-people or perfect ones by any means. You will notice little was said about roles but rather an emphasis on feelings and attitudes.

If roles or ways of relating are chosen by the individuals and are comfortable within the couple framework, it doesn't matter if they are traditional or contemporary. If they are imposed by "shoulds, guilts, outside pressure or cultural experiences" then, unnatural stress is placed on the relationship, and the individual and couple needs of the persons involved are not being listened to or met.

In summary,

Each person is of equal importance in and to the relationship.

Each trusts in the essential goodness of the other and so looks for no insidious desire to inflict pain.

Each is a person of deep integrity and expects the same of the spouse.

Each takes responsibility for his own success and happiness as a human being and expects the same of his spouse.

Each is committed to the relationship and to creatively helping it to grow.

Each is committed to genuineness and authenticity with each other.

These are not empty words or foolish promises. They do not seek to control an unforeseeable future. They are not looking for loopholes and escape clauses. These are the meaningful commitments of reasonable people.

"I'll love you forever or till death do us part" is not ours to commit. We cannot predict the circumstances of tomorrow or control the consequences of today.

We can commit to give the best that we have.

When two growing, actualizing people find each other and share each other in the ways described, it will be enough.

Did you test your marriage against the above points? How did you do?

Throughout this book, we have maintained that you cannot separate individual well-being from marital success, that marital growth is based on personal growth, that problems reflected in a relationship are those found within each individuals, that love for others is based on love of self, that the healthier the individuals, the healthier the marriage. This is the struggle to be me with you, what love as an expression of self is all about.

Chapter 18

Seven Pillars that Support the House of Self

This is a book about SELF: The looking at, seeing, acknowledging, accepting, loving, and sharing of the self. In order to successfully accomplish that we must suspend judgement, become an objective observer, and see total truth for what it is.

Think of the total self as a house supported by seven strategically placed pillars in perfect balance and harmony.

These areas combined contain all that you need to be a healthy self. They are the sum of all we have tried to present in this book. They are not of equal importance and will require various shifting of priorities as to time and energy invested in them, but it is still essential to maintain a balance of growth patterns in all seven areas to keep "the roof of the house on straight and true."

PILLAR #1

Let's start with an inventory of SELF. What are the facts:

1. Physical

    Height, weight, eyesight, color of skin, hair, eyes, general health, best features, worst features, average features.

2. Mental

   Intelligence, education, training, experience.

3. Emotional

   Dependency, independence, strengths, weaknesses, warm, cold, sensitive, insensitive, caring, uncaring, feeling or turned off.

Once this inventory is taken, we have a good beginning toward seeing "who I am now, in the moment, acceptable and unacceptable as that may be."

But there are two more steps to completing our inventory. The next step is the truth of how OTHERS see us. What do others perceive as the truth of who I am? You may complain that this is unfair. "They can't possibly see the total me, the factors I see, the hidden facts I don't want to share. I show them my social mask, the way I want to be seen."

That's what you believe you are doing and to some degree it is true. But we are often experienced by others in a far different manner than we think we are projecting. We are constantly emitting clues, vibrations, and messages to others that we are not necessarily aware of at all. No one lives in a vacuum. You do not exist solely as a self within a self. You also exist as you interact with and respond to the many selves of others and to some degree are incomplete without this interaction. (Is there action without reaction? If a tree falls in a forest and no one hears, is there a sound?)

The third step in this triangular version of Self is **your perception of how others see you.** Others provide feedback. How can we honestly evaluate who and what we are, think and feel without feedback. And this constant feedback not only verifies and reveals us to us but constantly feeds new information into our computer that instantly and continuously helps adjust and CHANGE who we are. We are in constant process. Never static or finished, we are always **becoming**. And it is this three-way interaction that makes it so.

   A. Me perceiving me.

   B. You perceiving me.

   C. Me perceiving you perceiving me.

Think of those as color separations or negatives, each laid carefully over the others. If slightly ajar or off center, they become distorted or unclear as a total picture. When in perfect overlay or harmony, we have perfect self.

That is why "perfect self" cannot be **selfish** or **selfless**. This is self-love, self-acceptance, inner peace, perfect atunement with oneself and universe. They cannot be separated. To separate is to be selfish or selfless. To be selfish says, I don't care what happens to you. We become adversaries rather than support systems and **I cheat myself** out of the harmony and feedback I need from you. I cannot see you or be seen by you, I can't love or be loved." There is NO benefit to me.

To be selfless and put you first, denying my own feelings, and rights also takes BOTH of us out of focus. I am not revealing my true self or properly reflecting you. WE ARE INTERTWINED IN THE REFLECTION AND A VIOLATION OF ONE IS VIOLATION OF THE OTHER - THEY CANNOT BE SEPARATED.

That is why SELF LOVE is the ultimate state of spiritual union and harmony with the universe. It is the perfect overlay of the relationship between self and others. We do not function alone - we are part of a complex organism and loving self is loving GOD, SOULMATES, PARENTS, CHILDREN, FRIENDS, AND MANKIND, appropriately being and expressing that love in all that we do and are.

PILLAR #2

Step number two in this evolvement and attainment of self is finding and experiencing that ultimate SOUL-MATE. Is there such a creature? The literature romanticizes about our "one and only" and everyone searches for the ultimate mate, while recent research implies that most people reach a point in life where they feel a need to get married and whoever happens to be available at the time is "it." A recent article discussed a 36-year-old single professional woman with a college degree suddenly faced with that statistic mentioned prior that women like herself over thirty had less than a 20 percent chance of every marrying. She was engaged in two weeks. How nice that she found her "one and only" so opportunely and fell in love so quickly.

Most people "fall in love" and get married to feel complete. They tend to feel unsatisfied, unloved, and missing part of self without a mate or partner. They, therefore, expect this new love to "fill in the blanks" of all that's been missing in life and become extremely agitated and upset when it doesn't happen, usually blaming the spouse for not living up to expectations.

A healthy, self-loving person has already found a sense of completeness. While none of us attain perfection, he has fairly well brought into focus his self perception, through the interaction with important others, including romantic love affairs, which have helped shape and define self image and worth.

Now he seeks a perfect complement to what he has discovered he is. Not just ANYONE, but someone special and unique who will more particularly fit and blend and harmonize when they overlay their self perceptions with other.

We have already discussed in detail compatibility, complementary, and noncomplementary opposites. This would be one of those rare, unique, special, "one of a kind" fits.

Once found, you might imagine a silver cord binding the two of you together like a long umbilical cord. Except that this cord is a two-way flow and neither is dependent upon the other for life. Let your imagination explore the possibilities of where **your** cord attaches to each partner. Is it head to head, or hand, genitals, or heart? What is the major connection between you? Allow the cord to be long and flexible, note how powerful and strong it is. It is powerful enough to keep you connected, to weather differences and difficulties and overcome obstacles and storms. It is long and flexible enough to allow freedom of movement, differences of opinion or approach, to include the love and caring of others without strain or damage to the cord itself.

And last of all, the cord is an open, flowing organ of subsistence and nurturing. Through this cord is a two-way ebb and flow of love, concern, information, and affirmation. Through this cord flows negative and positive current. There is a plus and minus, loss and gain, anger and softness, pleasure and pain. And all this nurtures and expands the people and the relationship. Make sure your silver cord stays open and flowing, valves functioning securely and well, maintaining a harmony and balance between you that minimizes exploitation or resentment. The flow need not always be in total balance. Life is rarely neat and compartmentalized. Needs vary, circumstances change, bio-rhythms fluctuate. But, we can be alert to keep a flow that has overall balance and harmony. Listen to the music of the flow, correct the discord, add the notes that beautify and expand.

Can it happen for you? Finely tune your own instrument and then listen and tune in to the others around you. The more in tune you are, the more you will notice discordant warnings to back off or go slow. Also, the more apt you are to pick up the sounds that most perfectly and completely blend, harmonize and beautify your own.

PILLAR #3

The natural consequence of love and mating is the building of family. Children are the abundant and delightful symbols of our love. As true lovers unite, they are creating a new entity or unit of life. They are now a couple and **this** coupling is unique and never existed before. The physical component of that major miracle is expressed in the birth of our child. We often lose sight of what a miracle that is. A miracle **is** a miracle, even if it happens every day.

It is a beautiful metaphysical belief that our children choose **us** as parents. Looking down over the ramparts of eternity, a child chooses **you** to nurture, love and bring to fruition the many lessons and experiences needed for a lifetime.

What a delightful thought. What would YOUR child have looked for in you? Children learn from who you **are**, not from what you do or say. Teach them harmony, balance and love by providing yourself as an ongoing example of your own evolving existence.

Admit your truth and imperfections and allow the children theirs. Children tune in to vibrations, feelings and experiences. BE THERE in unspoken bonding, as you gladly invite them to share the abundance of affection and caring that is you. Let them experience the unconditional reverence and love that can flow between husband and wife, parent and child.

Listen to each child's uniqueness. What is the need of THIS child? What is the experience necessary for new growth and understanding? Is he crying for discipline or concern, direction or exploration, release or demand? When does he need anger that says I care and softness to comfort pain?

We are the Master teachers of each child's life. What he learns and how he applies it is often his alone to determine. Don't "make in your own image" - share your image as a reflection of life to be learned and experienced. And, hopefully, the child will paint a portrait of which you can be proud.

PILLAR #4

We have stated elsewhere that the things we DO are symptoms or symbols of what we ARE, rather than being a direct expression of what we are.

Nowhere is this principle more important than in the area of career or profession. Doing and Being become tightly interlocked at this point. We joke about removing clothing, identity tags, and labels so that we can relate as people - human beings, unaffected by the biases of knowing someone's profession or education but it's not an entirely empty bias.

A woman once mused in my office, "I wonder if Joe would love me if I were not a successful woman with income and property of my own?"
My answer was somewhat jarring at first. "Probably not. If you were not a successful woman - a professional with income and property - what would you be? Would you dress as well, have as much confidence, be as independent or forceful? Those are the factors of and results of your success. Is he marrying you for your money and income or for the traits that enabled you to create success?" It has been said that "nothing is

as unsexy as an unemployed man." Do women marry for money, greed, prestige? Is power the great aphrodisiac, as Henry Kissinger once bragged?

How can you separate the person from his success - or failure? What have you chosen to do with your life? How have you chosen to spend or invest your time, energy, interests and lifestyle? How accurately does it reflect what you want it to reflect about you? The home you live in, car you drive, clothes you wear, are all reflections of your work, your income, your success.

Some people choose to downgrade this as materialistic and superficial. Others over-emphasize it to the point of obsession. Where does it fit for you?

The perfect job, career or profession is one that most closely fits and harmonizes with your image of self and the statement you are making to the world. "I am living a lifestyle totally within my COMFORT ZONE as to input and outgo. This is who I am and want to be. What you see, is what you get." All this is closely aligned to step one. This is the wordly statement of who I am. This is the manner I have chosen of contributing to my world - being a good steward of that which I have been given, supporting my existence, becoming an important part of the whole, expressing my need to accomplish and produce. Being happy and in balance with what is.

As in step one, there are two other sections: How others perceive me in the workplace and my perception of their perception.

As people feed back and respond to my contribution to society it validates my feelings of self worth and brings gratification that I am appreciated and admired. As this focus between us comes into play, there is a pleasure and satisfaction but not to the point of stagnation, in accepting what is done; but a continual need to improve, advance and succeed; integrating and fine-tuning of self and the profession.

PILLAR #5

You will notice that all these steps reach out to others, even step one, the beginning point. We do not exist without others and have no measure for ourselves without others. In the process of selection, we both give and receive back and thereby have more to give. Those vibrations of giving resonate out to others of like mind. We tune into the same frequency of life, hear the same music and find ourselves fine tuning with **close** friends, intimates, extended or **chosen** family if you will. This is different from lovers or our children.

We draw to ourselves experiences and people important to the moment. We fit into each other's grand scheme of life. Sometimes we meet in grade school and are lifetime friends; some relationships are intense but brief. This is all part of growth and being - the need to share and reflect those very intimate and private parts of self that cannot be common currency in the marketplace exchange. We need new and different reactions - not from family or spouse - an objective observation or a variation of subjectivity. Sometimes we teach and share our wisdom - at other times, we become pupil or receive. There is an ebb and flow that enhances and encircles as we reflect to each other the selves we experience and how that adds to each of our own lives.

PILLAR #6

A further extension of the previous step is taking our true balance and harmony out into the world at large, populated by many fringe players we are not really sure that we effect. They are not as special or important. They do not impact our daily lives, but they are there, relating and being related to. What messages or vibrations do each of us impart to this world at large? Famous people become heroes or infamous. All of us have extended contact we rarely notice. Let the world see you as a gracious, open, caring being - with integrity and good will. The returns will be significant.

PILLAR #7

This is somewhat complex in nature but often a final step of completion of self - parenting one's parents. First we are parented. As adults, we must then learn to be the good parents to ourselves and continue the process within. Now we return to complete the cycle.

Our parents shared in our lessons for life. They have helped to shape our values and promote our lifestyles. They had much to do with our view of self and others and how we have become what we have become. Our roots and beginnings are tied to theirs. We are a reflection of those early beginnings.

As adults watching our parents grow older and decline, we need to reflect back to them once more, from a different perspective, who we now are and how this fits for them. Let them see you fresh and new, who you are and what you have learned.

All our lives we have needed their love, comfort, support and understanding. We wanted to know we were unconditionally loved when we didn't deserve it, belonged to a family that would always be there for us and no matter the age or success, wanted reassurance that they respected, admired and pleased themselves in the essence of what we were.

Now the tables are turned and twilight time has somewhat reversed this need. They need to know they are unconditionally loved though they sometimes blow it, having loving children who care and will never be too busy to be there for them. They need the re-assurance that life has not slipped them by, it wasn't a waste, the sacrifices were seen and appreciated, the kids not only turned out OK, but are appreciative of the many loving contributions made to their lives.

"Here I am - revel in what you created. Enjoy the fruits of your labor. Be proud of what we did together - you in your life and me in mine!" If you have truly made peace with your parents, it's a rewarding experience as they pass into that second chance at childhood to slip on the roles of parenthood and give back the little favors so graciously bestowed upon you.

I have tried to summarize in this final chapter in seven steps, the essence and message of what loving self is all about. You will note that "being spiritual" is not included as one of the seven pillars. Spirituality like happiness, is a by-product, a result of living correctly. There is nothing as spiritual as simply "being" the person you were created to be. Keeping the seven pillars in focus and balance is the essence of fulfilling the highest self.

The ultimate love affair is with the self. As you revel in, experience, enjoy and appreciate who and what you are and then reflect this out for the world to see and share in, it comes reflecting back to you. As you relate to God, life, nature, people and the majesty of experience you are being nurtured and fed by the reflection of yourself even as they all are experiencing their own reflections as well. I love, you experience, - I experience, you experience - this we do for each other and the world. The better we do it, proclaiming trust, affirming self, the more we receive what we affirm - LOVE, SATISFACTION, MEANING OF LIFE and INNER PEACE, knowing we have served and loved our universe well.

I have tried to be simple without being naive enough to imply that it is easy. This is a lifetime job and fortunately, we are given the entire life to do it. There is no other task. And, it leaves nothing out.

LOVE AND LIFE TO YOU!!!

Name _____

Time Your Class Meets _____

Worksheet A
FOR YOURSELF

I have provided you with a checklist of common personality traits listed under the headings of mother, father, me, spouse, spouse's mother, spouse's father. Check off all the words - even list them in priority order, 1 to 10, that most fit each person. Do it with a minimum of thought, on an emotional level, otherwise we tend to rationalize, excuse or feel guilty about our answers. Remember, most of us have desirable and undesirable traits and contradictory ones. Spouse is defined as the person you are now in a relationship with or a pattern description of the kind of person you usually date or mate with.

	Mother	Father	Me	Spouse	Spouse's Mother	Spouse's Father
Warm	☐	☐	☐	☐	☐	☐
Cold	☐	☐	☐	☐	☐	☐
Touching	☐	☐	☐	☐	☐	☐
Distant	☐	☐	☐	☐	☐	☐
Angry	☐	☐	☐	☐	☐	☐
Loving	☐	☐	☐	☐	☐	☐
Critical	☐	☐	☐	☐	☐	☐
Supportive	☐	☐	☐	☐	☐	☐
Bright	☐	☐	☐	☐	☐	☐
Dumb	☐	☐	☐	☐	☐	☐
Alcoholic	☐	☐	☐	☐	☐	☐
Conservative	☐	☐	☐	☐	☐	☐
Liberal	☐	☐	☐	☐	☐	☐
Dominant	☐	☐	☐	☐	☐	☐
Submissive	☐	☐	☐	☐	☐	☐
Aggressive	☐	☐	☐	☐	☐	☐
Passive	☐	☐	☐	☐	☐	☐
Stubborn	☐	☐	☐	☐	☐	☐
Lenient	☐	☐	☐	☐	☐	☐
Generous	☐	☐	☐	☐	☐	☐
Stingy	☐	☐	☐	☐	☐	☐
_____	☐	☐	☐	☐	☐	☐
_____	☐	☐	☐	☐	☐	☐
_____	☐	☐	☐	☐	☐	☐

Fill in your adjectives not previously listed.

Summarize what you have learned about yourself and your spouse - strengths and weaknesses of each - how this is good or bad for the relationship - positive or negative attraction, etc.

Name _____

Worksheet A
FOR YOUR SPOUSE

I have provided you with a checklist of common personality traits listed under the headings of mother, father, me, spouse, spouse's mother, spouse's father. Check off all the words - even list them in priority order, 1 to 10, that most fit each person. Do it with a minimum of thought, on an emotional level, otherwise we tend to rationalize, excuse or feel guilty about our answers. Remember, most of us have desirable and undesirable traits and contradictory ones. Spouse is defined as the person you are now in a relationship with or a pattern description of the kind of person you usually date or mate with.

	Mother	Father	Me	Spouse	Spouse's Mother	Spouse's Father
Warm	☐	☐	☐	☐	☐	☐
Cold	☐	☐	☐	☐	☐	☐
Touching	☐	☐	☐	☐	☐	☐
Distant	☐	☐	☐	☐	☐	☐
Angry	☐	☐	☐	☐	☐	☐
Loving	☐	☐	☐	☐	☐	☐
Critical	☐	☐	☐	☐	☐	☐
Supportive	☐	☐	☐	☐	☐	☐
Bright	☐	☐	☐	☐	☐	☐
Dumb	☐	☐	☐	☐	☐	☐
Alcoholic	☐	☐	☐	☐	☐	☐
Conservative	☐	☐	☐	☐	☐	☐
Liberal	☐	☐	☐	☐	☐	☐
Dominant	☐	☐	☐	☐	☐	☐
Submissive	☐	☐	☐	☐	☐	☐
Aggressive	☐	☐	☐	☐	☐	☐
Passive	☐	☐	☐	☐	☐	☐
Stubborn	☐	☐	☐	☐	☐	☐
Lenient	☐	☐	☐	☐	☐	☐
Generous	☐	☐	☐	☐	☐	☐
Stingy	☐	☐	☐	☐	☐	☐
_____	☐	☐	☐	☐	☐	☐
_____	☐	☐	☐	☐	☐	☐
_____	☐	☐	☐	☐	☐	☐

Fill in your adjectives not previously listed.

Summarize what you have learned about yourself and your spouse - strengths and weaknesses of each - how this is good or bad for the relationship - positive or negative attraction, etc.

Name _____

FOR YOURSELF

Answer the Following Questions:

1. What (1-2-3) changes is my spouse constantly asking for that I don't want to give or have difficult giving?

2. What (1-2-3) changes do I want from my spouse that I feel would change the relationship in a postive manner?

3. What do I feel would realistically be the result of my changing the above as requested of my spouse?

4. What does my spouse say would be the result of this change?

5. What is my conscious, stated reason for NOT giving this change?

6. What do I feel would realistically happen if my spouse changed as requested?

7. What does my spouse feel happen if she/he changed?

8. What is my spouse's stated reason for not changing?

Summarize what you have learned about yourself and your motivations and your spouse and his/her motivations from answering these eight questions.

Name _____

FOR YOUR SPOUSE

Answer the Following Questions:

1. What (1-2-3) changes is my spouse constantly asking for that I don't want to give or have difficult giving?

2. What (1-2-3) changes do I want from my spouse that I feel would change the relationship in a postive manner?

3. What do I feel would realistically be the result of my changing the above as requested of my spouse?

4. What does my spouse say would be the result of this change?

5. What is my conscious, stated reason for NOT giving this change?

6. What do I feel would realistically happen if my spouse changed as requested?

7. What does my spouse feel happen if she/he changed?

8. What is my spouse's stated reason for not changing?

Summarize what you have learned about yourself and your motivations and your spouse and his/her motivations from answering these eight questions.

Worksheet C
FOR YOURSELF

Another approach to creatively improving relationships is deciding what you wish to CREATE, not CHANGE. First read the questions - then answer them. Two weeks later summarize what happened and why.

1. What change would I like to offer myself and my spouse that I believe would make a positive affect on the relationship. Example: spend more time at home with my spouse, take my spouse out for entertainment more, be less critical, do more thoughtful things such as notes or flowers. This is AUTONOMOUS CHANGE - one person choosing to change as a gift of love without concern that my partner has to respond in a certain way or give an equal change to mine.

2. How can I create the environment I want in my life? Do you want happy - BE HAPPY. Do you want less criticism - BE LESS CRITICAL. Change your attitude and approach to a more pleasant, upbeat and positive one. You might respond, "that sounds phony". It could start that way but if you decide to be warm, pleasant, positive and giving, and act that way, it generally brings a positive response and reaffirms your actions, and literally changes your feeling to conform to the behavior.

3. Pick something your spouse has asked for in the past that you've had trouble giving, and make a point to give it consistently for two weeks, without telling your spouse what you are doing. Be an objective observer and try to notice if your spouse is aware of the change and be aware of how your spouse consciously or unconsciously responds to your change.

Name _____

Worksheet C
FOR YOUR SPOUSE

Another approach to creatively improving relationships is deciding what you
wish to CREATE, not CHANGE. First read the questions - then answer them.
Two weeks later summarize what happened and why.

1. What change would I like to offer myself and my spouse that I believe
   would make a positive affect on the relationship. Example: spend more
   time at home with my spouse, take my spouse out for entertainment more,
   be less critical, do more thoughtful things such as notes or flowers. This is
   AUTONOMOUS CHANGE - one person choosing to change as a gift of
   love without concern that my partner has to respond in a certain way or
   give an equal change to mine.

2. How can I create the environment I want in my life? Do you want happy -
   BE HAPPY. Do you want less criticism - BE LESS CRITICAL. Change your
   attitude and approach to a more pleasant, upbeat and positive one. You
   might respond, "that sounds phony". It could start that way but if you
   decide to be warm, pleasant, positive and giving, and act that way, it
   generally brings a positive response and reaffirms your actions, and literally changes your feeling to conform to the behavior.

3. Pick something your spouse has asked for in the past that you've had trouble giving, and make a point to give it consistently for two weeks, without telling your spouse what you are doing. Be an objective observer and try to notice if your spouse is aware of the change and be aware of how your spouse consciously or unconsciously responds to your change.

NOTES

NOTES

NOTES

NOTES

NOTES

NOTES

NOTES

NOTES

NOTES

NOTES